About This Book

Why is this topic important?

Continuing education and development lie at the very heart of any successful organization. Time and time again, studies show that the best organizations, those that deliver better-than-average return on investment, also happen to be the ones with the highest commitment to training and development. Moreover, training has become a powerful ally in the war for talent. Job seekers frequently cite a strong commitment to development as one of the principal reasons for joining or remaining with an organization.

What can you achieve with this book?

In your hands is a working toolkit, a valuable source of knowledge for the training professional. Offering entirely new content each year, the Pfeiffer Training *Annual* showcases the latest thinking and cutting-edge approaches to training and development, contributed by practicing training professionals, consultants, academics, and subject-matter experts. Turn to the *Annual* for a rich source of ideas and to try out new methods and approaches that others in your profession have found successful.

How is this book organized?

The book is divided into four sections: Experiential Learning Activities (ELAs); Editor's Choice; Inventories, Questionnaires, and Surveys; and Articles and Discussion Resources. All the material can be freely reproduced for training purposes. The ELAs are the mainstay of the *Annual* and cover a broad range of training topics. The activities are presented as complete and ready-to-use training designs; facilitator instructions and all necessary handouts and participant materials are included. Editor's Choice pieces allow us to select material that doesn't fit the other categories and take advantage of "hot topics." The instrument section introduces reliable survey and assessment tools for gathering and sharing data on aspects of personal or team development. The articles section presents the best current thinking about training and organization development. Use these for your own professional development or as lecture resources.

About Pfeiffer

Pfeiffer serves the professional development and hands-on resource needs of training and human resource practitioners and gives them products to do their jobs better. We deliver proven ideas and solutions from experts in HR development and HR management, and we offer effective and customizable tools to improve workplace performance. From novice to seasoned professional, Pfeiffer is the source you can trust to make yourself and your organization more successful.

Essential Knowledge Pfeiffer produces insightful, practical, and comprehensive materials on topics that matter the most to training and HR professionals. Our Essential Knowledge resources translate the expertise of seasoned professionals into practical, how-to guidance on critical workplace issues and problems. These resources are supported by case studies, worksheets, and job aids and are frequently supplemented with CD-ROMs, websites, and other means of making the content easier to read, understand, and use.

Essential Tools Pfeiffer's Essential Tools resources save time and expense by offering proven, ready-to-use materials—including exercises, activities, games, instruments, and assessments—for use during a training or team-learning event. These resources are frequently offered in looseleaf or CD-ROM format to facilitate copying and customization of the material.

Pfeiffer also recognizes the remarkable power of new technologies in expanding the reach and effectiveness of training. While e-hype has often created whizbang solutions in search of a problem, we are dedicated to bringing convenience and enhancements to proven training solutions. All our e-tools comply with rigorous functionality standards. The most appropriate technology wrapped around essential content yields the perfect solution for today's on-the-go trainers and human resource professionals.

Pfeiffer *Essential resources for training and HR professionals*
www.pfeiffer.com

The Pfeiffer Annual Series

The Pfeiffer Annuals present each year never-before-published materials contributed by learning professionals and academics and written for trainers, consultants, and human resource and performance-improvement practitioners. As a forum for the sharing of ideas, theories, models, instruments, experiential learning activities, and best and innovative practices, the *Annuals* are unique. Not least because only in the *Pfeiffer Annuals* will you find solutions from professionals like you who work in the field as trainers, consultants, facilitators, educators, and human resource and performance-improvement practitioners and whose contributions have been tried and perfected in real-life settings with actual participants and clients to meet real-world needs.

The Pfeiffer Annual: Consulting
Edited by Elaine Biech

The Pfeiffer Annual: Training
Edited by Elaine Biech

Michael Allen's e-Learning Annual
Edited by Michael Allen

Call for Papers

How would you like to be published in the *Pfeiffer Training* or *Consulting Annual*? Possible topics for submissions include group and team building, organization development, leadership, problem solving, presentation and communication skills, consulting and facilitation, and training-the-trainer. Contributions may be in one of the following three formats:

- Experiential Learning Activities

- Inventories, Questionnaires, and Surveys

- Articles and Discussion Resources

To receive a copy of the submission packet, which explains the requirements and will help you determine format, language, and style to use, contact editor Elaine Biech at Pfeifferannual@aol.com or by calling 757-588-3939.

Elaine Biech, EDITOR

The *2012*
Pfeiffer
ANNUAL

TRAINING

Pfeiffer
A Wiley Imprint
www.pfeiffer.com

ISBN: 978-1-118-07390-2
ISSN: 1046-333-X
978-1-118-12462-8 ebook; 978-1-118-12463-5 ebook; 978-1-118-12464-2 ebook

Acquiring Editor: Marisa Kelley
Director of Development: Kathleen Dolan Davies
Development Editor: Susan Rachmeler
Production Editor: Dawn Kilgore
Editor: Rebecca Taff
Manufacturing Supervisor: Becky Morgan

Printed in the United States of America

Printing   10 9 8 7 6 5 4 3 2 1

Contents

Experiential Learning Activities

Editor's Choice

†Cutting-Edge Topics
**Learning in the Moment Topics

Website Contents

Our readers are invited to download customizable materials from this book related to the experiential learning activities and the instruments, as well as a PDF of the book text. The following materials are available FREE with the purchase of this book at: www.pfeiffer.com/go/training2012.

The following username and password are required for accessing these materials:

Username: training

Password: 2012

Experiential Learning Activities

Twenty-Five Ways to Include Others: Taking Action,
Julie O'Mara

Twenty-Five Ways to Include Others

Practice Role Play: Experiencing Emotional Intelligence,
Shri S.S. Roy

Practice Role Play Instructions

Practice Role Play Case 1: Boss

Practice Role Play Case 1: Assistant

Practice Role Play Case 2: Marketing Manager

Practice Role Play Case 2: Marketing Executive

Practice Role Play Case 3: Finance Manager

Practice Role Play Case 3: Accounts Officer

Practice Role Play Case 4: Supervisor

Practice Role Play Case 4: Worker

Editor's Choice

Inventories, Questionnaires, and Surveys

Three Dimensional Emotional Competence Inventory (3D-ECI),
Sethu Madhavan Puravangara

Three-Dimensional Emotional Competence Inventory (3D-ECI): Self

Three-Dimensional Emotional Competence Inventory (3D-ECI): Other

3D-ECI Score Prediction and Interpretation Sheet

3D-ECI Scoring Sheet

3D-ECI Profile Graph

Classroom Instructor Skills Survey,
Jean Barbazette

Classroom Instructor Skills Survey

Classroom Instructor Skills Survey Scoring Sheet

Classroom Instructor Performance Plan

Institutional Climate Survey,
K.S. Gupta

Institutional Climate Survey

Institutional Climate Survey Scoring Sheet

PDF

The book text is available in PDF format.

Preface

Happy 40th anniversary! Yes, the Pfeiffer *Annuals* have been published since 1972. For forty years the *Annuals* have set the standard in form, format, and functionality for experiential learning activities (ELAs).

Experiential learning can be traced back to 500 BC when Confucius, China's most famous teacher, philosopher, and political theorist, is purported to have claimed, "I hear, I know. I see, I remember. I do, I understand." Experiential learning has been recognized as critical to human development by experts such as Carl Rogers, Maria Montessori, John Dewey, David Kolb, and scores of others.

Although experiential learning has been around for eons, the Pfeiffer *Annuals* are recognized as the most definitive source for describing a precise model for ELAs, now the basis of work for every trainer, consultant, and facilitator. The *Annuals'* first editors had an "interest in providing a distinctive model of human relations training . . . toward experiences that produce generally predictable outcomes." That model lives today between the covers of the Pfeiffer *Annuals*. The model includes two parts: (1) how to design ELAs on paper so that everyone can understand the process, as well as (2) how to conduct a true ELA using the recognizable Pfeiffer Experiential Learning Cycle: experiencing, publishing, processing, generalizing, and applying.

Many leaders from academia, business, consulting, and training have published some of their best work in the *Annuals*. Some names you may know include Karl Albrecht, Jean Barbazette, Richard Beckhard, Geoff Bellman, Warren Bennis, Ken Blanchard, Warner Burke, Jack Canfield, Marshall Goldsmith, Len Goodstein, Paul Hersey, Bev Kaye, Jim Kouzes, Ed Lawler, III, Karen Lawson, Ron and Gordon Lippitt, Julie O'Mara, Udai Pareek, Bob Pike, Allison Rossett, Ed Schein, and Thiagi. Readers have been loyal to a resource that publishes the best of the best, like these authors.

During the forty years, the *Annuals* have grown from one volume to two and have introduced features and changes that ensure ease of use by readers. For example, most recently the *Training* and *Consulting Annuals* have presented themes. Our profession covers a wide variety of topics, and the themed *Annuals* have been successful with our readers and our authors because they help to narrow the focus; we can also publish several related articles and activities in one concentrated space. The theme for 2012 is "Learning in the Moment."

Both *Annuals* present a broad array of activities and articles that support the theme this year. The *Training Annual* presents eight Learning in the Moment submissions and the *Consulting Annual* provides ten Learning in the Moment submissions. In addition to the themed submissions, both *Annuals* continue to present other topics that help you do your job: teamwork, leadership, communication, problem solving, and so forth. The Learning in the Moment theme helps to focus some of our master contributors' talents in the 2012 volumes. Please let us know if you have suggestions for a theme in future years.

What is the meaning of our 2012 theme? How do we define "Learning in the Moment"? Everyone is bombarded with an overflow of information. The most successful people know what to do with that information. This occurs when the information is coupled with the knowledge and skills of implementation; "just-in-time" learning is what it was called back in the 1970s.

The introduction of the "blended" learning concept a decade ago legitimized the idea that learning occurs anyplace and any time; learning doesn't just happen in a classroom. A broad range of learning activities may be described as a part of Learning in the Moment: web search tools, mentoring, coaching, e-coaching, communities of practice, various e-learning events, chat rooms, blogging, yammering, and tweeting.

Why is this theme meaningful? Learning in the moment, just-in-time learning, learning on the fly, whatever you call it, is critical for everyone in the workplace: customer-service professionals, sales people, manufacturing line workers, military, supervisors, managers, dairy farmers, and even executives. What truly makes this theme critical are the statistics. To begin, ASTD's *State of the Industry* data shows that instructor-led training has decreased to just over 60 percent of total training. But that only refers to formal, planned learning. Other statistics suggest that talent development is better described using a 70-20-10 model. That is, 70 percent of learning and development occurs on the job, 20 percent occurs through coaching and mentoring relationships, and 10 percent occurs through formal training.

The profession recognizes the importance of moving away from time-constrained methods that include lengthy needs assessments, multiple-step design efforts, numerous pilot programs, and extended interventions. Both trainers and consultants are aware that providing ways to learn skills and knowledge at the moment when the learner needs them is critical. They know that prolonging the solution prevents their organizations from maintaining a competitive advantage.

This means that the biggest question is not what or why, but how? How can we as internal and external trainers and consultants ensure that we have the tools to use to help employees develop skills and knowledge in the moment?

Many trainers and consultants have already changed their learning philosophy to adapt to Learning in the Moment. Exploring and considering a few of these ideas will help you continue to make a strong transition:

- Recognize that learning is a day-to-day activity, not a singular event.

- Find ways to change behaviors and attitudes, not just enhance skills and knowledge.

- Identify how to embed learning on the job in a natural, easy-to-use process.

- Prepare peers and supervisors to support learning after the formal training has been delivered.

- Deliver learning in discrete bite-sized morsels, as opposed to setting aside multiple hours or days for learning.

Our authors lived up to the challenge of addressing Learning in the Moment with a variety of experiential learning activities (ELAs) and articles. *The 2012 Pfeiffer Training Annual* includes submissions in the facilitation, leadership, communication, coaching, and life/career planning categories. *The 2012 Pfeiffer Consulting Annual* includes Learning in the Moment submissions in problem-solving alternatives, team roles, leadership style, coaching, change management, personal growth, and interface with clients.

The *Training Annual* includes two ELAs you won't want to miss. In Pair/Share, Lou Russell wastes no time getting into the training topic. Jan Schmuckler's activity helps participants identify the relationships that have influenced them. Learning in the Moment occurs when this ELA is used by coaches and mentors. There are six articles relating to the theme. Homer Johnson and Anne Reilly present a 4R model that helps managers learn and maintain their skills on the job. Chris Hipple and Zane Berge present the opportunities and risks of incorporating user-created content in organizations. Brittany Ashby reminds us of the Socratic Method to teach employees to think. Gary Wise's article addresses the theme, but also is a cutting-edge topic that examines the urgency to reinvent training organizations. Jim Gary and Michele Summers discuss creating a playbook for delivering successful results for hazardous oversight programs, an area in which Learning in the Moment can mean the difference between life and death.

This year we are also honored to have an article submitted by Dr. Donald Kirkpatrick. Don discusses the four levels of evaluation, relating how they came about over fifty years ago. You will be excited to read how evaluation fits with our theme, identifying more than a dozen ways to evaluate learning in the moment. We are grateful that Don took time to share this contribution with us.

The *Consulting Annual* includes four ELAs on the theme topic. Karen Dietz and Lori Silverman demonstrate the use of storytelling to solve immediate problems. Linda Bedinger and Charlotte Waisman show us how teams can explore roles and qualities in short order. Diane Hamilton's ELA helps people define a vision of leadership and assess their own strengths and needs immediately. Antoine Gerschel and Lawrence Polsky have participants up on their feet practicing one-minute change messages. The *Consulting Annual* also includes five Learning in the Moment articles. Travis Russ explains how to conduct a 360 to gain in-the-moment feedback. Jean Lamkin is with us again to ensure that we all use coaching assessments for maximum and immediate learning. Linda Raudenbush relates a successful team-building experience that can easily be transferred to your situations. Leonard Goodstein discusses how executives learn in the moment through coaching practices. Mohandas Nair discusses a continuous process for developing managerial skills. Deborah Thomas is our editor's choice; she connects corporate values to learning, as learning occurs.

What Are the Annuals?

The *Annual* series consists of practical materials written for trainers, consultants, facilitators, and performance-improvement technologists. We know the materials are practical, because they are written by the same practitioners that use the materials.

The *Pfeiffer Annual: Training* focuses on skill building and knowledge enhancement and also includes articles that enhance the skills and professional development of trainers. *The Pfeiffer Annual: Consulting* focuses on intervention techniques and organizational systems. It also includes skill building for the professional consultant. You can read more about the differences between the two volumes in the section that follows this preface, "The Difference Between Training and Consulting: Which *Annual* to Use."

The *Annuals* have been an inspirational source for experiential learning activities, resource for instruments, and reference for cutting-edge thinking for forty years. Whether you are a trainer, a consultant, a facilitator, or a bit of each, you will find tools and resources that provide you with the basics and challenge (and we hope inspire) you to use new techniques and models.

Annual Loyalty

The Pfeiffer *Annual* series has many loyal subscribers. There are several reasons for this loyalty. In addition to the wide variety of topics and implementation levels, the *Annuals* provide materials that are applicable to varying circumstances. You will find instruments for individuals, teams, and organizations; experiential learning activities to round out workshops, team building, or consulting assignments; ideas and contemporary solutions for managing human capital; and articles that increase your own knowledge base, to use as reference materials in your writing, or as a source of ideas for your training or consulting assignments.

Many of our readers have been loyal customers for decades. If you are one of them, we thank you. And we encourage each of you to give back to the profession by submitting a sample of your work to share with your colleagues.

Just as our theme this year is Learning in the Moment, the *Annuals* are Ready in the Moment. The *Annuals'* success is primarily due to the fact that they are immediately ready to use. All of the materials may be duplicated for educational and training purposes. If you need to adapt or modify the materials to tailor them for your audience's needs, go right ahead. We only request that the credit statement found on the copyright page (and on each reproducible page) be retained on all copies. Our liberal copyright policy makes it easy and fast for you to use the materials to do your job. However, if you intend to reproduce the materials in publications for sale or if you wish to reproduce more than one hundred copies of any one item, please contact us for prior written permission.

If you are a new *Annual* user, welcome! If you like what you see in the 2012 edition, you may want to consider subscribing to a standing order. By doing so, you are guaranteed to receive your copy each year straight off the press and receive a discount off the cover price. And if you want to go back and have the entire series for your use, then the *Pfeiffer Library*—which contains content from the very first edition through the 2007 *Annuals*—is available on CD-ROM. You can find information on the *Pfeiffer Library* at www.pfeiffer.com.

I often refer to many of my *Annuals* from the 1980s. They include several classic activities that have become a mainstay in my team-building and strategic planning designs. But most of all, the *Annuals* have been a valuable resource for forty years because the materials come from professionals like you who work in the field as trainers, consultants, facilitators, educators, and performance-improvement technologists, whose contributions have been tried and perfected in real-life settings with actual participants and clients to meet real-world needs.

To this end, we encourage you to submit materials to be considered for publication. We are interested in receiving experiential learning activities; inventories, questionnaires, and surveys; and articles and discussion resources. Contact the Pfeiffer Editorial Department at the address listed on the copyright page for copies of our guidelines for contributors or contact me directly at Box 8249, Norfolk, VA 23503, or by email at pfeifferannual@aol.com. We welcome your comments, ideas, and contributions.

Acknowledgments

Kathleen Dolan Davies, Marisa Kelley, Dawn Kilgore, Susan Rachmeler, Rebecca Taff: Every year you produce one of the most valuable resources in the industry, delivering value to our dedicated readers. We all owe you a debt of gratitude. Thank you to Lorraine Kohart, of ebb associates inc, who pokes, prods, and cajoles our authors into submitting the best for you, the readers. She keeps us all organized, provides submission information, compiles the *Annuals'* content, keeps authors in the loop, and is the go-between with the editing team to ensure all the deadlines are met.

And the paramount thank you goes to our contributors, who continue to create new and exciting activities and materials so that trainers and consultants everywhere have fresh materials to deliver to their internal and external clients. I invite everyone who is reading this to join these prestigious professionals in our next *Annual*. We are always looking for new authors who have creative yet practical ideas to share with the rest of the profession.

Tribute to J. William Pfeiffer, Ph.D., J.D.

As we go to print with this forty-year anniversary *Pfeiffer Annual*, we are saddened to learn of the death of J. William (Bill) Pfeiffer, one of the *Annuals'* creators, on October 2, 2011. University Associates, Inc., and later Pfeiffer & Associates, Inc., started publishing the *Annuals* in 1972. Bill Pfeiffer, John E. Jones, and Leonard D. Goodstein all served as early editors of the *Annuals*. Jossey-Bass purchased Pfeiffer in 1996.

Bill grew up in Wallace, Idaho, graduated from the University of Maryland, and received his Ph.D. in adult education from the University of Iowa. He and John E. Jones founded University Associates in 1969 in Iowa City, and they later moved the company to San Diego. The company had a positive impact on the field of human resource development. In addition to the *Annuals*, Bill authored and edited dozens of books on a wide range of topics. Bill was also a consultant, specializing in managing change, strategic planning, management and leadership development, and organization development.

The company was founded on the belief that resources should be shared by peers, inviting readers to freely reproduce the materials for educational or training purposes. University Associates, its contributors, and its customers maintained this unique professional value at a time when many others were protecting all content and information with copyrights. This concept lives on and is embodied in the *Pfeiffer Annuals*.

Bill was a man of immense talent, who took advantage of "learning in the moment." I met Bill in 1986, a quarter of a century ago, and I still recall the entire three-hour session he led. Bill had an uncanny way of singling out people who were oblivious to the world around them (that would be me in this case) and then using any unorthodox way to help them become more cognizant. It was not comfortable, but was certainly a turning point in my life. I learned more "in the moment" during that three-hour session with Bill at the helm than at almost any other time in my life.

I suspect Bill may have used his unconventional approaches to help many others learn in the moment, and through his company and publications he was able to influence thousands of others like me with knowledge about OD, team building, consulting, training, communication, speaking skills, facilitating, problem solving, and leadership. All of these topics continue to carry his name in the *Pfeiffer Annuals*. Bill's legacy will carry on.

Elaine Biech
Editor
September 2011

The Difference Between Training and Consulting

Which Annual to Use?

Two volumes of the *Pfeiffer Annuals*—training and consulting—are resources for two different but closely related professions. Each *Annual* serves as a collection of tools and support materials used by the professionals in their respective arenas. The volumes include activities, articles, and instruments used by individuals in the training and consulting fields. The training volume is written with the trainer in mind, and the consulting volume is written with the consultant in mind.

How can you differentiate between the two volumes? Let's begin by defining each profession.

A *trainer* can be defined as anyone who is responsible for designing and delivering knowledge to adult learners and may include an internal HRD professional employed by an organization or an external practitioner who contracts with an organization to design and conduct training programs. Generally, the trainer is a subject-matter expert who is expected to transfer knowledge so that the trainee can know or do something new. A *consultant* is someone who provides unique assistance or advice (based on what the consultant knows or has experienced) to someone else, usually known as "the client." The consultant may not necessarily be a subject-matter expert in all situations. Often the consultant is an expert at using specific tools to extract, coordinate, resolve, organize, expedite, or implement an organizational situation.

The lines between the consulting and training professions have blurred in the past few years. First, the names and titles have blurred. For example, some external trainers call themselves "training consultants" as a way of distinguishing themselves from internal trainers. Some organizations now have internal consultants who usually reside in the training department. Second, the roles have blurred. While a consultant has always been expected to deliver measurable results, now trainers are expected to do so as well. Both are expected to improve performance; both are expected to contribute to the bottom line. Facilitation was at one time thought to be a consultant skill; today trainers are expected to use facilitation skills to train. Training one-on-one was a trainer skill; today consultants train executives one-on-one and call it "coaching." The introduction of the "performance technologist," whose role is one of combined trainer and consultant, is a perfect example of a new profession that has evolved due to the need for trainers to use more "consulting" techniques in their work. The "performance consultant" is a new role supported by the American Society for Training and Development (ASTD). ASTD has shifted its focus from training to performance improvement.

As you can see, the roles and goals of training and consulting are not nearly as specific as they once may have been. However, when you step back and examine the two professions from a big-picture perspective, you can more easily differentiate between the two. Maintaining a big-picture focus will also help you determine which *Pfeiffer Annual* to turn to as your first resource.

Both volumes cover the same general topics: communication, teamwork, problem solving, and leadership. However, depending on your requirement and purpose—a training or consulting need—you will use each in different situations. You will select the *Annual* based on *how you will interact with the topic, not on what the topic might be.* Let's take a topic such as teamwork, for example. If you are searching for a lecturette that teaches the advantages of teamwork, a workshop activity that demonstrates the skill of making decisions in a team, or a handout that discusses team stages, look to the Training *Annual.* On the other hand, if you are conducting a team-building session for a dysfunctional team, helping to form a new team, or trying to understand the dynamics of an executive team, you will look to the Consulting *Annual.*

The Training Annual

The materials in the Training volume focus on skill building and knowledge enhancement as well as on the professional development of trainers. They generally focus on controlled events: a training program, a conference presentation, a classroom setting. Look to the Training *Annual* to find ways to improve a training session for ten to one thousand people and anything else that falls in the human resource development category:

- Specific experiential learning activities that can be built into a training program;

- Techniques to improve training: debriefing exercises, conducting role plays, managing time;

- Topical lecturettes;

- Ideas to improve a boring training program;

- Icebreakers and energizers for a training session;

- Surveys that can be used in a classroom;

- Ideas for moving an organization from training to performance; and

- Ways to improve your skills as a trainer.

The Consulting Annual

The materials in the Consulting volume focus on intervention techniques and organizational systems as well as the professional development of consultants. They generally focus on "tools" that you can have available just in case: concepts about organizations and their development (or demise) and about more global situations. Look to the Consulting *Annual* to find ways to improve consulting activities from team building and executive coaching to organization development and strategic planning:

- Skills for working with executives;

- Techniques for solving problems, effecting change, and gathering data;

- Team-building tools, techniques, and tactics;

- Facilitation ideas and methods;

- Processes to examine for improving an organization's effectiveness;

- Surveys that can be used organizationally; and

- Ways to improve your effectiveness as a consultant.

Summary

Even though the professions and the work are closely related and at times interchangeable, there is a difference. Use the following table to help you determine which *Annual* you should scan first for help. Remember, however, there is some blending of the two and either *Annual* may have your answer. It depends . . .

Element	Training	Consulting
Topics	Teams, Communication, Problem Solving	Teams, Communication, Problem Solving
Topic Focus	Individual, Department	Corporate, Global
Purpose	Skill Building, Knowledge Transfer	Coaching, Strategic Planning, Building Teams
Recipient	Individuals, Departments	Usually More Organizational
Organizational Level	All Workforce Members	Usually Closer to the Top
Delivery Profile	Workshops, Presentations	Intervention, Implementation
Atmosphere	Structured	Unstructured
Time Frame	Defined	Undefined
Organizational Cost	Moderate	High
Change Effort	Low to Moderate	Moderate to High
Setting	Usually a Classroom	Anywhere
Professional Experience	Entry Level, Novice	Proficient, Master Level
Risk Level	Low	High
Professional Needs	Activities, Resources	Tools, Theory
Application	Individual Skills	Usually Organizational System

When you get right down to it, we are all trainers and consultants. The skills may cross over. A great trainer is also a skilled consultant. And a great consultant is also a skilled trainer. The topics may be the same, but how you implement them may be vastly different. Which *Annual* to use? Remember to think about your purpose in terms of the big picture: consulting or training.

As you can see, we have both covered.

Introduction
to *The 2012 Pfeiffer Annual: Training*

The 2012 Pfeiffer Annual: Training is a collection of practical and useful materials for professionals in the broad area described as human resource development (HRD). The materials are written by and for professionals, including trainers, organization-development and organization-effectiveness consultants, performance-improvement technologists, facilitators, educators, instructional designers, and others.

Each *Annual* has three main sections: Experiential Learning Activities; Inventories, Questionnaires, and Surveys; and Articles and Discussion Resources. A fourth section, Editor's Choice, has been reserved for those unique contributions that do not fit neatly into one of the three main sections, but are valuable as identified by the editorial staff. Each published submission is classified in one of the following categories: Individual Development, Communication, Problem Solving, Groups, Teams, Consulting, Facilitating, Leadership, and Organizations. Within each category, pieces are further classified into logical subcategories, which are identified in the introductions to the three sections.

The Training *Annual* and the Consulting *Annual* for 2012 have a slightly different focus from past years. Both focus on the theme of Learning in the Moment, a topic that permeates our organizations and pervades all that we do as professionals in the learning and consulting arena.

The series continues to provide an opportunity for HRD professionals who wish to share their experiences, their viewpoints, and their processes with their colleagues. To that end, Pfeiffer publishes guidelines for potential authors. These guidelines are available from the Pfeiffer Editorial Department in San Francisco, California.

Materials are selected for the *Annuals* based on the quality of the ideas, applicability to real-world concerns, relevance to current HRD issues, clarity of presentation, and ability to enhance our readers' professional development. In addition, we choose experiential learning activities that will create a high degree of enthusiasm among the participants and add enjoyment to the learning process. As in the past several years, the contents of each *Annual* span a wide range of subject matter, reflecting the range of interests of our readers.

Our contributor list includes a wide selection of experts in the field: in-house practitioners, consultants, and academically based professionals. A list of contributors to the *Annual* can be found at the end of the volume, including their names, affiliations, addresses, telephone numbers, email addresses, and, when available, websites. Readers will find this list useful if they wish to locate the authors of specific pieces for feedback, comments, or questions. Further information on each contributor is presented in a brief biographical sketch that appears at the conclusion of each article. We publish this information to encourage "networking," which continues to be a valuable mainstay in the field of human resource development.

We are pleased with the high quality of material that is submitted for publication each year and often regret that we have page limitations. In addition, just as we cannot publish every manuscript we receive, you may find that not all published works are equally useful to you. Therefore, we encourage and invite ideas, materials, and suggestions that will help us to make subsequent *Annuals* as useful as possible to all of our readers.

Introduction
to the Experiential Learning Activities Section

Experiential learning activities ensure that lasting learning occurs. They should be selected with a specific learning objective in mind. These objectives are based on the participants' needs and the facilitator's skills. Although the experiential learning activities presented here all vary in goals, group size, time required, and process, they all incorporate one important element: questions that ensure learning has occurred. This discussion, led by the facilitator, assists participants to process the activity, to internalize the learning, and to relate it to their day-to-day situations. It is this element that creates the unique learning experience and learning opportunity that only an experiential learning activity can bring to the group process.

Readers have used the *Annuals'* experiential learning activities for years to enhance their training and consulting events. Each learning experience is complete and includes all lecturettes, handout content, and other written material necessary to facilitate the activity. All these materials can be found in a downloadable format on the Pfeiffer website using the code provided in this edition. In addition, many include variations of the design that the facilitator might find useful. If the activity does not fit perfectly with your objective, within your time frame, or to your group size, we encourage you to adapt the activity by adding your own variations. You will find additional experiential learning activities listed in the "Experiential Learning Activities Categories" chart that immediately follows this introduction.

The 2012 Pfeiffer Annual: Training includes sixteen activities, including two that are critical to this year's theme of Learning in the Moment: Pair/Share: Identifying Triggers to Negative Emotions and Role Montage: Discovering Leadership Influencers.

The following categories are represented:

Individual Development: Sensory Awareness

Are You Aware? Forming Impressions, by K.M. Tripathi, Rajinder Kaur Sokhi, and Mitu Mandal

Individual Development: Diversity

Twenty-Five Ways to Include Others: Taking Action, by Julie O'Mara

Communication: Awareness

Barnyard Basics: Avoiding Communication Foibles, by M.K. Key and Brenda Barker

Number Recall: Positioning Emphasis for Influence, by Paul H. Pietri and Teresa G. Weldy

Practice Role Play: Experiencing Emotional Intelligence, by Shri S.S. Roy

Communication: Listening

I See What You Mean: Sending and Receiving Messages, by Sharon Dera

Communication: Styles

†Who's in Control? Exploring an Emotional Intelligence Competency, by Dennis E. Gilbert

Groups: How Groups Work

Logos for You: Understanding Different Perspectives, by David Piltz

Groups: Negotiating/Bargaining

Rough Day @ Work: Resolving Conflict Through an Online Simulation, by Noam Ebner and Yael Efron

Consulting, Training, and Facilitating: Facilitating: Opening

**Pair/Share: Identifying Triggers to Negative Emotions, by Lou Russell

Cheering a Community: Opening with Energy, by Robert Alan Black

Consulting, Training, and Facilitating: Facilitating: Skills

Subject-Matter Expert: Learning Factual Material, by Linda M. Raudenbush

---

†Cutting-Edge Topics
**Learning in the Moment Topics

Consulting, Training, and Facilitating: Facilitating: Closing

Crossword Conundrum: Reviewing Concepts, by Margie Parikh

Leadership: Styles and Skills

**Role Montage: Discovering Leadership Influencers, by Jan M. Schmuckler

The Fugitive: Assessing the Style of a Leader, by Guido R. Britez

Organizations: Vision, Mission, Values, Strategy

Values in Leadership: Understanding the True Drivers, by Mohandas Nair

To further assist you in selecting appropriate ELAs, we provide the following grid that summarizes category, time required, group size, and risk factor for each ELA.

Category	ELA Title	Page	Time Required	Group Size	Risk Factor
Individual Development: Sensory Awareness	Are You Aware? Forming Impressions	15	80 minutes	15 to 20	Moderate
Individual Development: Diversity	Twenty-Five Ways to Include Others: Taking Action	19	25 to 30 minutes	24	Low
Communication: Awareness	Barnyard Basics: Avoiding Communication Foibles	27	Approximately 45 minutes	Any, in four groups	Moderate
Communication: Awareness	Number Recall: Positioning Emphasis for Influence	31	20 to 30 minutes	More than 15	Low
Communication: Awareness	Practice Role Play: Experiencing Emotional Intelligence	35	50 to 75 minutes	15 to 30, in groups of 3	Moderate
Communication: Listening	I See What You Mean: Sending and Receiving Messages	51	40 minutes	16 to 20 in pairs	Low
Communication: Styles	Who's in Control? Exploring an Emotional Intelligence Competency	55	60 to 70 minutes	5 to 25	Low to Moderate
Groups: How Groups Work	Logos for You: Understanding Different Perspectives	63	60 to 90 minutes	Unlimited in groups of 3 to 5	Moderate
Groups: Negotiating/ Bargaining	Rough Day @ Work: Resolving Conflict Through an Online Simulation	67	About 3 1/2 hours	Any, in groups of 3	Moderate to High
Consulting, Training, and Facilitating: Facilitating: Opening	Pair/Share: Identifying Triggers to Negative Emotions	77	15 to 60 minutes	12 to 40 in groups of 4 or 5	Low
Consulting, Training, and Facilitating: Facilitating: Opening	Cheering a Community: Opening with Energy	81	10 to 15 minutes	15 or more	Low
Consulting, Training, and Facilitating: Facilitating: Skills	Subject-Matter Expert : Learning Factual Material	83	100 minutes	24	Moderate
Consulting, Training, and Facilitating: Facilitating: Closing	Crossword Conundrum: Reviewing Concepts	87	90 minutes	Any	Low
Leadership: Styles and Skills	Role Montage: Discovering Leadership Influencers	93	45 to 60 minutes	5 to 12	Moderate
Leadership: Styles and Skills	The Fugitive: Assessing the Style of a Leader	101	60 minutes	Any	Low
Organizations: Vision, Mission, Values, Strategy	Values in Leadership: Understanding the True Drivers	105	Approximately 90 minutes	Up to 12 in trios	Moderate

Experiential Learning Activities Categories

Note that numbering system was discontinued beginning with the 2004 *Annuals*.

Are You Aware?
Forming Impressions

Activity Summary

An activity to help participants understand how impressions are formed.

Goal

- To develop participants' awareness of the ways in which they judge and form opinions about others.

Group Size

15 to 20 participants.

Time Required

Approximately 80 minutes.

Materials

- Pen and paper for each participant.

- Flip chart for posting discussion points.

- Markers.

Physical Setting

A large room with tables and chairs where the participants can be seated comfortably.

Facilitating Risk Rating

Moderate.

Process

1. Introduce the session by stating the goal of the activity. Divide the entire group into dyads randomly.

2. Tell participants to talk with their respective partners about anything personal or professional, but to keep the conversation about themselves.

   (20 minutes.)

3. Provide each participant with paper and a pen. Ask the participants to write descriptions of the impressions they have formed about their partners from the conversations.

   (15 minutes.)

4. When all the pairs have finished, form groups of four and ask each participant to present his or her description to the other three.

   (15 minutes).

5. After the presentations in the foursomes, ask the group members to discuss among themselves how each of them formed impressions about his or her partner.

   (10 minutes.)

6. Ask participants to reconvene as a large group and summarize the activity by answering these questions:

   - Which of the following features were mentioned in forming impressions?

     - Facial features, body build.

     - Vocal qualities, including speech, loudness, pitch, tone, accent, or grammatical errors.

     - Posture, facial expressions, gestures, management of body, eye contact, or other nonverbal behaviors.

     - Overall appearance, clothing, or other visual items

   - Which aspect(s) was the strongest?

   - How does past experience influence us in forming impressions of others?

   - What impact do first impressions have?

- What did you learn about yourself during this activity?

- How will you use this information in the future?

(20 minutes.)

7. During the group discussion, write the main points on the flip chart.

Submitted by K.M. Tripathi, Rajinder Kaur Sokhi, and Mitu Mandal.

K.M. Tripathi *has worked with the Defence Institute of Psychological Research as a senior research fellow since 2006. His areas of interest are organizational behavior and organizational science. He is currently pursuing his doctorate in the area of organizational trust.*

Rajinder Kaur Sokhi, Ph.D., Sc.E., *is head of the organizational behavior division and HRD at DIPR, Delhi. She completed post-graduate work in psychology from Kurukshetra University and has a master's degree in philosophy from Delhi University and a Ph.D. in psychology from M.D. University, Rohtak. She has made numerous contributions to the field of organizational behavior.*

Mitu Mandal *is senior research fellow at DIPR. She completed post-graduate work in psychology from Banaras Hindu University. She is pursuing a Ph.D. from Bharthiar University in appreciative inquiry and is involved in various research projects related to organizational behavior in DIPR.*

Twenty-Five Ways to Include Others
Taking Action

Activity Summary

A session-closing activity that facilitates individuals making a commitment to take action to include others in the workplace.

Goals

- To increase understanding of behaviors needed to create and sustain an inclusive work environment.

- To enable individuals to select one or more concrete actions they can take to include others.

- To improve the quality of actions individuals take to include others.

Group Size

24 participants.

Time Required

25 to 30 minutes.

Materials

- One copy of Twenty-Five Ways to Include Others for each participant.

- Pencils for all participants.

Physical Setting

Writing surfaces should be supplied.

Facilitating Risk Rating

Low.

Process

1. At the beginning of the session announce that at the end of the session all participants will be asked to state one action they will take to include others in the workplace. Mention that you will provide a list of twenty-five actions to select from, but that they are welcome to state any action they wish to take to include others. Suggest that throughout the session they think about what actions they may want to take.

2. At the end of the session, announce that they will now be asked to make a commitment to take action to include others in the workplace.

3. Tell participants they will have 8 minutes to read Twenty-Five Ways to Include Others and place a check mark by any action that they could reasonably take back on the job.

   (10 minutes.)

4. Say that the next step is to select one of the actions they have checked and make a commitment to start this within the next week. Tell them to write the statement and some notes about exactly what they will do in the space provided on the sheet. If they have a different action in mind, they should write it in the space provided. Remind participants that they will be asked to share their choices with the large group. Announce when 1 minute remains.

   (5 minutes.)

5. Thank participants for making their commitments and ask for a volunteer to be the first to share his or her action. Ask the person to share the action in 15 seconds or less. After that, go around the room until all have been heard from.

6. After all have shared their actions (about 8 minutes or less for 24 participants), say that you wish them success in accomplishing the actions they have selected. Suggest that they place their action statements in a prominent place at their work location or on their computers as a reminder to

complete them. If appropriate, suggest they share the selected actions with their managers and ask for assistance from the manager or others in their organizations.

7. If appropriate, summarize with some discussion of the following questions.

   - What came to mind as you were selecting your action?

   - How might this commitment change what you do daily?

Variations

- Go over the handout earlier in the session and ask participants to be thinking about which one they will commit to doing as the workshop proceeds.

- Ask participants to select two or three actions instead of only one.

- Put each action on a 5 x 8 index card and ask table groups to select five or six actions they think are most relevant for their situations and then limit their choices to one of the five or six they selected.

Submitted by Julie O'Mara.

Julie O'Mara is president of O'Mara and Associates, an organization development consulting firm specializing in leadership, facilitation, and the managing diversity process. Julie is co-author of Managing Workforce 2000: Gaining the Diversity Advantage, *author of* Diversity Activities and Training Designs, *and co-author of* Global Diversity and Inclusion Benchmarks. *She is a former national president of ASTD and currently serves as a reviewer of ASTD's Excellence in Practice Awards.*

Twenty-Five Ways to Include Others*

Step 1: Read the following actions and place a check mark by any that you could reasonably do in your organization under current circumstances.

☐   1.   Identify and be aware of my biases, assumptions, and prejudices. Consider how they may affect my attitude and behaviors at work. Recognize that prejudice is often subtle. It is quite natural to make assumptions and to possess biases toward others. When I know I'll be in a challenging situation, plan to question my biases and make decisions based on being as objective as I can.

☐   2.   Take a course or read about how to listen more effectively to understand how people hear things differently. Use my enhanced ability to listen effectively, especially with people who may have views different from mine. Listen to others as if they are wise.

☐   3.   Learn as much as possible about what happened before taking a stand on news accounts of events related to diversity. Sometimes news accounts present a one-sided view. Strive to learn other views. Discuss others' perceptions (especially those different from mine) to help me see multiple points of view.

☐   4.   Try eating different foods than I usually do. Influence the managers of our organization's cafeteria to offer vegetarian, ethnic, kosher choices, or other choices that a majority of people wouldn't normally select. An expanded menu offers additional choices for persons who regularly eat a certain type of food, and it helps others become more familiar with a culture through its food.

☐   5.   Read about cross-cultural communication, sexual orientation, and other diversity issues and apply this knowledge as I communicate with others. Sources include newspapers, business magazines, books, popular movies, etc. When reading non-business books, consider selecting those that discuss diversity-related issues. Examples are *Bury My Heart at Wounded Knee* by Dee Brown, *The Joy Luck Club* by Amy Tan, *The Kite Runner* by Khaled Hosseini, and *Breaking the Surface* by Greg Lougainis. Discuss with others the insights I gain.

☐   6.   Take a personal stand against racial or sexual jokes and storytelling. Don't tell them and don't participate or laugh at such jokes or stories told by

---

*This list of twenty-five actions is an excerpt from *101 Actions You Can Take to Include Others* by Julie O'Mara.

others. Encourage co-workers to refrain from participating in joke telling by explaining the personal and legal implications on the workplace and the workers. Expand my repertoire of jokes that are not sexist, not racist, and that don't belittle others.

☐   7. Learn effective assertive techniques to suggest others stop using the word "girls" when referring to women in the workplace, to curtail white male bashing, or to stop negative and stereotypical comments about LGBTQ persons. Generally, assertive—not aggressive—techniques are the most effective for expressing wants, needs, and ideas. Read about or take a course on assertiveness.

☐   8. Write and speak in language that is non-sexist and non-racist. Sometimes use "she" instead of "he" in written and oral communications, including videos and advertising. When using fictitious names in writing or speaking, use names from various cultures. Keep in mind the need to counter stereotypes in writing and speech. Avoid using names from one ethnic group to describe good performers and names from another group to describe poor performers. Be sure I am sensitive and vary the use of names.

☐   9. Encourage my office to celebrate and decorate for many cultural events and holidays, not just for traditional holidays, such as Christmas. Read my organization's policy regarding celebrating religious holidays.

☐ 10. Create opportunities for discussions with others about including others. Bring the topic up in one-on-one conversations, meetings, and social activities. Share my views and learn those of others.

☐ 11. Participate enthusiastically in the celebration of someone else's heritage (Black History Month, Hanukkah, Cinco de Mayo, etc.), or attend a religious service or event different from mine.

☐ 12. Have lunch or coffee once a week with a person different from me in race, age, department, education or discipline, level, and so forth. Invite others into our break and lunch circle.

☐ 13. Learn to increase my level of empathy by thinking about times in my life when I have felt different. Recalling these experiences and feelings may help me understand the difficulties others have in being different and keep me focused on sustaining a culture in my organization that values and includes others.

☐ 14. Mentor someone of a different race, gender, age group, or personality. Learn about the various types of mentoring: formal, informal, or facilitated.

☐ 15. Be flexible. The phrase "one size fits all" or procedures that treat everyone the same may have worked in the past, but often don't work with today's workforce, which wants to be treated equitably, but not the same. For example, some employees want time off, while others prefer money or an opportunity to make a presentation for a job well done. Provide choices rather than offer the same reward to all.

☐ 16. Learn to give feedback in a way that recognizes different cultures and styles.

☐ 17. Involve others in decisions that until now have been made only by those in higher levels in the organization. Strive to change the mindset that some people "aren't paid to think."

☐ 18. During a presentation or speech, share the spotlight with others who have worked on the project.

☐ 19. Form pairs or teams of people who are different in style, age, viewpoint, race, gender, or other visible differences to co-present, co-lead, or co-train. If needed, coach them in how to work collaboratively. Great teamwork facilitates inclusion.

☐ 20. Hold your peers and those who report to you accountable for exhibiting behaviors that include others.

☐ 21. Examine my assumptions about whether or not a particular person might be interested in an assignment. Sometimes I assume that single parents, people highly involved in the community, and others may not want to take on additional work or travel or that those who are younger and single are eager to take on additional work or travel or that men do not have childcare responsibilities. Give individuals an opportunity to say "yes" or "no" to assignments. Don't make decisions based on my assumptions.

☐ 22. Assess our worksite for access to persons with disabilities. Are there ramps, wide entrances? Are restroom facilities, including mirrors, sinks, towels, available to people with disabilities? Is the salad bar or buffet accessible to wheelchair users? Do emergency evacuation procedures take into account the special needs, if any, of employees with disabilities? Is technology accessible to all?

☐ 23. Be an ally by speaking up for people who are sometimes not included or are overlooked because they don't seem to "fit" the dominant culture of our organization.

☐ 24. Learn to distinguish between a performance issue and one that may be based on diversity. Honestly assess why I view the performance of each person the way I do. Be sure my assumptions and hidden biases don't get in the way of my objective view of performance.

☐ 25. Observe the social interactions of my work group to determine whether some of my colleagues feel excluded from these events. Find out why and strive to resolve these issues.

Step 2: Either select one of the actions you checked or write another action below and make a commitment to start doing this within the next week.

Barnyard Basics
Avoiding Communication Foibles

Activity Summary

An opener for meetings and training events that teaches the importance of communication and ways to improve it.

Goals

- To discuss communication foibles created by lack of a common language, no intention to communicate, and not giving the process a time and place.

- To allow group members to experience the misery of miscommunication, before addressing its solutions.

- To have some fun.

Group Size

Any, divisible into four groups.

Time Required

Approximately 45 minutes, depending on the size of the group.

Materials

- Four message cards customized for the training topic prior to the workshop.

- Flip chart and paper.

- Markers.

Physical Setting

Room for all participants to sit as well as stand and move about easily. A flip chart in the front of the room.

Facilitating Risk Rating

Moderate.

Preparation

Prepare four cards crafted for your audience or topic. Some examples might include:

- You have made an important breakthrough discovery that will revolutionize your industry. You want to tell others.

- You have discovered a very dangerous practice that will cost many lives. You want to warn others.

- You see a group (family) that is in desperate need of help, and want others to come to their rescue. Formulate your plea.

- Your group has made incredible progress and you want your patrons to know. You have an opportunity to meet with the press and officials. Tell your story with enthusiasm.

Process

1. Challenge the group by saying, "You have something very important to tell others (in _____, e.g., your organization, community, the world, or other place). Sometimes we need to consider how we deliver our messages."

2. State that you have assigned four areas in the room to four different animals: chickens, dogs, sheep, and cows. Point to each area. Ask them to select an animal and move to the area, keeping the four groups approximately the same size.

   (5 minutes.)

3. Hand out one card to each group. Tell them not to let other groups see their cards.

4. State that each of the four groups will have 5 minutes to formulate its message *in the language of the animal their group represents*. Participants will

need to use some creative thinking to speak to each other in the language of the animals. For example, for a pig, they could use grunts, oinks, and other nonverbal communication to "speak" to each other.

(10 minutes.)

5. Call time and ask the participants to mingle with the other groups and communicate their messages in the language of their assigned animals. Allow several attempts to run about 5 minutes each, and encourage additional mingling.

(15 minutes.)

6. Call time after about 15 minutes.

7. Ask, "What is required for us to get important data and messages to one another?" Record their answers on a flip chart. Responses might be:

   - Time.

   - A common language—learning others' languages.

   - Willingness to be open and earnestly listen to each other.

   - The power and significance of nonverbal communication.

   (5 minutes.)

8. Lead a discussion of the group's major learning points.

   - What skills are most critical to good communication?

   - What is the most important idea you are taking away from what happened here today?

   - How will you incorporate this idea in other situations?

   (10 minutes.)

Variations

   - Ask each subgroup to communicate its message to the whole room all at one time, using their assigned animal language and nonverbal gestures.

   - Change the animal subgroup titles to relevant subgroups of their organization or different language groups (for diversity training).

- Ask everyone to use Pig Latin. See www.idioma-software.com/pig/pig_latin.html.

- Ask subgroups to use only nonverbals, no language—mainly grunts, sighs, and gestures.

Submitted by M.K. Key and Brenda Barker.

M.K. Key, Ph.D., *is a licensed psychologist and the founder and principal of Key Associates in Nashville, Tennessee. She is a nationally recognized speaker on leadership, releasing the creative spirit, mediation of conflict, and team development. She has authored more than thirty publications on such topics as change management, continuous quality improvement, strategic business issues, and leadership during turbulent times. Her most recent releases are Corporate Celebration: Play, Purpose, and Profit at Work, with Terrence E. Deal (1998), and Managing Change in Healthcare: Innovative Solutions for People-Based Organizations (1999). She has also served as an adjunct professor of organization and human development at Vanderbilt University.*

Brenda Barker, M.Ed., *is the project manager of the Tennessee Initiative for Prenatal Care (TIPQC). She has been an educator, speaker, author, counselor, and social worker for the last fourteen years and has worked in international medical relief and adoptions as the southeast regional director of one of the largest U.S. children's humanitarian and adoption organizations, overseeing four U.S. offices and a team in eleven states. She has worked extensively around the world with government officials and orphanages and at-risk children and their families. Brenda has been an activist on women's issues, serving on President Carter's National Advisory Committee for Women and has received numerous honors, including a U.S. Congressional Award. Brenda was chosen the Ambassador of the Year and Volunteer of the Year, and her family was honored as the Family of the Year for the Tennessee Leukemia and Lymphoma Society.*

Number Recall
Positioning Emphasis for Influence

Activity Summary

Unusual activity that takes only a few minutes for participants to experience a critical communication skill.

Goals

- To explore the role of emphasis in communicating.

- To demonstrate the degree of emphasis in the beginning, middle, and end of a message.

Group Size

More than 15 works best.

Time Required

20 to 30 minutes.

Materials

- Paper and pen or pencil for each participant.

- Flip chart or whiteboard and markers.

Physical Setting

Any comfortable room where a flip chart or whiteboard is visible to the entire group.

Facilitating Risk Rating

Low.

Process

1. Tell the group: "We are going to conduct an experiment to see who has the best memory. I am going to call out a series of eight numbers, which I want you to try to remember. Each will be a two-digit number, and I will pause after calling each. You do not need to remember the sequence of the numbers, only the numbers called. You may not write the numbers down or do anything special to remember the numbers after I've called them out. Just try to remember as many as you can."

2. Call out the numbers to the group. Pause for about half a second before calling each number in the sequence. Pause slightly after calling the last number. The numbers are as follows. (*Note:* any numbers may be used. These are listed only as an illustration).

   23   97   62   58   84   73   32   45
   (5 minutes.)

3. Reinforce the instructions by saying, "Now don't write these down or mention the numbers to anyone else. Just hang on to them for a while. We'll get back to them shortly."

4. It's important to distract participants before having them recall the numbers. Perhaps continue with the subject being discussed for about 5 minutes or let the group take a short break. If giving a break, however, remind participants that they may not mention a number to anyone, write any numbers down, or do anything to specifically help them recall a number(s).

5. After 5 to 10 minutes, say to the group, "Ok, let's see how many of the numbers you can remember. Please write down any of the eight numbers that you remember. It's ok to guess, and the numbers don't have to be in order." While the participants are writing, draw Chart 1 on the board with the number of participants in the group on the Y axis and leave the X axis

blank. You will use this template to record the number of individuals who correctly remembered each number.

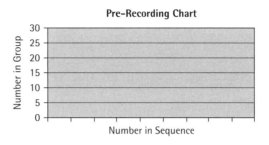

Pre-Recording Chart

6. Ask the participants to raise their hands if they have the number 23 written down. Write the number 23 on the X axis and record the number of people who remembered it. Do the same for each of the remaining numbers by calling the numbers out in sequence and recording the number of participants who recalled each number. (*Note:* the number most remembered will be the first number, likely followed by the second number. The series will then drop off, with an increased number of participants recalling the last number.) Results for a typical group of thirty people might look something like Chart 2.

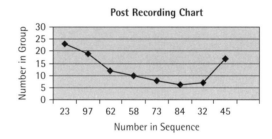

Post Recording Chart

(5 minutes.)

7. Circle the scores for the first two numbers in the sequence. Also circle the score for the last number.

8. Tell the group that unless you called out a number that coincided with a participant's age or a local highway number, the numbers should not have any significant meaning for them. The only variable affecting their recall was the sequence in which the numbers were called.

9. Debrief the activity using the following questions:

   • What positions seem to be the most memorable in communications? The least memorable?

- So what does that tell you about messages you want to deliver?

- Can you think of any common expressions or examples that reflect what you've experienced? Examples might be:

  - "First impressions are lasting."

  - "You never get a second chance to make a good first impression."

  - "Most juries make up their minds about a case's outcome after hearing the opening arguments."

  - "If you need to cover yourself by being on record, but want to bury it, stick it somewhere in the middle."

  - "Rules for giving instructions: tell them what you're going to tell them, then tell them, then tell them what you told them."

- What will you do differently when communicating information to others based on what you learned from this activity?

  (15 minutes.)

10. Conclude by saying, "Strategically, where we position information in our messages is instrumental in achieving our communication goals."

Submitted by Paul H. Pietri and Teresa G. Weldy.

Paul H. Pietri, D.B.A., *is a professor of management at the University of South Alabama in Mobile, Alabama. He has been a consultant and trainer for over thirty years. Dr. Pietri is author of ten books, including the current* Management: Leadership in Action *and* Supervisory Management: The Art of Inspiring, Empowering, and Developing People *(7th ed.).*

Teresa G. Weldy, Ph.D., *is an associate professor of management at the University of South Alabama in Mobile, Alabama. She has conducted training sessions in communication, leadership, conflict management, and organizational change. Dr. Weldy's research has been published in the* Journal of Education for Business, Journal of Business Communication, *and the* Learning Organization, *and the* Journal of Academic Administration in Higher Education.

Practice Role Play
Experiencing Emotional Intelligence

Activity Summary

An activity that allows participants to experience the impact of emotional intelligence.

Goal

- To experience the impact of emotional intelligence in the workplace.

Group Size

15 to 30 participants who are familiar with the concepts of EI, in groups of 3.

Time Required

60 to 75 minutes.

Materials

- One copy of the Practice Role Play Instructions for each participant.
- Sets of Practice Role Play Cases 1 through 6, one set per triad.
- Flip chart and markers.

Physical Setting

A room large enough for the groups to work without disturbing one another.

Facilitating Risk Rating

Moderate.

Process

1. Explain the objective of the activity. You may tell participants that they are about to do something interesting that will be fun and also will provide them with practical learning.

2. Divide the participants into groups of three. Any persons remaining can be observers.

3. Have each trio sit away from the other trios in different parts of the room. Give every participant in all trios a copy of the instructions. Then give one member of each trio the boss role and the other two members the *same* subordinate role. (There are six cases provided, enough for eighteen participants, three per case. Additional participants can be given duplicate role plays. The number of participants to complete the role plays can be adjusted based on the group size and time available.)

4. In each trio, one person plays the boss or manager twice and the other two participants switch off playing the second role. One time the "boss" plays someone with high EI and the other time plays a person with low EI. Ask each trio to decide who will play the "boss" role.

   (5 minutes.)

5. Tell the trios that the "boss must decide how to play the role two ways" and that each role play should take about 2 minutes. Answer any questions and allow preparation time of about 10 minutes.

   (15 minutes.)

6. Ask the participants to act out their plays for the entire group. Participants will experience someone dealing with a person with high EI and someone with low EI.

   (5 minutes per trio, up to 30 minutes for six trios.)

7. At the end of the role plays, reconvene participants into one large group and ask them to share what they have learned. Some of the debriefing questions may include:

   • How did you feel playing someone with high EI?

   • How did you feel playing someone with low EI?

   • How did you feel dealing with the person with high EI?

   • How did you feel dealing with the person with low EI?

- What differences did you observe between the two?

- What is the importance of emotional intelligence in our lives?

- How does what happened during the role plays relate to some of your experiences in real life?

- Based on what you have learned, how do you think we should respond to others?

- What positive or negative qualities did the role players display?

- What is the most important thing you learned today?

- How will you implement what you learned back on the job?

(20 minutes.)

Variation

- You may wish to conclude with conceptual input on the EI models by Daniel Goleman, Claude Steiner, or others.

Submitted by Shri S.S. Roy.

Shri S.S. Roy, MBA, *is a senior faculty in BHEL, HRD Institute, Noida, India, in the area of marketing, contracts, behavioral sciences, negotiation skills, and team building. He holds a B.S. in mechanical engineering from Delhi College of Engineering and an MBA in marketing management. Shri is a proficient public speaker and presenter. Trained under several eminent faculty of India, including the late Professor Ramanathan, he has trained more than fifteen hundred people from all parts of India. He is a certified NLP practitioner and a certified T-group trainer of ISABS. Shri believes strongly that adults learn better through experience. Therefore, all his programs are highly oriented toward role play, case discussions, and experiential methods—learning by doing.*

Practice Role Play Instructions

Instructions: You will prepare two short plays of about 2 minutes each. One person will play the supervisor role both times. The other two will take turns playing the subordinate. The "boss" will play his or her role as a person with high emotional intelligence the first time and as a person with low emotional intelligence the second.

Practice Role Play Case 1: Boss

You feel like you are on top of the world. Such fine days come rarely.

It started with the news that your son was admitted to the most prestigious engineering college in the country. You had just entered the office when the general manager called you and informed you of a substantial raise in salary due to your excellent work. Just now your doctor called to say that your medical reports are fine and all your anxiety of some serious ailment are unfounded.

You are feeling absolutely relaxed and joyful and would like to share your happiness with someone. You were thinking of calling your assistant to tell him/her the good news. Just then your assistant walked in.

Practice Role Play Case 1: Assistant

You were working in the office on a very important task when you received a phone call that your son has met with an accident. You are extremely worried because the caller only told you the hospital address and asked you to come there at once. He did not give you any information about how your son is or the problem.

You must inform your boss of the situation and rush to the hospital.

Practice Role Play Case 2: Marketing Manager

The market is very tough and orders are not coming in. You are doing your best and also telling your people to put in more effort. Your superiors are constantly pressurizing you to show better results, as the position of your company is declining. While they appreciate your difficulties, the situation is very embarrassing for you. You are constantly under stress in your job. You think your people are most likely giving too many concessions to strike deals. You are thinking of calling your marketing executive and giving him/her a piece of your mind. Just then he/she walks in.

Practice Role Play Case 2: Marketing Executive

You have been working very hard for the last six months to secure a large contract of a very high value. It is also a very prestigious job. The client knows it well and has been acting difficult. He is also unethical at times and goes back on some agreements. Because of this, you have been finding it very difficult to strike a deal.

Despite all odds and due to your perseverance and persuasive skills, you have finally managed to beat all your competitors and have bagged the contract. Although you made concessions, it is still a very attractive deal. You are highly excited about it and you rush to your boss to break the news.

Practice Role Play Case 3: Finance Manager

You have had a bad day what with all the problems you have had since morning. The alarm clock did not ring; you cut yourself badly while shaving in a hurry; the door to your house jammed; and the car had a flat tire. To top it off, you missed an appointment with the CEO and he was furious. Things could not have been worse.

The CEO wants to see the accounts statement first thing in the morning. You have asked your accounts officer to prepare the statement quickly because it will take at least one hour for you to check it.

You have a splitting headache and you feel like leaving everything and rushing home. It is just 10 minutes to closing time and your accounts officer is still not ready with the statement.

Practice Role Play Case 3: Accounts Officer

It is 6 p.m. You are preparing an urgent statement of trial balance. It is to be cleared by the finance manager and then presented to the CEO first thing tomorrow. The finance manager told you to finish it quickly because he/she was not feeling well and wanted to go home early. But there are many loose ends and, in spite of your best efforts, you just completed the draft.

It is a four-page statement and you know it will take a minimum of an hour to check. Your boss has called you and wants to see the statement immediately.

Practice Role Play Case 4: Supervisor

Work on the shop floor is very high-pressure. There are too many orders and the delivery schedule is also very tight. Some slippages have taken place in commitments to customers, and management is not happy about it. The production manager called you this morning and made it clear that every worker must be supervised very strictly. Close watch is to be kept so that people do not waste any time on the machines. You have been asked to make regular rounds of the shop floor to maintain strict discipline. You are making a round and see one worker sitting idle. The person's machine is even turned off. This is just too much!

Practice Role Play Case 4: Worker

You are a hard worker. Just now while you were working on the lathe, you received a message that one of your dearest friends has been admitted to a hospital. He is in the last stage of terminal cancer and is not expected to make it through the week.

You are shocked and shaken. Your hands are unsteady and you are afraid that if you continue work in this state of mind you may spoil the job on the machine, so you shut off the machine and are taking a two-minute break to compose yourself.

Just then, your supervisor walks in and sees you sitting idle.

Practice Role Play Case 5: Boss

You believe that all people are truthful and sincere and have been treating your subordinates accordingly, with respect. You have, however, been told by your superior that some people are taking undue advantage of this. You have therefore decided to be stricter now and want to enforce discipline. Your first target is your subordinate, Anna, whom you have observed coming late, leaving early, missing from her desk at times, and also spending time on personal business while important work is piling up. You call Anna.

Practice Role Play Case 5: Subordinate

Your spouse is not well and is currently bedridden. This puts much pressure on you. Besides managing the house, you also have to go to the doctor, pathology lab, and pharmacy and have other responsibilities connected to his treatment. You would like to take leave and be with your spouse but there are very important jobs at the office. You are somehow managing to deal with both your home and office responsibilities simultaneously. You have been taking some work home to stay on top of it all. You have not, however, shared this with your colleagues, thinking that they would not understand.

You have not been able to come to the office on time on three or four occasions this month and had to reschedule or cancel some of your appointments. Today again you came in about half an hour late and have heard that the boss is looking for you. Your boss has called you to his office and you guess that he wants to talk to you about this issue.

Practice Role Play Case 6: Block Development Officer

You are responsible for appraising loan applications and disbursal of loans for development activities in your department. The responsibility requires you to thoroughly study the loan applications so that loans are given to truly deserving individuals, are utilized properly, and are also repaid on time. Your work requires you to deal with several types of people, including farmers, entrepreneurs, industrialists, and others. You come across people who are smooth talkers but may be unscrupulous and also people who have very poor communication skills but who are genuine. There cannot be any generalization, and you have to assess each case patiently and painstakingly on merit.

Today you have had a bad time—nothing went right. Things could not have been worse. Your work for the day is just finished and you are getting ready to leave this mess for today. Just now, a new client walks in. He looks like a tramp, with an overgrown beard, crumpled clothes, and rough manners.

The 2012 Pfeiffer Annual: Training.

Practice Role Play Case 6: Entrepreneur

You started your own company. Although the idea was good, you suffered losses due to a breakup with your business partner. This has left you shaken, but you are confident that, with some financial support, you will be able to put your business back on track and make a reasonable profit after recovering your losses and paying back the loan. You are approaching the block development officer for your case to ask for a loan.

You were running late to make it today and have not had time to clean up.

I See What You Mean
Sending and Receiving Messages

Activity Summary

A hands-on activity that demonstrates the importance of complete and correct communication from both the sender's and receiver's perspectives.

Goals

- To articulate the difficulty of communication.

- To practice listening and following directions.

- To experience both the sender and receiver roles when communication is difficult.

Group Size

16 to 20 participants, in pairs.

Time Required

40 minutes.

Materials

- Deck of playing cards.

- One clipboard per pair.

- Copyright-free clipart images, each on a separate sheet of paper, one image per pair (see examples).

- One copy of the I See What You Mean Image Examples for the facilitator.

- One blank sheet of paper for each participant.
- One pencil for each participant.

Physical Setting

Room for pairs to sit back-to-back, spaced comfortably away from others.

Facilitating Risk Rating

Low.

Preparation

Select pairs of cards from the deck of playing cards, e.g., 2 aces, 2 kings, 2 queens, 2 jacks, 2 tens, equal to the number of people in the session.

Process

1. Shuffle the playing cards to mix playing card pairs. Fan out the cards. Holding them face toward you, move around the room asking participants to each select one of the playing cards, until everyone has one card.

2. Ask participants to look at their cards and find the people holding the cards that complete the pairs. Ask each pair to move their chairs to form back-to-back seats.

3. Ask each of the pairs to sit in one of the back-to-back seats and hand a clipboard to each pair.

4. Assign activity roles. One person will be the sender and give instructions. The other person will be the receiver and draw the image being described. To be equitable, select sender roles by stating, "The person whose first letter of his or her first name appears in the alphabet first will be the first sender." Give each person blank paper and a pencil.

   (5 minutes.)

5. Tell the pairs the receiver can ask questions, but neither sender nor receiver can look at the other or look at the other person's paper during the activity.

6. Give each pair a different image and tell the senders that they have 5 minutes to describe what the receiver is to draw.

7. Allow 5 minutes, then stop the activity and ask the senders to look at the receivers' rendition of the communicated instructions.

   (5 minutes.)

8. Ask the pairs to switch roles.

9. Collect the clipart images from the pairs, shuffle the images, and redistribute them, ensuring each pair is working with a different image. Tell the new senders to begin giving directions to their receivers.

(5 minutes.)

10. Again, allow 5 minutes for the activity, then stop the activity and ask the senders to look at the receivers' renditions of the communicated instructions.

(5 minutes.)

11. Allow a few minutes for the pairs to examine the results. Debrief the activity using questions such as these:

   • What happened? Why?

   • How does this activity relate to communication?

   • What worked well?

   • Did pairs change their approach after seeing the first results? In what way?

   • What could you have done differently?

   • How can you translate what you did here to communication on a daily basis?

   • What will you do differently as a result of experiencing this activity?

   (15 minutes.)

Submitted by Sharon Dera.

Sharon Dera, MBA, CPLP, *has more than seventeen years of experience in needs assessment, human performance, process improvement, and organization development. Her broad experience was acquired by working in the retail, finance, healthcare, government, manufacturing, hospitality, and travel industries in operations, business management, customer service, sales, communications, marketing, succession planning, leadership, coaching, and training. Sharon is owner and CEO of The Proficience Group, Inc., working in partnership with organizations to identify the root cause of performance deficiencies and determine the best solutions/interventions that close the performance gap. The company lends a "fresh set of eyes," exposing possible blind spots.*

I See What You Mean Image Examples

Who's in Control?
Exploring an Emotional Intelligence Competency

Activity Summary

An individual discovery activity that stimulates thought and encourages participants to gain a deeper understanding of self-control and its relationship to emotional intelligence in the workplace.

Goals

- To develop awareness about self-control and its relationship to emotional intelligence.

- To discover how self-control and the management of our emotions affect individual and group performance in the workplace.

- To discover relationships between self-control and motivation.

Group Size

Best suited for 5 to 25 participants.

Time Required

60 to 70 minutes.

Materials

- One copy of the Who's in Control Mini-Assessment for each participant.

- One copy of the Who's in Control? Debriefing Guide for the facilitator.

- Whiteboard or flip chart and paper for the facilitator.

- Markers.

- Pen or pencil for each participant.

Physical Setting

Participants should have a writing surface and enough space to form pairs or small groups for break-out discussions without interfering with one another.

Facilitating Risk Rating

Low to Moderate.

Process

1. Introduce the session by presenting the activity goals and state that this activity is designed to expand the participants' consideration of self-control, to learn its relationship to emotional intelligence, and to discuss how to properly manage emotions in the workplace. Say that the activity is not about right or wrong answers but is intended to stimulate discussion and to help them discover a greater appreciation for self-control. Additionally, participants may consider the role self-control and emotion management play in groups and teams. Answer any initial questions before beginning.

   (2 or 3 minutes.)

2. Explain to participants that the first task in this activity is to individually complete the self-assessment. Distribute the Mini-Assessment and writing instruments and ask participants to circle the word after each statement that seems to best match their typical behavior. The objective is not to answer "correctly" but to provide honest answers as they assess themselves. Ask participants to place their pencils/pens down and to remain quiet until all have completed the assessment.

   (6 to 8 minutes.)

3. When all participants have completed the Mini-Assessment, debrief by using the Debriefing Guide. Keep in mind that some participants may challenge the suggested results. This is acceptable and an integral part of the knowledge exchange and transfer for this activity. You may ask the participants to "shout out" which way the statement should lean before

providing your response. This keeps the participants engaged and adds excitement to the activity. Facilitate discussions as appropriate, using the guide as a reference.

(15 minutes.)

4. Break the group into subgroups or partners. Ask participants to select three statements in the Mini-Assessment that they find most interesting or relevant to their own experiences. Each partner or subgroup member should spend a few minutes to discuss his or her selections and what actions could be taken to improve in that area.

(20 minutes.)

5. Bring the entire group back together. Using a whiteboard or flip chart to capture insights, ask the following questions to debrief the activity:

   • What statements, if any, were also selected by several within your subgroup? Why are there similarities or differences among your selections?

   • What statement best matches the area in which you would like to improve the most? Why?

   • In what additional ways does this assessment relate to emotional intelligence in the workplace?

   • What will you do differently in the future as a result of what you have learned by participating in this activity?

(15 minutes.)

6. Wrap up the activity by aligning discussions and observations to the opening activity goals. Address any final questions.

(5 minutes.)

Facilitator's Note

Additional ways that this assessment may relate to emotional intelligence could include the idea that emotional intelligence is not just about being nice. It is not about entirely suppressing emotions; in fact, in some cases you may be trying to draw out emotions. Occupations such as bill collectors, retail clerks, flight attendants, and others that require you to improve relationships with people represent examples where drawing out emotions may be helpful. Everything is about balance. The trouble with our emotions, and those of others, is that in high-stress or uncomfortable situations we sometimes react inappropriately. When we have more knowledge about emotional control and intelligence, we can work more effectively together and better manage our environment in the workplace.

Variations

- Partnered pairs instead of small groups will typically process faster.

- This activity can be shortened by not breaking out into the subgroup activity (Step 4).

Submitted by Dennis E. Gilbert.

Dennis E. Gilbert *is the president of Appreciative Strategies, LLC, a human performance improvement training and consulting business. He combines his expertise in private for-profit business management with his experience in the non-profit educational sector to deliver outstanding results through training and consultation. An accomplished consultant, trainer, and coach, he delivers exceptional human performance improvement solutions to businesses and organizations. His focus is on leadership development, communication, and group dynamics.*

Who's in Control? Mini-Assessment

Instructions: Circle the word after each statement that best matches your typical behavior. Your first reaction is probably best.

1. When I receive unexpected bad news I patiently think before I speak.
   Usually   Occasionally   Seldom

2. If I feel my emotions kicking in, I mentally regroup and control my impulsive reactions.   Usually   Occasionally   Seldom

3. I feel agitated about new ideas and directions; I feel they detract from our productivity.   Usually   Occasionally   Seldom

4. In stressful confrontational situations, I thrive, always being prepared to turn an issue into a debate.
   Usually   Occasionally   Seldom

5. When someone critiques my work (unfavorably), I seek additional feedback instead of immediately defending my position.
   Usually   Occasionally   Seldom

6. I accept change to a plan by staying flexible.
   Usually   Occasionally   Seldom

7. My work is not affected by my mood. I stay on task and I am not lured into time-wasting pleasures or insignificant distractions.
   Usually   Occasionally   Seldom

8. So many disruptions happen in my work life that I become very upset and feel like quitting.   Usually   Occasionally   Seldom

9. During workplace discussions I feel swamped by anxiety and avoid contributing.   Usually   Occasionally   Seldom

10. When I am angry about work issues, I stay focused on fixing the problem in a positive, forward-thinking manner.
    Usually   Occasionally   Seldom

11. At work I suppress all feelings and spontaneity about upsetting issues.
    Usually   Occasionally   Seldom

12. To avoid making situations worse, I remain silent about my true thoughts on subjects or issues.   Usually   Occasionally   Seldom

The 2012 Pfeiffer Annual: Training.
Copyright © 2012 by John Wiley & Sons, Inc. Reproduced by permission of Pfeiffer, an Imprint of Wiley. www.pfeiffer.com

Who's in Control? Debriefing Guide

After all participants have completed the Mini-Assessment, utilize the following guide to debrief each statement.

1. When I receive unexpected bad news, I patiently think before I speak.

   Your response: "This answer should lean toward *usually.*" This is a great example of effectively utilizing emotional intelligence to practice self-control. This could be labeled one of the golden rules of effective communication.

2. If I feel my emotions kicking in, I mentally regroup and control impulsive reactions.

   Your response: "This answer should lean toward *usually.*" Persons who are effective at self-control can feel their emotions starting to boil and take appropriate action to contain strike-outs and strike-backs based on impulse. If we react on impulse, we may make big mistakes.

3. I feel agitated about new ideas and directions; I feel they detract from our productivity.

   Your response: "This answer should lean toward *seldom.*" Being receptive to change (transition is emotional) is important in most workplace environments. Even though in some cases we cannot control the change itself, we can control our responses or reactions.

4. In stressful confrontational situations, I thrive, always being prepared to turn an issue into a debate.

   Your response: "This answer should lean toward *seldom.*" Debates typically create winners or losers; a person well skilled in emotional intelligence would most likely not want to create a win/lose situation.

5. When someone critiques my work (unfavorably), I seek additional feedback instead of immediately defending my position.

   Your response: "This answer should lean toward *usually.*" We should consider seeking additional feedback first, before reacting. Not that we should never defend ourselves, but we should consider reactions as feedback and not as a strike at us; and if it is, we should still keep our composure.

6. I accept change to a plan by staying flexible.

   Your response: "This answer should lean toward *usually*." Most work-place strategies should allow for the change process to be somewhat fluid. Employees who embrace change while staying flexible will not only process the change more quickly but they will help the entire team improve trust and morale.

7. My work is not affected by my mood. I stay on task and I am not lured into time-wasting pleasures or insignificant distractions.

   Your response: "This answer should lean toward *usually*." Good emotional self-control means we can stay focused on the task at hand. We avoid day-dreaming, gossiping, Internet surfing, or other non-productive activities.

8. So many disruptions happen in my work life that I become very upset and feel like quitting.

   Your response: "This answer should lean toward *seldom*." If this is happening to you, you may feel that you don't have control over your fate. You do, but it starts by managing the situations around you. Sometimes a difficult boss may make life very challenging.

9. During workplace discussions, I feel swamped by anxiety and avoid contributing.

   Your response: "This answer should lean toward *seldom*." We have to learn to control anxiety; in some cases anxiety can even be a motivator. Avoiding issues will almost never resolve them.

10. When I am angry about work issues, I stay focused on fixing the problem in a positive forward-thinking manner.

    Your response: "This answer should lean toward *usually*." Anger, when well managed, can be a powerful source of positive motivation.

11. At work I suppress all feelings and spontaneity about upsetting issues.

    Your response: "This answer should lean toward *seldom*." This may be called over-control. While thinking before we speak is good, suppressing all emotions can be very harmful. Find the right balance.

12. To avoid making situations worse, I remain silent about my true thoughts on subjects or issues.

    Your response: "This answer should lean toward *seldom*." As with Question 9, avoiding issues altogether can be counterproductive and may cause many other problems, including harm to our physical health.

Logos for You
Understanding Different Perspectives

Activity Summary

A creative activity that allows participants to actively create, apply, and synthesize learning material.

Goals

- To discuss differences in perspective.

- To practice a creative and practical application of content.

Group Size

An unlimited number of subgroups of 3 to 5 who have attended a workshop on a specific topic.

Time Required

60 to 90 minutes.

Materials

- Participants' notes from a workshop.

- Flip-chart paper and felt-tipped markers for each subgroup.

- (Optional) Additional craft material can be provided for each group, such as Play-Doh, craft sticks, pipe cleaners, etc.

- One electronic device per group to take still pictures that can be downloaded to a computer for viewing.

- Evaluation criteria for each subgroup.

Physical Setting

A room large enough for the groups to work without disturbing one another. Ideally, a location in which groups can easily access other areas than the training room, such as hotel lobbies and outdoor places.

Facilitating Risk Rating

Moderate.

Process

1. Explain that the goal of the activity is to create a still picture representing either an ad campaign or a scene that clearly illustrates the training content being reviewed.

2. Ask participants to examine their notes from the training session. If they are to concentrate on only one area of learning, assign the area. Groups can be assigned the same content to illustrate diversity in perspectives, or groups can have different portions of the content.

3. Divide the participants into teams of three to five (or smaller depending on the number of participants). You can do this by traditional numbering or by asking participants to form groups with those next to them.

4. Tell participants that the activity has two rounds plus a debriefing session. Neither round will have a strict time limit, although Round 1 will take the longest.

   (5 minutes.)

5. Tell participants that during Round 1, each group decides whether they are going to create an ad or a scene to fully illustrate their assigned content.

6. Ask each group to be as creative and original as possible. Each ad or scene that is captured by a photo should:

   • Have everyone as part of the photo in some way.

   • Use whatever is around but not break any laws.

   • Clearly illustrate the group's content.

7. Tell them that the ad or scene can be anything illustrative of the training content. Provide examples of common ads. Examples could be:

- An Olympic sporting event in which the winner is clearly identified.

- A crime scene in which the crime is very obvious.

- A movie blooper.

8. Start Round 1. Depending on the amount and complexity of content each group has to summarize, give them from 30 to 60 minutes. Remind everyone that the end result of Round 1 is a still picture of an ad or scene that can be downloaded to a computer for viewing in the large group.

   (30 to 60 minutes.)

9. At the end of the time allotted, ask groups to provide their photos of their ad or scene. Lead applause as each group displays its photo.

10. Start Round 2 by asking for a volunteer from each group. Ask the volunteers to form their own (new) group. They are now the "evaluators." Provide everyone with evaluation criteria such as:

    - Originality.

    - Creativity.

    - Clearly illustrates the content.

    - Easy to interpret.

11. Ask the evaluator group to agree on how they will use the criteria to judge each group's submission. Will they use a yes/no or a Likert-type scale?

12. Have groups share their photos and allow about 10 minutes for the evaluators to evaluate/score the photos.

    (10 minutes.)

13. While the evaluators are completing their task, have the original subgroups discuss their own products and evaluate them against the same criteria.

14. Have the evaluators share the scores and announce the winner.

    (5 minutes.)

15. Lead a processing discussion based on the following questions:

    - What made this activity difficult?

    - Are these types of challenges a factor when you are learning or reviewing information in the workplace? Why or why not?

- What was easy about this activity? When is learning information easy for you?

- What different perspectives came out within your group?

- How do these different perspectives represent what happens daily back on the job?

- Did needing to describe the content through a photo present a challenge? How was this situation similar or dissimilar to your workplace?

- How did introducing evaluators change the dynamic?

- What role does individual perspective play in daily life?

- How is this similar or dissimilar to your work environment?

- What is your greatest learning from this activity?

  (10 minutes.)

Variation

- Instead of using material that needs to be learned, consider the content to be goals, strategy, or tactics for visioning and strategic planning.

Submitted by David Piltz.

David Piltz *is an associate of CapitolMed, a company experienced in creating learning games and experiences for all ages in areas such as sales training and specialty- industry-focused topics. He has been creating and offering programs in leadership, organizational and educational change, communication, teamwork, customer service, and personal and professional effectiveness for more than fifteen years. He developed* The House That Cards Built *and* Picture This.

Rough Day @ Work
Resolving Conflict Through an Online Simulation

Activity Summary

An online role-play simulation designed to help managers improve and increase their skills in managing intra-organizational conflict.

Goals

- To allow participants to practice their negotiation and communication skills.

- To give participants an opportunity to explore conflict management.

- To encourage individuals to use online communication for negotiation and conflict management.

Group Size

Any number, divided into small groups of 3 participants each.

Time Required

Participant Preparation Time: 20 to 30 minutes.

Running Time: This depends on the communication method. If performed asynchronously, such as by email, any period from five days to two weeks can be allotted to the simulation; one week is recommended. If performed in a synchronous fashion (such as by instant messaging), it is recommended to have participants clear two hours for the activity.

Debriefing Time: A face-to-face or online synchronous debriefing of this simulation can take 45 to 60 minutes.

Materials

Each participant receives an instruction sheet or an email with role material, according to the role he or she is assigned:

- Rough Day @ Work: Instructions for Party A

- Rough Day @ Work: Instructions for Party B

- Rough Day @ Work: Instructions for the HR Mediator

Physical Setting

In the framework of an online training program or between sessions of a face-to-face training program.

Facilitating Risk Rating

Moderate to High.

Facilitator's Note

The following steps can all be conducted in pre- or post-simulation face-to-face sessions, or they can be conducted online by posting notices through a course management system or via email.

Participants are usually quite comfortable in their roles and capable of managing this simulation with very little external tweaking. It is recommended that you let participants play it out in whatever way they see fit. You might choose to intervene with process tips or reminders (for example, reminding the HR representatives they might like to initiate private sessions or behind-the-scenes communication with each party).

Process

1. Explain to participants that this activity is a simulation designed to help them learn conflict-management skills. In the scenario, two co-workers suffer intense clashes of style and personality. Their constant bickering is affecting not only their own productivity, but that of the entire department. Their manager refers them to a new online mediation program administered by the human resources department.

2. Divide participants into groups of three to play the two parties and a mediator. Extra participants can be assigned to be co-mediators in an existing group. Assign one participant in each group to each role, and distribute

the role material. Make sure that all participants in each group have sufficient contact information for others in their group.

3. Explain the procedure you expect participants to follow for communication and the platform or medium you intend them to conduct this simulation through. While the story line indicates email exchanges, you can give instructions to conduct the negotiation through videoconferencing or via a text-based medium such as a threaded discussion forum. Instruct participants on any technological issues they need to know about and the timeframe for conducting the simulation.

4. Instruct participants to read their role material carefully and to try to flesh out their instructions with their own knowledge, emotions, and experience. Explain that through "owning" the roles in this manner, the simulation will not only become more lifelike, but it will also enable them to understand what parties to a conflict managed online by a third party truly experience, enabling them to transfer insights to real-life situations.

5. Instruct the mediators to consider the type of process they wish to manage, its ground rules, the stages of the process, and the atmosphere they wish to create. Remind them that they are not being tested; rather, they are being given a chance to try out their skills and to improve them. If mediators are working together in pairs (co-mediation), suggest they take time to coordinate their efforts.

6. Instruct the mediators that it is their job to initiate the process by reaching out to the parties; they are responsible for making first contact.

7. The simulation ends when parties reach either an agreement or an insurmountable impasse. If time constraints demand, the simulation can be cut off at any point in time.

8. Afterward, collect the mediation results from participants in one of the following ways:

   • Have them send you an email showing only the outcome. To ensure that the outcome you receive is an accurate representation of the parties' agreement, ask that one participant in the mediation group (or the mediator) email the outcome to you, sending a copy to the other parties so that they can follow up on any inaccuracies.

   • Have them provide the chain of emails leading to the outcome. Most email-reading programs embed a previous note in a reply; accordingly, the mediation conversation is "captured" as the chain of emails comprising the mediation grows. You might prefer to see not only the final outcome, but also the back-and-forth email chain. The last participant to agree to the final outcome, or the mediator, can simply forward you the whole email chain, including the outcome (being sure to cc the other parties).

- Have them copy (cc) you on every message sent to the other parties. Although this might inflict heavy incoming email volume upon your inbox, it allows you to keep an eye on simulation progress in case any special intervention is required.

9. If you are using a full-featured email client program (such as Microsoft Outlook) that allows the user to create rules for handling incoming mail, here's a way to make the heavy email traffic a little more manageable:

- Instruct participants to include a particular keyword (e.g., "RoughGroupA") in the subject line of all emails during the simulation, and

- Create a rule that automatically moves emails having that word in the subject line into a designated folder. This kind of rule automatically steers negotiation email traffic into a separate place, away from your other inbox messages.

10. Debrief the process in one of four ways: face-to-face; online synchronously; online asynchronously; or through individual reflection. See the hints below for each type:

- *Face-to-Face/Online Synchronous Debriefing.* Begin by asking which of the groups reached agreement and ask a couple of them for the main points of their agreements; ask a group that did not reach agreement whether there had been a last refused offer on the table (this is done mainly to allow participants still engrossed in the simulation to join the group, others to vent a bit, and to stress in general the joint-but-separate experience of the groups, transforming them back into one large learning-group). Afterward, focus the discussion on specific themes, according to training goals and the dynamics that unfolded in the different groups' processes. Some possible questions by category include:

  - *Negotiation Strategy:* How would the parties define their overall beginning strategy? (Help participants frame a short strategic definition, such as "working cooperatively" or "trying to humiliate the other guy.")

  - *Online Communication Skills:* What communication tools did the parties and the mediators use throughout the discussions? What communication techniques did the mediators employ for the purposes of trust-building and information-gathering? Was it difficult to utilize these techniques due to the online setting? Did any communication problems arise over the course of the negotiation? What was their source? How did the parties or the mediator address them? Was there anything pertaining to the online environment that made communication in this mediation especially challenging?

- *Information Sharing:* Was an atmosphere of trust built between the parties? Did parties share information openly, or did they play their cards close to their chests? Why was that? Was it effective? What actions or circumstances proved conducive to information sharing, and what actions or circumstances inhibited it? What did the mediators do in order to allow information sharing? Did the online environment pose any challenges to information sharing? Did the mediators employ different forms of caucusing (such as through separate emails), or was all communication handled publicly (such as through joint e-mails)? How did this affect the process? If caucusing was employed, did the mediators find it an effective tool in the online setting? What were its advantages or disadvantages, as opposed to face-to-face caucusing?

- *Exploring Options:* How did the process of problem solving and searching for options begin? Did the mediators take an active role in generating or evaluating options for agreement? What effect did this have on the process? What might have been done differently? Did the search for options (or the final agreement) focus on elements that were very much on the table, or were attempts made to expand the pie?

- *Online Mediation Process Management:* Did the mediators set/discuss process management rules, such as ground rules (time frame, permitted language) or communication rules (order in which to post messages; whom to address messages to; limit on the length of a posting)? Was there any need to remind parties of these rules or to enforce them throughout the process? Do the mediators feel they managed the process "by the book," moving from one stage of the model they learned to the next in a conscious and controlled manner? Do they feel that the structured process they tried to manage was taken away from them every so often? How did the online environment affect this issue? Do the parties feel that their relationship shifted somehow at different stages of the mediation? What was the

mediator's role (if any) in bringing this about? What did the mediators do in order to help parties face their problem constructively?
Did the mediators make use of the online environment to work
efficiently (word processing possibilities, shared documents, simul-
taneous caucusing, etc.)? What was the greatest challenge posed to
the mediators by the online environment?

- *Online Dispute Resolution for Workplace Conflict:* Do parties feel that
  the online process was a suitable one for working out their differences? Do mediators feel that the online process was a suitable one
  for assisting the parties? Do parties or mediators feel that the process may have benefited from incorporating face-to-face meetings?
  Do participants feel that an online dispute resolution program such
  as the one provided in the scenario might be a productive mecha-
  nism for resolving workplace conflict? Do they think this method
  would work best along with a face-to-face program or when operating as a stand-alone program? Did any element in this scenario
  make it particularly suitable or unsuitable for an online resolution
  process? Can participants identify any particular elements or char-
  acteristics of typical workplace disputes that might make them suitable for an online dispute resolution process?

- *Online Asynchronous Debriefing:* Using threaded message boards or group
  emails, start off conversations on specific topics, such as the questions raised above, or on more general subjects, such as those below.
  Encourage participants to reflect on their own experiences as well as
  comment on others' experiences.

  - The greatest challenge in this mediation was:

  - Communication difficulties:

  - Techniques I used:

  - The major lesson I learned was:

  - This happened online and could never have happened offline because:

  - My impressions regarding use of online dispute resolution for work-
    place conflict:

- *Individual Self-Reflective Debriefing:* Instruct participants to write self-
  reflective papers based on their own experiences and insights or pose
  several questions such as those above, instructing them to respond
  on several questions with one or two paragraphs each and to choose

one of the questions to elaborate on in one or two pages. Completed assignments can be sent in to you by email. If course technology allows this, papers might be posted publicly for all participants to read and perhaps comment on (if choosing this option, be sure to inform students ahead of time that their comments will be made public). Another possibility might be instructing participants to send their assignments to other participants, who will comment on them.

Variation

- The simulation can be conducted as a negotiation scenario by cutting out the mediator role and by instructing parties that the head of the department has told them they have to work things out on their own on their own time online. In this case, the process and debriefing will focus on participants' online negotiation and communication skills.

Submitted by Noam Ebner and Yael Efron.

Noam Ebner *is an assistant professor at the Werner Institute at Creighton University's School of Law, where he chairs the online master's program in negotiation and dispute resolution. He has written widely on the topic of negotiation and mediation pedagogy and, in practice, specializes in negotiation and mediation processes conducted online.*

Yael Efron *is assistant to the dean of the Safed College School of Law. She is at the forefront of dispute resolution in Israel, having consulted to the Ministry of Justice, private mediation initiatives, and community mediation centers, in addition to her own private practice as an attorney and a mediator.*

Together, Noam and Yael direct Tachlit Mediation and Negotiation Training, located in Jerusalem, Israel, which provides mediation services as well as negotiation and conflict management training in Israel and abroad.

Rough Day @ Work: Instructions for Party A

You completed your MBA last year and began working in the sales department of a large import company. You know that the job is beneath you; with your abilities and education you could be running the department better than its current head does. However, you long ago decided you wanted to start at the bottom, gaining as much experience as possible by the time you reach the top.

One of the workers in the department, a junior client manager like yourself, has been giving you a hard time since your first day on the job. You feel he is constantly measuring the length of your breaks and listening in on your phone calls. Besides making comments about how you waste company time, he has also repeatedly laughed at you for your "fancy education" and for wearing a tie to work every day.

He is a good example of everything wrong with the company. He has no business education, yet has been in the department forever, is responsible for a large budget, and makes decisions affecting employees' lives. He is always raising his voice at people, his desk is a mess, and his presence really makes the office an unpleasant place to be. When you tried to make friends with him and help him out with some advice to make his job easier, he shouted at you to mind our own business. At a staff meeting last week, when you mentioned that in most leading companies upper management positions are reserved for MBAs, he screamed at you to shut up in front of the whole department.

The department head requested you to make another effort to work things out, as the friction is taking its toll on the whole department. He told you he was turning the issue over to the human resources department, which is operating a pilot program for settling in-house conflict online. He doesn't know much about the process, but knows that parties participate in talks by email, from the quiet of their own homes, helped out by an expert from the HR department. You will be contacted shortly by this expert, who will introduce him- or herself and explain the process. While the department head wants to let you work this out in whatever way you see fit, he does want you to give this process your best shot.

Rough Day @ Work: Instructions for Party B

You have worked in the sales department of a large import firm for the past ten years. Having proved yourself as a salesman, you worked your way up to the position of junior client manager. You lack university education (you've been supporting yourself since you were sixteen) and you know this position may be as high as you will go; still, you aspire for more and work hard in order to earn it.

About six months ago the company hired a new junior client manager. He really annoys you; this kid is straight out of business school and is starting off at the position it took you seven years to earn! He is always talking about his school and offering you and everyone else the wisdom of his professors. As if that has anything to do with the real world! He's made annoying comments about your work and personal habits, as if he were your boss, while he himself takes long lunch breaks and is always on the phone. You feel he is stuck up and disrespectful, and his rich-kid university manners are making the office an unpleasant place to be.

When you complained to the department head, he suggested you teach the kid how things are done around here. You've tried to do so, but he always starts lecturing you about the changes he thinks should be made until you lose patience and walk off. At last week's staff meeting, he proposed that only managers with MBAs should be assigned mid-level positions in the department. With your own job threatened, you lost your temper and shouted at him.

The department head asked you to make another effort to work things out, as the friction is taking its toll on the whole department. He told you he was turning the issue over to the human resources department, which is operating a pilot program for settling in-house conflict online. He doesn't know much about the process, but knows that parties participate in talks by email, from the quiet of their own homes, helped out by an expert from the HR department. You will be contacted shortly by this expert, who will introduce him- or herself and explain the process. While the department head wants to let you work this out in whatever way you see fit, he does want you to give this process your best shot.

Rough Day @ Work: Instructions for the HR Mediator

You have been working at the company for two years, specializing in organizing in-house training and handling individual personnel problems. After studying a mediation course, you tried to implement an in-house conflict resolution program within the firm to settle internal conflicts at all levels. Although you were able to help in a few cases, you realized that most processes failed to get off the ground due to the parties having time constraints. You suggested to your department head that she let you run a pilot program for conducting online mediation in which parties could participate on their own free time and at their convenience. You have decided that, in this pilot stage, you would run the process entirely by email communication, trying to mirror the offline mediation process as closely as possible. You are now working at writing a description of the process, as well as mapping out how it would work.

Sooner than you expected, you have just received your first case. The head of the sales department called you saying he has two employees, both of whom he values, who have personality clashes and work-style differences. Their constant bickering is driving the whole department nuts and lowering productivity. While he could impose a solution from above (such as firing one or both of them or transferring one or both to another department), he feels that the firm would be better off if they were able to work it out between them. He thinks email mediation might be a suitable process in this case, as the two are rarely in the same room together without fighting. He has told them he expects them to partake in the process and that you will be in contact with them to explain the purpose and rules of the process.

Consider how you want to run the process from your initial opening letter to the parties and get to work.

Good luck!

Pair/Share
Identifying Triggers to Negative Emotions

Activity Summary

An activity to bring out the real experiences and concerns of participants in order to map them to the intended learning of the session.

Goals

- To customize the learning experience to the needs of participants.

- To lay out the course objectives to meet the needs of the participants.

Group Size

Works best in groups of 4, so requires at least 12 (see Variations for how to modify for a smaller group). From a debriefing perspective, fewer than 40 participants is best.

Time Required

15 to 60 minutes, depending on number of participants and discussion.

Materials

- One blank piece of paper for each participant.

- Writing utensils for all participants.

- A computer, flip chart, or whiteboard to list instructions.

- Markers.

Physical Setting

This is primarily a walking/standing activity, so the challenge is to have enough room for people to work in standing teams of 4 or 5.

Facilitating Risk Rating

Low.

Facilitator's Note

This activity can be used for almost any topic. The sample presented here is for leadership training. This is a completely intrapersonal activity. Do not encourage discussion with others, and allow people the quiet space they need to remember what the situation was really like. The experience pushes them into things that have really triggered strong emotions for them in the past, so they are more likely to remember vividly the actual triggers or causes of the situations.

Topics you can use include:

- *Project Management:* List a negative emotion you have had on a recent project.

- *Communication:* List a negative emotion you have had while trying to communicate with someone recently.

- *Sales:* List a negative emotion you experienced during a sales situation recently.

- *Training:* List a negative emotion you experienced while leading a workshop recently.

- *Team Building:* List a negative emotion you experienced recently during a team meeting.

Preparation

Before participants arrive, write the following instructions on a PowerPoint slide or flip-chart page (don't reveal it yet):

- List a negative emotion you have had as a leader.

- Rank the emotion (1 = hardly any, 10 = intense).

- List three things that triggered this emotion for you.

Process

1. Welcome everyone to the session and state the goals of the workshop. Say that you will use an activity to help them focus on the topic today so everyone will be engaged in setting personal learning goals.

2. Give a blank piece of paper and pen or pencil to each participant. Show them the instructions on the screen/flip chart and say they will have about 5 minutes to write their lists. Ask them to concentrate only on their own lists and not to discuss their remembered emotions with others.

   (4 or 5 minutes.)

3. Ask participants to pair up with someone at another table or someone they don't know. Say that each person will have 1 minute to share his or her remembered emotion and the triggers. The other person will *just listen*, without asking questions or commenting in any way. After 1 minute, you will tell them to switch roles. Say, "First person, BEGIN!" Watch the time and have them switch after about 1 minute.

   (5 minutes.)

4. After the pairs have completed their discussions, ask them to partner with another pair, forming a foursome. For this round, each member of a pair will share the other person's emotion and triggers with the new pair. Again, say that you will tell them when to switch. Say, "First person, BEGIN!" Remind them to switch roles after 30 seconds and then for the other pair to take turns sharing each other's emotions and triggers until all four have shared.

   (5 minutes.)

5. When the quads are finished, ask each quad to come up with a word that expresses an emotion that they can all agree is important for discussion during the workshop. Give them 30 seconds. (It is likely that they will all come up with *frustration*, or something close.)

   (1 minute.)

6. Debrief by calling on one quad at a time. Ask one person to tell you the shared emotion, and then ask each of the other three people to briefly introduce him- or herself and share one of his or her own triggers. Capture this list on a flip chart and work them into the goals for the workshop.

7. Tell participants that, because of participating in this activity, they will be able to:

    •   Revisit and identify the emotions associated with challenges that impeded their leadership effectiveness.

    •   Identify the triggers that created the emotions.

    •   Accurately identify their most important unique leadership challenges.

8. Review at the end of the session using the original lists. Ask participants to share how what they learned during the session helped them with the triggers.

Variations

•   If you do not have groups of four exactly, use a couple of teams of three instead of two in Step 3 and then combine them into groups of five instead of four in Step 4.

•   If you have a very large group, debrief by having teams collect one common trigger and one common emotion. Record the common trigger on the flip chart, and don't do introductions—or do them very briefly.

Submitted by Lou Russell.

Lou Russell is *the CEO of Russell Martin & Associates and L+earn, an executive consultant, speaker, and author whose passion is to create growth in companies by guiding the growth of their people. In her speaking, training, and writing, Lou draws on thirty years of experience helping organizations achieve their full potential. Lou is the author of six popular and practical books and is a sought-after international speaker to leaders. Lou serves on the boards of Butler University and ITT Technical Institute. Her background includes an "expired" B.S. from Purdue University in computer science and an M.S. in instructional systems technology from Indiana University. She is the original queen mother of the local "Wine and Whine" group in Indianapolis and past president of the local SIM chapter. In her spare time, she learns from her three daughters and husband, teaches religious education, and plays and coaches soccer (and occasionally sleeps).*

Cheering a Community
Opening with Energy

Activity Summary

A series of physical exercises to begin to create a community from a large group at a conference or workshop.

Goals

- To reconnect and energize people attending a program.

- To challenge participants to meet and connect with as many people at a large workshop or conference as possible.

Group Size

Any size from 15 to hundreds.

Time Required

10 to 15 minutes, depending on the size of the group.

Materials

- None.

Physical Setting

A room large enough for the groups to work without disturbing one another with seating and tables or without.

Facilitating Risk Rating

Low.

Process

1. Ask all the participants to stand and push chairs under tables if sitting at tables. Ask them to face the front of the room.

2. Have the group do a WAVE, as they would do in a stadium, starting from one side to the other side of the room. Then have them do it from the front to the back of the room and back again.

3. Challenge the entire group to demonstrate the *hidden energy* in the group by first dividing them into two or three groups from the right side to the middle to the left side. Ask them to demonstrate how they would cheer for their favorite sports team in a stadium. After the first group cheers, challenge the second and third groups to outdo the first one.

4. Then ask the entire group to cheer for the conference, the workshop, the presenters, their organization, or themselves.

5. State that before they sit down they should introduce themselves to at least five people they have not met before.

Submitted by Robert Alan Black.

Robert "Alan" Black, Ph.D., CSP, *is an international speaker and consultant who focuses on developing Cre8ng Communities throughout entire organizations from the front and back doors to the top floors. He has written and co-written more than thirty books and published more than 450 articles on creative thinking, leading, communicating, and teamwork.*

Subject-Matter Expert
Learning Factual Material

Activity Summary

An energizing learning activity especially well-suited for teaching dry or required factual material.

Goals

- To communicate concepts contained in assigned reading material.

- To evaluate the effectiveness of the planning and communications processes used to deliver new information.

Group Size

Any number, ideally 24.

Time Required

100 minutes per session.

Materials

- Original factual content (book, article, handouts, web postings) should be given to the participants for required reading prior the participating in the experiential learning activity.

- Flip chart and paper.

- Markers of several different colors.

- Blank paper and pens or pencils for participants.

- (Optional) Projector.

Physical Setting

One large room with moveable chairs.

Facilitating Risk Rating

Moderate.

Preparation

Introduce the required content as assigned reading material for all participants to complete by a specific time and date. This can be a book, articles, handouts, online information, or other materials. Be sure to tell them they need to know it well and ask them to bring the material with them to the workshop, with any notes they may have made.

Process

1. At the beginning of the session, introduce the activity by saying, "This is an activity that will enable you to recall and interpret the information you have read. Half of you will become subject-matter experts (SMEs) on half of the material, and you will help other participants to understand the content. The other half of you will become SMEs for the rest of the content, and in the same way help others to understand it."

2. Inform the participants of the activity's learning goals, displayed on a flip chart or PowerPoint slide.

3. Ask participants to form two groups, A and B. Direct the A participants to one side of the room and the B participants to the other side.

4. When everyone has settled into one of the groups, tell them: "You will now plan as a group how to explain the material you have been assigned to one or two other people so that they will be able to recall and interpret the information accurately."

5. Designate half of the reading material for the A participants and the other half for the B participants. Use appropriate flip charts or slides to clearly show the assigned readings, for example:
   • A Participants—Chapter 1 and Article 1

   • B Participants—Chapter 2 and Articles 2, 3

6. Hand out paper and writing instruments. Advise each group to outline the steps they will take to prepare and then communicate the assigned

material to others. Say: "I will give you 20 minutes for this planning process, the end result of which will be a chart of the steps your group members will take to prepare and to communicate the assigned content to others."

7. Track time and circulate between the two groups to answer any questions and coach participants as needed.

    (20 minutes.)

8. Announce the end of the planning session and invite each group to post its chart and have a spokesperson explain how they plan to become SMEs on their assigned content material and how they will communicate the concepts to others. (*Note:* They do not deliver content at this time; they describe "how" they will deliver the content, not "what" the content covers.)

9. After both subgroups present their charts, lead a discussion to highlight their good ideas and take suggestions to help them make improvements.

    (20 minutes.)

10. Direct the A and B participants to meet in their subgroups for about 10 minutes to prepare, ensuring that all members will be ready individually to execute the steps described on their subgroup's chart.

    (10 minutes.)

11. When the two groups are ready, ask participants to form pairs (or trios if there is an uneven number) with one A and one B participant in each.

12. When all pairs (or trios) are formed and seated together, direct them to take about 20 minutes to use their plans to communicate the information that was assigned to them. Each person will have 10 minutes.

13. Monitor the pairs' progress during this phase by visiting each pair at least twice in order to observe and listen to each speaker. This ensures all participants are accurately portraying the required content. Announce the halfway point so the second person can deliver his or her content. When all pairs have completed the task, call time.

    (20 minutes.)

14. Direct participants to return to their A and B subgroups.

15. Begin debriefing by giving each subgroup its initial planning chart and a marker of a different color than previously used.

16. Ask the participants to "Evaluate the effectiveness of your subgroup's planning and communication processes by discussing the questions I have posted." Post the following on a flip chart or display on a PowerPoint slide.

     • How was the experience? What worked well? What did not work well?

     • Did all of you follow your group's plan? Describe any deviations, why they were made, and the results.

     • What feedback did you receive from your partner?

     • What would you do differently next time?

17. Tell them to make any changes they would like to make to their charts using a different color marker. Give them time to do this.

     (20 minutes.)

18. Invite each subgroup to post its revised chart and have a spokesperson explain the highlights of their discussion to the total group.

19. Summarize and close the session by reviewing the learning objectives and the benefits of participating in this experiential activity.

Submitted by Linda M. Raudenbush.

Linda M. Raudenbush, Ed.D., *holds a BA in mathematics and secondary education from St. Joseph College, an MS in applied behavioral science from Johns Hopkins University, an Ed.D. in human resource development from The George Washington University, a certificate of professional development in leadership coaching from Georgetown University, and an associate's certificate in project management from The George Washington University. Linda has more than thirty years of experience in training, organization development, project management, and leadership coaching in both private and public sectors. She is an adjunct professor at the University of Maryland, Baltimore County. She is currently employed as an internal HRD/OD consultant and leadership coach at the U.S. Department of Agriculture in the National Agricultural Statistics Service. Linda is an active volunteer in her community and was awarded the Maryland State 2005 Volunteer of the Year Award for Faith-Based Initiatives.*

Crossword Conundrum
Reviewing Concepts

Activity Summary

An activity in which the participants create a crossword puzzle using the concepts that they have learned.

Goals

- To reflect on learned content.

- To encourage participants to communicate and share their learning.

Group Size

No limit, divided into subgroups with up to five participants per group.

Time Required

90 minutes.

Materials

- Crossword Conundrum Instructions for Round 1 for each subgroup.

- Crossword Conundrum Instructions for Round 2 for each subgroup.

- Materials that can be used for reference.

- Many sheets of graph paper with 5 x 5 mm grid.

- Pencil with an eraser for each participant.

- A flip chart and markers.

Physical Setting

A large room with plenty of light. Groups need common writing space. The distance between tables should be sufficient so that the discussion among members of one group does not disturb others.

Facilitating Risk Rating

Low.

Process

1. Near the end of a training session, introduce the activity as one intended to help them to review and have some fun at the same time.

2. Divide the participants into subgroups with up to five members in each subgroup. Give a copy of the Instructions for Round 1 to each subgroup and ask them to begin.

   (30 minutes.)

3. Alert the groups when 5 minutes are left, and then when the time is over. Say, "Now you are going to start the next phase of this activity. Using the concepts and their definitions, you will build a crossword puzzle in a way that the chosen concept is the word, and the definition or its creative, funny, or factual definitions become the clues. You have 40 minutes to do so. The smallest acceptable puzzle is five words across and five words down. Crossword puzzles that are larger than that will be evaluated more favorably. Arrange your words horizontally as well as vertically. You will not be using computers to build your crossword puzzle." Hand out a copy of the Instructions for Round 2, graph paper, and pencils to each subgroup.

   (40 minutes.)

4. Collect the completed crossword puzzles.

5. Ask questions about and encourage participants to share their experiences.

   • What did you gain from this activity?

   • What insights did you experience from the way your group built the crossword puzzle?

   • How did your group decide to make the puzzle? What problems did you encounter? What were the positive points of the experience?

- What did the majority members in your group prefer—the "fun" way to present the concepts or the "classic" way? Why?

- What is the learning from this activity for you? How will you use it back on the job?

(10 minutes.)

6. After participants have shared their responses, explain to them that, as they first went through their materials in order to make a list of the concepts they found most relevant, useful, interesting, thought-provoking, or even controversial, it encouraged *abstract conceptualization or comprehension*. It is one of the ways in which learning can occur. Abstract conceptualization plays a critical role in the four-stage learning cycle (the other three being *active experimentation, concrete experience,* and *reflective observation*). Post these terms on the flip chart.

7. Next, tell them that when they were discussing possible concepts within their groups, verifying, validating, looking for funny and creative expression of those definitions, *reflection* took place. Reflection is a mental process that challenges learners to use critical thinking to examine information, question its validity, and draw conclusions.

8. Continue by saying that, when the participants presented their selected concepts, often in their funny or creative derivative forms, the group engaged in *critical reflection*, a process in which the social, cultural, and political contexts surrounding individual perceptions are questioned. Reflection can be about the content or the process, as well as about the premise of the problem solving.

9. Finally, ask why you asked them to make crossword puzzles. Take a few suggestions and then wrap up by saying that when the participants were asked to make their own crosswords, it changing the paradigm to how best to communicate what they had learned to others in fun and creative ways, intensifying debate and teamwork in the process.

Variations

- You may wish to hand out the newly created crossword puzzles to different teams and challenge them to complete them in a set amount of time.

- Create crossword puzzles using the terms and concepts derived from company policies, manuals, laws, or other corporate documents. The participants could be employees, new recruits, partners, and volunteers.

References

Brookfield, S.D. (2000). The concept of critically reflective practice. In A.L. Wilson and E.R. Heys (Eds.), *Handbook of adult and continuing education*. San Francisco: Jossey-Bass.

Hoyrup, S. (2004). Reflection as a core process in organizational learning. *Journal of Workplace Learning, 16*(8), 442–454.

Kolb, D.A. (1984). *Experiential learning: Experience as the source of learning and development*. Upper Saddle River, NJ: Prentice-Hall.

Submitted by Margie Parikh.

Margie Parikh *is on the core faculty of the BK School of Business Management, Gujarat University, India. She has been teaching organizational behavior since 1998 in diverse settings. Her case studies are published in such journals as the Asian Case Research Journal and Decision, the journal of the Indian Institute of Management. She is the lead author of a text on organizational behavior, presenting the Western as well as Indian perspectives and insights. Margie also teaches a course on human resource development.*

Crossword Conundrum: Instructions for Round 1

Review concepts from the session or assigned readings and create definitions for terms that are either factual or funny.

As a group, listen to the definitions and validate, correct, or improve the meanings.

You have 30 minutes to come up with as many definitions as possible.

Crossword Conundrum: Instructions for Round 2

Use the concepts and definitions you created earlier to build a crossword puzzle using definitions as the clues.

You have 40 minutes to create a crossword puzzle arranging words horizontally as well as vertically. You may not use computers to build your puzzle.

When you complete the crossword design, make two copies. On the first, present the crossword accompanied by horizontal and vertical clues. On the second, present a solved version of your crossword puzzle. Write the names of the group members on the back of each sheet.

Role Montage
Discovering Leadership Influencers

Activity Summary

An activity that helps participants to gain deeper insight into their professional and personal leadership styles and roles based on awareness of people, mentors, role models, fictional characters, and metaphors or stories that have influenced their lives.

Goals

- To show relationships that add value to participants' lives over time.

- To examine which influences, mentors, or role models are enduring.

- To identify differences among those who influence one in different life stages.

Group Size

5 to 12 participants who are leaders in an organization.

Time Required

45 to 60 minutes.

Materials

- One copy of the Role Montage Background for Trainers for the facilitator.

- One copy of the Role Montage Definition for each participant.

- One copy of the Role Montage Questions for each participant.

- Paper and colored pencils, pens, or fine felt-tipped markers for participants.

- Flip chart and felt-tipped markers.

- Masking tape.

Physical Setting

A room large enough for participants to work without disturbing each other and where there is space for drawing. Wall space is required for posting flip-chart sheets and for sharing montages.

Facilitating Risk Rating

Moderate.

Preparation

Read the Role Montage Background for Trainers.

Process

1. Introduce the activity by saying that a role montage is a concept that takes a more in-depth look at role models, mentors, and others who have influenced a person's leadership style. Give the Role Montage Definition to each participant and point out that a montage is like an art collage.

   (5 to 10 minutes.)

2. Distribute the Role Montage Questions and pens or pencils and ask participants to answer the questions to help guide them in designing their own role montages. Ask them to consider the *positive* influences only at this time.

   (10 to 15 minutes.)

3. Ask participants how they felt while answering the questions. Record their feelings on the flip chart and probe with these questions:

   - What did you learn about yourself?

   - What surprised you?

   - How did you feel when you had completed the assignment?

4. Give participants blank paper or other drawing materials. Have them write their own names in a circle in the center of a sheet of paper. They could

draw a box or balloon if desired. Then ask them to make more circles and label them with the names of people, characters, heroes, and others who have influenced their leadership and/or those who have recognized qualities of influence and leadership in them. Tell them to put those who had or have the biggest impact closest to themselves. Have them add a message or metaphor that most represents each influencer. For example, the page can be filled with balloons reaching out from the center box of the individual to the edges of the page.

(10 to 15 minutes.)

5. Hand out the colored pencils. Write these additional guidelines for the role montage page on a flip chart:

    - Use a blue pencil to circle names of those with personality aspects you aspire to.

    - Use a green pencil to circle names of those who helped you get where you are currently.

    - Use a plus sign to indicate that the person has had an influence on you that has lasted over time.

    - Use numbers (5 is high, 1 is low) to say what the relative strength of that person's influence has been.

    (5 to 10 minutes.)

6. Walk around and answer questions as they arise. Notice how the participants are doing in terms of time. Give more time if participants ask for it.

    (5 minutes.)

7. After everyone has completed his or her role montage, ask the group members to share as much as they like with the large group. Use the following questions to bring closure to the activity:

    - What themes stand out for you?

    - What did you learn about yourself?

    - What did this activity suggest to you about your leadership and influence?

    - How can what you have learned help you in the future?

8. Ask them what action steps they can take now to have more influence over others and to show leadership in their work lives.

9. Encourage participants to do role montages for every decade of their lives to see what has influenced their leadership at specific times. Ask them to consider whether they have the right number of influencers now or need to find others.

Variations

- A role montage can be used for coaching.

- Montages can be completed on the computer using colors and shapes in Word or Excel.

- Participants can also list their influencers in a timeline by the decades of their lives.

Submitted by Jan M. Schmuckler.

Jan M. Schmuckler, Ph.D., *is an organizational psychologist and dynamic coach. She works with global leaders and teams to develop high-performance workplace strategies and achieve outstanding business results in biotechnology, financial services, health care, and in the nonprofit sector. For more than twenty-five years, she has transformed organizations and changed lives with innovative ideas, energy, and expertise. She is working on a book about women leaders. Jan previously served as director of the Graduate Coaching Program at John F. Kennedy University. She received her Ph.D. in psychology from The Wright Institute.*

Role Montage Background for Trainers

A role montage is a way of looking at the influences, memories, imagination, and relationships that add value to us throughout our lifetimes. A role montage, an original concept, is a kaleidoscopic picture of elements, ideas, and values incorporated from various persons both real and imaginary that we internalize and so develop an image after which we pattern ourselves. It assumes that we have incorporated abstract principles about values, thinking, and meaning from many different sources. A role montage can be used as a developmental tool for leaders who want to explore who had an impact on their lives.

A role montage is comprised of people and characters who have impacted and influenced us. It is similar to an art collage. A montage could be made up of family members, real or fictional characters, and historical or political figures. In addition, part of the montage could come from entertainers, filmmakers, sports heroes, artists, cartoonists, bloggers, and others. For example, one business owner added Nancy Drew, teenage sleuth, from the Nancy Drew detective stories, to her montage. When probed, she responded that Nancy Drew was "spunky and always solved the problems of the day, just like me." We absorb parts of meaningful people and characters and weave a tapestry of those who influence our lives.

Role Models and Mentors

The role montage idea can be expanded to include role models and mentors. A role model is a person who serves as an example and whose behavior is worthy of imitation. Males have many examples of role models, especially in leadership positions. Many women leaders have a more difficult time with the concept of role models, because they feel as though they do not have as many choices. Although role models do not have to be gender-specific, many women want a female role model and, because they don't find them easily, a role montage allows them to open up to a wider range of choices.

A mentor focuses on helping the less experienced person in the relationship succeed. Many people choose mentors who have qualities that they would like to have or political clout that they need.

Thus, role montages provide a complete picture of all the mentor, role model, and influencers in one's life and allow us to reflect on the messages, the meaning, and the importance of certain people in our lives.

Role Montage Definitions

A *role montage* is a way of looking at the influencers and relationships with others that add value throughout our lifetimes. Role montage is a kaleidoscopic of elements, ideas, and values incorporated from various persons, both real and imaginary, that we internalize and so develop an image on which to pattern ourselves.

The concept of a role montage assumes that we have incorporated values and ways of thinking and given meaning to input from many different sources. A role montage is comprised of people who have influenced us. It is similar to an art collage. A montage can be made up of family members, real or fictional characters, and historical or political figures, role models (those who serve as examples and whose behavior is worthy of imitation), and mentors (those who focus on helping us succeed). In addition, some of the montage could come from entertainers, filmmakers, sports heroes, artists, cartoonists, bloggers, or others, just so they have influenced our lives in a significant way.

Role Montage Questions

- Who in my family has influenced me?

- What teachers (day care, preschool, elementary, middle, high school, college) were important in my development?

- In my room or office, what did/do I put on the walls? How did I decorate the room (posters, fabric, photos, quotes, cartoons) before I left home, in college, in my first apartment or home?

- What political person(s) influenced me and what were the messages that resonated with me the most?

- What were my favorite characters on TV, in movies, and in cartoons?

- Who were my sports heroes, favorite entertainers, or movie stars?

- Who is my favorite character in a book or favorite blogger? (If you are a reader, then you might want to answer beginning from ages ten to twelve years and include authors as well as fictional characters.)

- Who would I like to invite to a dinner party and why? Anyone can be included—dead or alive.

The Fugitive
Assessing the Style of a Leader

Activity Summary

Allows participants to appreciate the role of a leader through watching a movie clip.

Goals

- To understand the role of a leader.
- To discuss the concept of leadership.

Group Size

Suitable for any group that is studying leadership.

Time Required

60 minutes.

Materials

- Projection and screen large enough to be seen by everyone.
- Movie *The Fugitive* starring Harrison Ford and Tommy Lee Jones. Segment from 20:13 to 42:27. (*Note:* The Federal Copyright Act requires a performance license for showing films. Information about licensing can be obtained from the Motion Picture Association of America on their website at www.mpaa.org/Public_Performance.asp.)

Physical Setting

No special requirements.

Facilitating Risk Rating

Low.

Process

1. After the participants have discussed the role of a leader, particularly "working through others," planning, organizing, leading, and controlling, state that you will show them an example of a leader in action.

2. Provide a brief background of the movie plot up to the segment to be shown.

3. Request that participants focus on the behavior of Deputy U.S. Marshall Samuel Gerard (Tommy Lee Jones) and to draw parallels between the concepts they have learned previously in the workshop and his actions.

4. Show the 23-minute video segment.

   (30 minutes.)

5. Debrief what learners saw using the following questions:

   • When did Samuel Gerard plan, organize, and lead? When did he work through others? Control others or the situation?

   • What management behavior did Samuel Gerard use the most in the segment?

   • What might have happened if Samuel Gerard had not done all the things he did?

   • What is your opinion about him personally going after the fugitive in the tunnel? Should he have done that? Should he have delegated? What, if any, similar actions do managers take in real life?

   • What is your opinion of Samuel Gerard's leadership style?

   • Would you like to work for someone like Samuel Gerard? Why? Why not?

   • Examining your own leadership behavior, what steps can you take to become a better leader?

Variations

- Some scenes may be omitted.

- If time is available, debriefing can be first in triads and later as a whole group.

- The segment can be also used for discussing the concept of leadership in a critical situation.

Submitted by Guido R. Britez.

Guido R. Britez *is director of Sunergos, a corporate training firm. He earned his B.S. degree in business administration from the University of the Pacific, Stockton, California. He enjoys designing and delivering training in management, leadership, communication, and negotiation. He is a licensed master practitioner in neuro-linguistic programming, practitioner in human resources and organizational effectiveness from University Associates, and a qualified administrator of the MBTI. He has delivered training in Spain and Argentina and taught graduate courses in Paraguay.*

Values in Leadership
Understanding the True Drivers

Activity Summary

Allows a group of people to understand how values are strong drivers of the leadership process.

Goals

- To contemplate one's own values and how they drive leadership processes.

- To understand various value systems and how they drive leadership processes.

Group Size

A maximum of 12 participants clustered in trios. All participants should have had or will soon have leadership experience.

Time Required

Approximately 90 minutes.

Materials

- One copy of Values in Leadership Lecturette for the facilitator.

- One copy of the Values in Leadership: Spiritual Leader Case for each participant.

- Whiteboard or flip chart.

- Markers.

- Paper and pens or pencils for the participants.

Physical Setting

A room large enough for at least four groups of three to work together comfortably.

Facilitating Risk Rating

Moderate.

Process

1. Facilitate a discussion on leadership values. Use the lecturette as a basis.

   (10 minutes.)

2. Divide the participants into triads. Provide each participant with the Values in Leadership: Spiritual Leader Case.

   (5 minutes.)

3. Have the participants read the case and discuss it considering the values demonstrated. Tell participants to work together in their groups for 20 minutes to prepare a list of leadership values for presentation to the large group.

   (20 minutes.)

4. After the time is up, ask one participant from each group to present his or her small group's observations to the large group. Allow for discussion. Record the values on the flip chart.

   (20 minutes.)

5. Discuss each value listed on the flip chart with the large group and solicit participation through responses and experience sharing.

   (10 minutes.)

6. Bring closure through a discussion and a reinforcement of the message that leadership is truly driven by values. Debrief with the following questions:

   • What have you learned about values in leadership that you can apply when you are interacting with your followers?

   • Which value is most important to you? How do you demonstrate it now?

   • How can you be sure that what you have learned is not lost as you return to the workplace?

   (10 minutes.)

7. Ask participants to make arrangements with one another to check each other's progress via email at stated times in the future, such as in thirty days or three months. Give them time to exchange email addresses or make other plans.

8. Ask participants to share some of their ideas with the group and then close the session.

(10 minutes.)

Variations

- If the group is small, participants could share their responses within the large group rather than breaking into subgroups.

- If everyone is from the same organization, different case studies from within that organization could be used, enabling a better understanding of the value systems prevailing within the organization.

- The leadership of the organization's founding fathers could be used as a case to better understand the organization's ethos.

Submitted by Mohandas Nair.

Mohandas Nair *is a management educator, a teacher, trainer, writer, and facilitator of learning. He earned a B.Tech. (Mech.) from IIT Kharagpur, India, has a diploma in training and development, and has more than thirty years of experience in industry and consultancy in the field of industrial engineering and human resource development. He has published two books, written numerous articles, and facilitated many management development programs.*

Values in Leadership: Lecturette

Values guide human action and are assumed to be positive and import to the person holding them. They may vary with culture, but some fundamental values such as honesty, credibility, and strength of character are enduring and fit all cultures uniformly. When they are perceived to be held by an individual, the individual is believed, respected, and followed willingly.

Values determine the importance an individual places on how he or she interacts with his or her environment. Demonstrating values through appropriate behavior enables leaders to build connections with followers and build bonds of trust and commitment to the processes the leader facilitates.

A leader is primarily a facilitator of processes that drive the business. Followers continue the processes through their own actions. Because followers are dependent on the leader, the effectiveness of their actions will be proportionate to the bonds they share with their leader. If a follower is not satisfied with the support provided by nor perceived values of a leader, he or she will not be very effective in his or her work and will not be optimally utilized.

To satisfy followers, a leader has to connect well with them. Values are the primary way a connection is made. Leaders have to ensure that his or own value system and those of followers are in sync.

Often an open and continuous dialogue will enable leaders and followers to see both their commonalities and differences. The relationship needs to be taken seriously and remain stable over time so that followers achieve optimum output.

All people are unique in the values they hold. It is incumbent on leaders to share theirs and know what values are important to their followers. When there is a major disconnect in expectations between an organization and an employee, it is appropriate to let the employee move on. If the disconnect is between a leader and employees, the issue is more serious. Unless the leader can get onboard, the organization may fail to perform effectively the processes that leader controls.

Values in Leadership: Spiritual Leader Case

Chinnapillai is an illiterate farm worker from a poor village in the state of Tamil Nadu in South India. She was being presented with the Indian Merchant Chambers (IMC) Ladies Wing–Jankidevi Bajaj Award for rural entrepreneurship in 2000 in the Indian capital, New Delhi. After presenting her with the award, Ms. Sumitra Kulkarni, granddaughter of Mahatma Gandhi, remarked: "Chinnapillai doesn't need our awards; she just needs us to allow her space to carry on the fantastic work she is doing."

Her work? Women's empowerment in village India, feudal India.

The diminutive Chinnapillai, a fifty-year-old landless laborer from Tamil Nadu, won the annual award for promoting a unique savings-and-loan scheme for village women in her region. The program, which she launched informally thirty-five years ago, now covers nearly fifty thousand village women in Tamil Nadu and the neighboring state of Andhra Pradesh. The movement, called *Kalajiam* (savings, credit, self-help), now also conducts campaigns against alcoholism and child labor and runs a primary school.

"I've always been a daredevil. Perhaps that's why God has been on my side," said Chinnapillai to a journalist after the award ceremony. Not that her achievement came easily. "But can you accomplish anything in this world without a hard fight?" asked Chinnapillai, who has taken on the ferocious feudal lords, ruthless money lenders, bloody minded politicians, obstreperous bankers, and bureaucrats in her long struggle to give the downtrodden their due.

Chinnapillai's struggles started when she was only thirteen. "We women would work long days in the fields but go home with only a bag full of grain, or occasionally a few rupees. It used to burn my heart. I was a leader of a group of women workers and decided to use my position to demand our due. I started calling women's meetings to discuss the issue. Everyone was terrified in the beginning, including my husband, but I persuaded them to demand a hike in wages."

Chinnapillai asked the landlord for a wage hike and got a kick instead. Nonetheless, she persisted until they relented and agreed to a two-rupee hike. "I felt that was a signal from God to carry on. I soon started urging the women to put aside a little money as savings. Of course, they didn't listen. How could they? They needed food for their families and liquor for their men. But again, I kept at it. Eventually, they agreed to keep aside a few rupees—not at home, where it could be spent at any minute, but safely in our *Kalajiam*.

Chinnapillai then decided that these collective savings could be used to give small loans to women at a low rate of interest—24 percent against the 60 to 120 percent charged by local money lenders. "My dream was to free us peasants from the stranglehold of money lenders. City people will not understand how that feels. It's like walking around with a tight noose around your neck."

She also organized the women to seek jobs in new and non-women-oriented projects. For instance, she obtained fishing rights in the local pond for her village women (which had for decades been controlled by local landlords and corrupt politicians). "We petitioned the local government authority in this regard, and the sympathetic officer took up cudgels on our behalf," she explained.

The *Kalajiam* movement began to spread and women from other villages joined in. As the corpus of savings grew, a local non-government organization (NGO) called DHAN (Development of Humane Action) came in to help them bank their money, liaise with officialdom, and establish local committees to disburse loans meant to pay for house construction, marriage expenses, farming materials, and seeds.

"We started with two hundred rupees collected from twenty women in my village some thirty years ago. Now our *Kalajiam's* savings run to several hundred thousand rupees in the local district alone and nearly fifty million rupees in the two states of Tamil Nadu and Andhra Pradesh." She smiles. "But you know I have no idea how much money Rs. 100,000 is. I still cannot count more than 100."

The crusader is still as poor as, well, an Indian peasant, earning as she does twenty-five rupees a day for four hours' work in the fields. Her two sons and daughters-in-law toil all month, but Chinnapillai now works only ten days a month; the rest of the time she's busy with committee meetings in various villages. She has debts totaling 35,000 rupees. But she does not intend to touch her prize money of 100,000 rupees. "It will go to the *Kalajiam*, toward helping the more needy," she stated firmly.

Small wonder, then, that when he presented her with a special award during the special Women's Empowerment Year launch function in Delhi, the then–Prime Minister of India, Atal Behari Vajpayee, was sufficiently moved to bow down and touch Chinnapillai's feet.

[*Author's note:* In India you touch the feet of an elder to show respect. However, the prime minister of India is in a position where he or she is not constrained to do this as a formality. He or she would not have touched the feet of any top business executives of any organization in the world or of any politicians. He or she would have done it only in the presence of saints, sages, or spiritual leaders.]

Some Leadership Values Demonstrated in the Case Study

- Honesty
- Credibility
- Trust

- Respect

- Perseverance/Determination/Never give up/No concept of failure

- Courage

- Compassion/Love

- Humility

- Focused drive

- Sacrifice

- Others?

Introduction
to the Editor's Choice Section

Unfortunately, in the past we have had to reject exceptional ideas that did not meet the criteria of one of the sections or did not fit into one of our categories. So we created an Editor's Choice section that allows us to publish unique items that are useful to the profession rather than turn them down. This collection of contributions simply does not fit in one of the other three sections: Experiential Learning Activities; Inventories, Questionnaires, and Surveys; or Articles and Discussion Resources.

Based on the reason for creating this section, it is difficult to predict what you may find. You may anticipate a potpourri of topics, a variety of formats, and an assortment of categories. Some may be directly related to the training and consulting fields, and others may be related tangentially. Some may be obvious additions, and others may not. What you are sure to find is something you may not have expected but that will contribute to your growth and stretch your thinking. Suffice to say that this section will provide you with a variety of useful ideas, practical strategies, and creative ways to look at the world. The material will add innovation to your training and consulting knowledge and skills. The contributions will challenge you to think differently, consider a new perspective, and add information you may not have considered before. The section will stretch your view of training and consulting topics.

The 2012 Pfeiffer Annual: Training includes two editor's choice selections. Keep in mind the purpose for this section—good ideas that don't fit in the other sections. The submissions by Steve Sugar, Greg Williams, and Linda Raudenbush and by Philip Donnison are perfect examples of items that are valuable to the readers of the *Training Annual*, but simply do not fit in any of the other categories. These submissions feature a process to get the most out experiential learning activities and a great example of how to create your own. Enjoy these creative submissions. Both are presented by long time contributors and respected professionals in the training field.

Article

Playing to Learn: Engaging Learners with Frame Games, by Steve Sugar, Gregory R. Williams, and Linda M. Raudenbush

Activity

Preparing Participants to Get the Most from Experiential Learning, by Philip Donnison

Playing to Learn
Engaging Learners with Frame Games
Steve Sugar, Gregory R. Williams,
and Linda M. Raudenbush

Summary

Engaging learners is one of the most challenging aspects of teaching and training. This brief article introduces a simple way to incorporate a frame game, an extremely flexible game format, into a teaching situation. The article also provides guidelines and a checklist for successfully incorporating games into your teaching or training.

"What we play is life."

Louis Armstrong

The Experiment

It was painfully clear to the college instructor that her American history lecture was not nearly as exciting to the students as it was to her. For weeks students assumed chair postures that suggested interest, but were betrayed by a blank gaze that indicated they were enduring rather than enjoying the topic. After much soul-searching, the instructor decided to incorporate an educational forced-choice wall game she had experienced during her graduate UMBC instructional systems development (ISD) course. Conscious of the theory of adult learning pioneered by Malcolm Knowles, she wanted her game to have clear goals, require players to make decisions, and provide feedback to the learners (Knowles, Holton, & Swanson,

2005). She also wanted the game to be user-friendly, easy and fun to play, and focused on her content.

Preparing the Wall Game

For the forced-choice wall game, the instructor pulled the necessary game materials from her instructor's supply cabinet—three sheets of flip-chart paper, several felt-tipped makers, a roll of masking tape, and one stack of index cards—and produced her game in three steps.

- First, she created three sets of fifteen index cards, each with the name of a prominent political figure.

- Second, she made three simple "T" wall charts with "Democrat" and "Republican" on either side of the flip-chart pages, as shown.

Democrat	Republican

- Third, she wrote the rules of play (shown below) on three index cards, placing one index card near each chart.

Game Rules

- Form three teams.

- Each team receives one set of fifteen prepared index cards.

- Each team meets at a wall chart.

- First player turns over an index card and places it in the appropriate column.

- *Only after the first player plays* his or her card can the second player touch the next card.

- Continue to play until time is called.

- Teams receive a point for each correctly placed card; the team with the most points wins.

Before her next class, the instructor mounted the wall charts. As the class members were settling into their seats, she introduced them to the wall charts that the students had undoubtedly noticed entering the classroom. With minimal urging and instruction, the class split into three teams, each team going to a wall chart. Each team then received a set of index cards, placing the cards face down near the wall chart.

The instructor started play. At the end of 1 minute, time was called, but students continued placing their cards. Time was called again, and play finally stopped.

In 1 minute, energy and focus were returned to the classroom. The instructor, now with full student attention, proceeded to debrief the students with the correct responses, weaving the information into the tapestry of her lesson plan. The importance of debriefing students after game play cannot be over-emphasized. Providing effective feedback enables players to learn from their mistakes and builds on their success for improved performance (Hayes, 2005).

The Beauty of a Frame Game

The "beauty" of a frame game is that it is open to almost any topic. Think of the last time you purchased a picture frame; you removed the picture of the model family and replaced it with a picture of your own family. In the same way, a well-designed frame game allows you to insert your own content.

For the theorists, it is important to point out that frame games embrace a number of practices associated with effective adult learning (Oblinger, 2004), including:

- Activate prior learning;

- Expand the learning context;

- Provide opportunities for feedback;

- Transfer learning from the game to real life;

- Engage multiple senses;

- Engage multiple intelligences; and

- Foster a team approach.

The original version of this game can be traced back to elementary school forced-choice wall and table exercises. K-12 teachers used this game to demonstrate similarities and differences between topic items, ranging from kindergarten topics, such as shapes and word sounding, to the present high school version on identification of political parties. In the same way, this energizing game format has been used in adult training topics ranging from a popular version of plant safety, featuring item cards of "safe" and "unsafe" practices; and ethics, featuring ethical versus unethical situations; to any topic using item cards sorted into columns depicted as "true" or "false." To develop this frame game, simply prepare one "T" wall chart for every student team and then develop a set of true-false item cards for each wall chart.

Successful Game Checklist

To be successful, the game must:

- Address the instructional objectives of the overall course or program;

- Adhere to systematic instructional design principles;

- Engage students in the learning experience;

- Provide students safe opportunities to "fail";

- Provide performance feedback that can enhance learning; and

- Enable students to learn by doing.

Facilitating Classroom Games

These guidelines will help you facilitate successful games that promote team play, energy, and dialogue.

- Do not force people to play if they do not want to; give them the chance to be observers.

- Do not over-explain directions; let team members develop synergy by working toward game goals.

- Do not advise teams how to set up and distribute supplies; this is part of the team-development process.

- Decide whether you will allow teams to coach a player holding a card. Some instructors begin with no coaching, then change over to one or more coaches to demonstrate the power of team input.

- One Coach: Allow teams to select one coach; change coaches for each round of play.

- Team Coach: Allow ALL players to coach the card holder.

Pressure Points

- Don't give in to cries of "we need more time"; remind players that life doesn't allow unlimited time for any activity.

- Life does require thinking while acting, so this is a realistic constraint.

- Peer pressure is a normal real-life influence and/or distraction; game play allows players to experience this real-time stress element.

Team Roles

- Consider assigning special roles, especially for larger teams.

- Special roles include, but are not limited to:

  - Observer(s): one or two players who watch for specific words, behaviors, or roles identified by the instructor and report back to the group.

  - Card reader: reads each card aloud.

  - Team Recorder: tracks team process and records observations on chart paper.

Closing

While it is possible to learn by being a spectator, there is more to be learned by participating in the learning process. Classroom games add far more than just fun to the curriculum. They bring the real world, as we want it to be known, into a playful learning zone. Game play introduces the opportunity to demonstrate individual decision making under pressure and to successfully complete a competitive team activity—all in a non-threatening, observable learning environment. Educational games make players of participants, and to quote Louis Armstrong, "What we play is life."

References

Knowles, M.S., Holton, E.F., & Swanson, R.A. (2005). *The adult learner: The definitive classic in adult education and human resource development* (6th ed.). Amsterdam: Elsevier.

Oblinger, D. (2004). The next generation of educational engagement. *Journal of Interactive Media in Education, 8*. Special Issue on the Educational Semantic Web.

Hayes, R.T. (2005). *The effectiveness of instructional games: A literature review and discussion* (Technical Report 2005-004). Orlando, FL: Naval Air Warfare Center Training Systems Division.

Steve Sugar *is a writer and teacher of learning games. His writings include game collections for five books published by Pfeiffer and ASTD Press, articles featured in over forty books and journals, and the stand-alone games QUIZO, Maestro, and LearnIt! used in private- and public-sector training worldwide. Steve is currently an ISD adjunct faculty member at the University of Maryland, Baltimore County (UMBC).*

Gregory R. Williams, Ed.D., *has more than twenty years of experience in education and training. He has taught online and in-person courses at a variety of institutions, including the University of Maryland, Baltimore County (UMBC). He is currently the director of UMBC's program in instructional systems development and teaches as clinical assistant professor. Dr. Williams received his B.A. and M.S. degrees from the State University of New York and his Ed.D. from The George Washington University.*

Linda M. Raudenbush, Ed.D., *holds a B.A. degree in mathematics and secondary education from St. Joseph College, an M.S. degree in applied behavioral science from Johns Hopkins University, an Ed.D. in human resource development from The George Washington University, a Certificate of Professional Development in Leadership Coaching from Georgetown University, and an Associates Certificate in Project Management from The George Washington University. Linda has more than thirty years of experience in training, organization development, project management, and leadership coaching in both private and public sectors. She is an adjunct professor at the University of Maryland, Baltimore County. She is currently employed as an internal HRD/OD consultant and leadership coach at the U.S. Department of Agriculture in the National Agricultural Statistics Service.*

Preparing Participants to Get the Most from Experiential Learning

Activity Summary

A guided reflection to be undertaken prior to any experiential learning to ensure that participants get the most out of taking part in activities.

Goals

- To encourage participants to enter an experiential learning process in a spirit of engagement with the learning, making the most of the three stages of the experiential learning cycle: "doing," "reviewing," and "applying."

- To introduce experiential learning to participants.

- To encourage participants to examine their personal learning goals to help them use the activities as a vehicle for learning.

Group Size

Usually between 6 and 20, depending on the group size for the activity that will be used.

Time

25 to 30 minutes.

Materials

- One Experiential Learning Process handout for each participant.

- Pencils for participants.

- Flip chart and markers.

Physical Setting

A circle of chairs to enable discussion in a room that does not contain the activity or any related instructions.

Facilitating Risk Rating

Low.

Process

1. Before issuing the instructions for the first experiential learning activity in your workshop, give participants copies of the Experiential Learning Process handout and pencils and ask them to read the handout and list their goals for the workshop on it.

   (10 minutes.)

2. Discuss the nature of experiential learning with the group, being sure to bring out the following points:

   - Experiential learning allows participants to learn in an active way by doing rather than being taught what to do.

   - It assumes that most people learn from their experiences, from practice, and from hands-on experimentation, for example, learning to use computer software through trying things out rather than consulting the instruction manual.

   - The experiential learning cycle has three distinct stages: Do, Review, and Apply. This allows participants to review their participation in activities to identify lessons learned and to apply the learning to subsequent activities or real-life events.

   - Participants often go through the learning cycle several times during a training program through participation in several different activities.

   - An experiential activity is a vehicle for learning. It is to be treated seriously, and participants should respond as they would in real life. It is not a competition or a role play.

   - The actual activity will probably be completely unrelated to any work tasks that participants are familiar with, but their behavior in response to situations will likely be the same as it would be in real life.

   - The connection to participants' work is the nature of the "processes" rather than the content of the task. The emphasis is on *how* the task is undertaken. The debriefing is likely to center on processes such as how time was divided between planning and implementation.

- Because of the emphasis on learning, application, and processes, each activity must be followed by a discussion of what took place. For example, an activity that takes 30 minutes will often be followed by a 30-minute discussion.

3. Ask participants what their learning objectives will be for the day, the key reasons why they are attending the course or gaps in their skill sets they need to fill in for a future role.

4. Ask each participant to read his or her learning objectives to the group, so that everyone is are aware of what others want to practice, experiment with, or learn during the activity.

5. Remind participants that you will refer back to their learning objectives in the review discussion after the activity. For example, if someone's learning objective is to focus on planning discussions, you may ask whether the group gave the amount of time to planning that it intended to give.

Variation

- The whole group may have a single shared learning objective. This objective may be agreed on before the activities commence by following the same process.

_____

Submitted by Philip Donnison.

An occupational psychologist based in the UK, **Philip Donnison, Ph.D.,** *is retained as coach and mentor by organizations around the world. A strong advocate of active methods of learning, he uses many techniques he presented in a Ph.D. dissertation on experiential learning. His use of action-based approaches is founded on long-term experience of how experiential learning can bring about sustainable improvements in the performance of teams and individuals.*

The Experiential Learning Process

People learn by doing. They learn practical skills through hands-on experimentation to see what works and what does not work. They learn from experience and learn from their mistakes.

The experiential learning cycle is a process of doing something, reviewing it, and applying any lessons learned the next time a similar situation is encountered. The stages of the cycle are often referred to as Do, Review, and Apply.

During this training program, you will have a chance to learn from experience by taking part in some practical activities. These activities:

- Will form the Do stage of the learning cycle.

- Are not a competition, a test, or a role play.

- Will probably be unlike any tasks that you face at work.

The main reason for asking you to take part in an activity is so that you can learn from what happened. We will therefore hold a Review discussion after each activity, focusing on what lessons can be drawn from what happened during the activity and how they can be applied to future situations you may face.

At the end of the Review stage of the learning cycle, we will ask you to think about what you want to Apply—what you want to try out, practice, or experiment with during the workshop or when you return to the job. This should be something based on the lessons you have learned from the discussion of the activity.

Before taking part in the first activity, spend some time deciding what your learning objectives are for attending this session. Write these below and be ready to discuss them with the rest of the group.

Introduction
to the Inventories, Questionnaires, and Surveys Section

Inventories, questionnaires, and surveys are valuable tools for the HRD professional. These feedback tools help respondents take an objective look at themselves and at their organizations. These tools also help to explain how a particular theory applies to them or to their situations.

Inventories, questionnaires, and surveys are useful in a number of training and consulting situations: privately for self-diagnosis; one-on-one to plan individual development; in a small group to open discussion; in a work team to help the team to focus on its highest priorities; or in an organization to gather data to achieve progress. You will find that the use of inventories, questionnaires, and surveys enriches, personalizes, and deepens training, development, and intervention designs. Many can be combined with other experiential learning activities or articles in this or other *Annuals* to design an exciting, involving, practical, and well-rounded intervention. Each instrument includes the background necessary for understanding, presenting, and using it. Interpretive information, scales, and scoring sheets are also provided. In addition, we include the reliability and validity data contributed by the authors. If you wish additional information on any of these instruments, contact the authors directly. You will find their addresses and telephone numbers in the "Contributors" listing near the end of this volume.

The 2012 Pfeiffer Annual: Training includes three assessment tools in the following categories:

Individual Development

Three-Dimensional Emotional Competence Inventory (3D-ECI), by Sethu Madhavan Puravangara

Consulting, Training, Facilitating

Classroom Instructor Skills Survey, by Jean Barbazette

Organizations

Institutional Climate Survey, by K.S. Gupta

Three-Dimensional Emotional Competence Inventory (3D-ECI)

Sethu Madhavan Puravangara

Summary

The concepts of emotional intelligence (EI), emotional quotient (EQ), and emotional competencies have received widespread attention during the last fifteen years. Authors concur that cognitive intelligence or intelligence quotient (IQ) is not sufficient to explain the effectiveness of people at work and their success in life. According to the proponents of the EQ concept, emotionally intelligent people are more effective in managing themselves and others at work and in their personal lives. This self-report inventory was developed to assess respondents' emotional competency.

The concepts of emotional intelligence (EI), emotional competencies (EC), and emotional quotient (EQ) have received widespread attention since the publication of a book on the topic by Daniel Goleman (1995) and an article on the topic by Gibbs (1995).

Proponents of EQ have argued that IQ is not sufficient to explain the effectiveness of people at work and their success in life. Based on his research, Goleman (1998) said that emotional intelligence is twice as important as technical skills for outstanding performance at work. He further stated that EI assumes more importance as we are promoted in organizations and that it becomes the most important quality at the leadership levels. Goleman (1998) defined emotional competence (EC) as a learned capability based on emotional intelligence (EI) that results in outstanding performance at work.

Feldman and Mulle (2007) state that EI is the X-factor that separates average performers from outstanding ones. They observe that emotionally intelligent people are capable of knowing themselves well, managing their emotions, relating with others, collaborating with others, motivating themselves, and taking personal responsibility for their actions. Today, assessments of EI and related concepts are used by organizations for a variety of purposes such as recruitment, training, personal development planning, leadership development, succession planning, and so forth.

The Three-Dimensional Emotional Competence Inventory (3D-ECI) was developed to be used for assessing people on EC. It was developed over a period of two years and has been used successfully in management and leadership training programs to facilitate sessions on EI and EQ. The 3D-ECI offers a logical framework for understanding and elaborating on the practical applications of the EI concept.

Description of the Instrument

Dealing with self, dealing with others, and dealing with life have been identified as the three most important dimensions or "D"s of EC. It is conceptualized that these three dimensions interact and reinforce each other to enhance the EC of people (see Figure 1).

The twenty-one indices of emotional intelligence were identified by the author based on a detailed review of the literature and published assessment tools. These indices were then categorized into the seven factors, seven "M"s, based on their similarities. Definitions of the seven factors are provided on the Score Prediction and Interpretation Sheet. Finally, the seven factors were grouped under the three dimensions: dealing with self, dealing with others, and dealing with life (see Figure 1). The instrument contains sixty-three items distributed under the twenty-one indices.

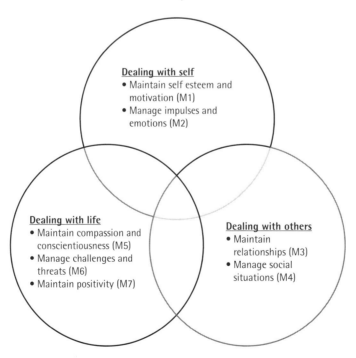

Figure 1. 3–D Model

Theory Behind the Instrument

When psychologists began to explore the concept of intelligence in more depth during the 1900s, most of them focused on cognitive aspects of intelligence such as abstract reasoning, logical thinking, memory, and problem solving. However, some of the early researchers had emphasized the importance of non-cognitive and emotional factors in intelligence. For example, during the 1920s, Edward Thorndike used the concept of "social intelligence" to describe the skill of understanding and managing other people (Thorndike, 1920, 1936). During the 1940s, David Wechsler described the influence of non-cognitive factors such as "affective" and "cognitive" abilities on intelligent behavior (Wechsler, 1940, 1943). Leeper (1948) stated that emotional thought is an important part of intelligence. In the 1980s, Howard Gardner proposed that "intrapersonal and interpersonal intelligences" are as important as the abilities covered by the traditional intelligence tests (Gardner, 1983, 1993).

The earliest uses of the term "emotional intelligence" is attributed differently by various authors. Mayer, Salovey, and Caruso (2004) note that the term was used in literary criticism as early as 1961 and in psychiatry in 1966. Payne (1986) used the term extensively in his dissertation. However, the concept became popular mainly due to the more recent works by Salovey and Mayer (1990) and Goleman (1995).

Many authors have attempted to define EI, identify its sub-factors, and develop measures of EI. The sub-factors identified by some authors are summarized in Table 1.

With steadily growing interest on the topic, there is an emerging need for user-friendly measurement tools that can be used for training and development. The 3D-ECI framework was developed based on a review and analysis of various existing EI frameworks and associated measurement tools.

Table 1. Sub-Factors of EI

Authors	Sub-Factors of EI
Goleman, Boyatzis, & McKee (2002)	Self-awareness (Personal competence) Self-management (Personal competence) Social awareness (Social competence) Relationship management (Social Competence)
Lynn (2005)	Self-awareness and self-control Empathy Social expertness Personal influence Mastery of purpose and vision

(Continued)

Table 1. (*Continued*)

Authors	Sub-Factors of EI
Salovey & Mayer (1990)	Perceiving emotions
	Understanding emotions
	Facilitating thought
	Managing emotions
Bar-On (1997)	Intrapersonal
	Interpersonal
	Stress management
	Adaptation
	General mood
Higgs & Dulewicz (1999)	Self-awareness
	Emotional resilience
	Interpersonal sensitivity
	Influence
	Motivation
	Intuitiveness
	Conscientiousness
Cooper & Sawaf (1996)	Emotional literacy
	Emotional fitness
	Emotional depth
	Emotional alchemy

Applications and Uses of the Instrument

The 3D-ECI is an excellent tool for improving the self-awareness of respondents and to enhance their understanding of the concept of EC. Some of the potential uses include:

- As a quick assessment, feedback, and training tool in behavioral and leadership training workshops;

- As a multi-rater, 360-degree assessment;

- As a tool in assessment and development centers;

- As a diagnostic assessment tool by coaches, mentors, and supervisors; and

- As a self assessment tool for those who would like to understand their own emotional competency levels.

The 3D-ECI is designed for use in work situations and is not for use in counseling. It was created primarily for developmental purposes and, therefore, the results may be used for leadership development, coaching and mentoring, succession planning, and behavioral training. However, because the 3D-ECI is valid across a broad array of situations and has been found to be reliable, it can also be used for selection and promotion decisions in conjunction with other assessments.

Administration of the 3D-ECI

Administration of 3D-ECI does not require any special training. Depending on the available time and the purpose of the assessment, the trainer may administer the inventory in a group situation, such as in a classroom, or individually, in a coaching situation.

Face-to-Face Administration

Explain the rating scale used in the inventory and remind the participants that there are no right or wrong answers. Encourage respondents to give genuine responses by stating that the scores will be treated with complete confidentiality unless they decide to share their scores with others. Encourage participants to complete the inventory within 30 minutes, as specified. Alternatively, you may just read the instructions given and encourage them to ask questions.

Indirect Administration

In some circumstances, you may decide to save time by sending the inventory in advance to participants. You may also decide to use the inventory as a multi-rater assessment tool by asking others who know the respondent to complete the inventory in order to obtain "other" scores. In either case, it is important to send the questionnaires in advance to the responders and remind them to read the instructions carefully before completing the inventory. The name of the person undergoing the assessment should be written on the "other" version of the inventory before sending to respondents.

The Scoring Process

A Scoring Sheet is provided. Respondents can score themselves, or you may score them either before or during a workshop. Depending on group size, the administration of the "self" version of the inventory, scoring, profiling, interpretation, and discussion of the scores will take 90 to 120 minutes. If the inventory is used as a multi-rater tool, the time will depend on the number of raters involved.

You may share the definitions given on the Score Prediction Sheet with the participants and encourage them to guess what their scores will be for each factor before starting the scoring process (or before sharing the scores with them). Alternatively, the participants may also ask close colleagues to predict their scores. The steps involved in the scoring are described on the Scoring Sheet. Scoring is simple when the 3D-ECI is used as a self-assessment tool. Participants will not need calculators.

When the inventory is used as a multi-rater assessment tool, it is important to complete the scoring before the session, either with or without the help of the respondents. In this case, you will need a calculator to find the average score for each category, subordinates, peers, supervisor, or customers, by adding the scores given by "others" and dividing by the total number of raters in each category.

When participants have finished scoring themselves, hand out the 3D-ECI Profile Graph and ask them to plot their totals on the graph. You may wish to project a slide showing some sample plots. After they have completed their Profile Graphs, give participants the Score Prediction and Interpretation Sheets so they can compare their actual scores with predicted scores.

Encourage participants to share any major differences between actual scores and predicted scores. You may also encourage them to analyze their results by looking at the scores of the individual items falling under each category. Participants can share their views of the possible reasons for differences between their predicted and actual scores. Some of the common reasons for the differences are lack of self-awareness, lack of frequent opportunities to gain feedback from others, differences in the understanding of the meaning of the factors, misunderstanding the items, and so forth. Tell participants that their actual scores are likely to be more accurate than their predicted scores and that if anyone has any doubts about an actual score, then he or she should review his or her responses to all the items in that category. You may wish to interpret some of the profiles from participants who are willing to share by highlighting the implications of the scores and interrelationships among them. Finally, you may encourage the participants to identify two or three actions for improving their behaviors and emotional competency.

Reliability and Validity

Reliability refers to the consistency of a measure internally across the items and subscales (for example, Cronbach alpha and split half reliability coefficients) as well as externally across time (test-retest reliability coefficient). The final items of the 3D-ECI were selected from an initial pool of items based on their contribution to the reliability indices (Cronbach alpha coefficients and item total correlations) of the seven factors. The 3D-ECI and its seven subscales were found to have high internal consistency as indicated by the Cronbach alpha coefficients, which ranged from 0.72 to 0.83. The split half reliability coefficient also was found to be high ($r = 0.76$).

The face validity of the 3D-ECI was ensured by using expert judges to evaluate the items used. Feedback from participants of the sessions using the 3D-ECI also indicated that it has high face validity. The 3D-ECI has reasonable content validity, as it was developed based on extensive review of existing literature and with the help of expert judges. Determination of other types of validities, such as predictive validity and construct validity, requires the scores of 3D-ECI to be correlated with other measures and tools. No attempt has been made to determine such types of validity for the 3D-ECI.

References

Bar-On, R. (1997). *The Emotional Quotient Inventory (EQ-i): A test of emotional intelligence.* Toronto: Multi-Health Systems, Inc.

Cooper, R.K., & Sawaf, A. (1996). *Executive EQ: Emotional intelligence in leadership and organizations.* New York: Grossett/Putnam.

Feldman, J., & Mulle, K. (2007). *Put emotional intelligence to work: Equip yourself for success.* Alexandria, VA: American Society for Training and Development.

Gardner, H. (1983). *Frames of mind: The theory of multiple intelligences.* New York: Basic Books.

Gardner, H. (1993). *Multiple intelligences: The theory in practice.* New York: Basic Books.

Gibbs, N. (1995, October 2).The EQ factor. *Time, 146,* 60–68.

Goleman, D. (1995). *Emotional intelligence.* New York: Bantam Books.

Goleman, D. (1998). *Working with emotional intelligence.* New York: Bantam Books.

Goleman, D., Boyatzis, R., & McKee, A. (2002). *Primal leadership: Learning to lead with emotional intelligence.* Boston: Harvard Business School Press.

Higgs, M.J., & Dulewicz, V. (1999). *Making sense of emotional intelligence.* Windsor, Ontario: NFER-Nelson.

Lynn, A. (2005). *The EQ difference.* New York: AMACOM.

Mayer, J.D., Salovey, P., & Caruso, D.R. (2004). Emotional intelligence: Theory, findings, and implications. *Psychological Inquiry, 15,* 197–215.

Mayer, J.D., & Salovey, P. (1993).The intelligence of emotional intelligence. *Intelligence, 17*(4), 433–442.

Payne, W.L. (1986). A study of emotion: Developing emotional intelligence; self integration; relating to fear, pain and desire. *Dissertation Abstracts International, 47,* 203A.

Salovey, P., & Mayer, J.D. (1990). Emotional intelligence. *Imagination, Cognition and Personality, 9*(3), 185–211.

Thorndike, E.L. (1920). Intelligence and its use. *Harper's Magazine, 140,* 227–235.

Thorndike, R.L. (1936). Factor analysis of social and abstract intelligence. *Journal of Educational Psychology, 27,* 231–233.

Wechsler, D. (1940). Non-intellective factors in general intelligence. *Psychological Bulletin, 37,* 444–445.

Wechsler, D. (1943). Non-intellective factors in general intelligence. *Journal of Abnormal Psychology, 38,* 100–104.

Dr. Sethu Madhavan Puravangara *is currently working with the Tawazun, Abu Dhabi. Earlier he worked with Ernst and Young, Larsen and Tubro, Abu Dhabi Company for Onshore Oil Operation, Indian Institute of Management, Centre for Organization Development, and Academy of HRD. He has rendered training and consulting services to many leading companies and has many publications to his credit. He has served as the editor of journals and as a member of the boards of several organizations.*

Three-Dimensional Emotional Competence Inventory (3D-ECI): Self

Sethu Madhavan Puravangara

Name: _____

Job title: _____

Instructions: In this survey you will find sixty-three phrases describing behaviors. Indicate how accurately each statement describes your behavior by agreeing or disagreeing with the statement using the 5-point rating scale below. Describe yourself as you generally are now and not as you wish to be in the future. Describe yourself as you honestly see yourself in relation to other people. Read each statement carefully and circle the appropriate number on the rating scale.

Please note that this is not a test and there is no right or wrong answer to any of the items. Complete this inventory in one sitting and within 30 minutes. Avoid pondering too much about any of the items.

Item	Strongly Disagree	Disagree	Undecided	Agree	Strongly Agree
I . . .					
1. Am not clear about my goals in life.	1	2	3	4	5
2. Feel proud of myself.	1	2	3	4	5
3. Am self-motivated.	1	2	3	4	5
4. Fail to control my moods.	1	2	3	4	5
5. Accept criticism from juniors.	1	2	3	4	5
6. Control gratification of my desires.	1	2	3	4	5
7. Return the support received from others.	1	2	3	4	5
8. Respect others' feelings.	1	2	3	4	5
9. Trust people, until they prove to not be trustworthy.	1	2	3	4	5
10. Do not enjoy parties and gatherings.	1	2	3	4	5

Item	Strongly Disagree	Disagree	Undecided	Agree	Strongly Agree
11. Am warm and kind to others.	1	2	3	4	5
12. Confidently interact with strangers at parties.	1	2	3	4	5
13. Am not sensitive to the rights of others.	1	2	3	4	5
14. Feel sorrow when I see others in distress.	1	2	3	4	5
15. Follow ethical and moral principles.	1	2	3	4	5
16. Look for win-win solutions.	1	2	3	4	5
17. Avoid problems rather than confronting them.	1	2	3	4	5
18. Remain balanced when faced with difficulties.	1	2	3	4	5
19. Am unhappy.	1	2	3	4	5
20. Dream about a positive future.	1	2	3	4	5
21. Freely express positive emotions to others.	1	2	3	4	5
22. Am aware of my feelings and emotions.	1	2	3	4	5
23. Am dissatisfied with my achievements in life.	1	2	3	4	5
24. Am not self-motivated to work.	1	2	3	4	5
25. Manage my anger and emotions well.	1	2	3	4	5
26. Become angry if a junior questions my views.	1	2	3	4	5
27. Fail to resist temptations.	1	2	3	4	5
28. Express gratitude to others for their support.	1	2	3	4	5
29. Feel superior to others.	1	2	3	4	5

Item	Strongly Disagree	Disagree	Undecided	Agree	Strongly Agree
30. Do not trust others until they prove worthy.	1	2	3	4	5
31. Enjoy attending social gatherings.	1	2	3	4	5
32. Am effective in my interactions with others.	1	2	3	4	5
33. Avoid mixing with strangers in gatherings.	1	2	3	4	5
34. Do not consider the needs of others.	1	2	3	4	5
35. Help people if they are facing any problems.	1	2	3	4	5
36. Am hard-working and reliable.	1	2	3	4	5
37. Prefer to collaborate rather than compete.	1	2	3	4	5
38. Confront difficult people without fear.	1	2	3	4	5
39. Cope with work stress effectively.	1	2	3	4	5
40. Maintain a friendly and positive mood.	1	2	3	4	5
41. Am optimistic.	1	2	3	4	5
42. Appreciate others for their strengths.	1	2	3	4	5
43. Am not aware of my weaknesses and limitations.	1	2	3	4	5
44. Feel ashamed of my achievements in life.	1	2	3	4	5
45. Am self-driven and need no pressure from others.	1	2	3	4	5
46. Do not shout or scream at others when upset.	1	2	3	4	5
47. Know that my ego gets hurt easily.	1	2	3	4	5

Item	Strongly Disagree	Disagree	Undecided	Agree	Strongly Agree
48. Act in an impulsive manner without thinking.	1	2	3	4	5
49. Fail to return the favors to others.	1	2	3	4	5
50. Am sensitive to people and their feelings.	1	2	3	4	5
51. Am suspicious of the intentions of others.	1	2	3	4	5
52. Like interacting with groups of people.	1	2	3	4	5
53. Make friends easily.	1	2	3	4	5
54. Fail to capture attention in groups.	1	2	3	4	5
55. Worry about the impact of my actions on others.	1	2	3	4	5
56. Feel sad when I see others suffering.	1	2	3	4	5
57. Avoid acting against my conscience.	1	2	3	4	5
58. Convert competition into collaboration.	1	2	3	4	5
59. Confront problems rather than avoiding them.	1	2	3	4	5
60. Cope with problems that are not in my control.	1	2	3	4	5
61. Am in a negative mood frequently.	1	2	3	4	5
62. Convert problems and threats into opportunities.	1	2	3	4	5
63. Feel jealous about the achievements of others.	1	2	3	4	5

Three-Dimensional Emotional Competence Inventory (3D–ECI): Other

Sethu Madhavan Puravangara

Your Name: _____

Your Job Title: _____

Person Being Assessed: _____

Your relationship with the person being assessed: _____

Instructions: This survey contains sixty-three phrases describing behaviors. Indicate how accurately each statement describes the behavior of the person you are rating by agreeing or disagreeing with the statement using the 5-point rating scale below. Describe the person as he or she generally is now and not as you wish he or she would be in the future. Describe the person as you honestly see him or her in relation to other people. Read each statement carefully and circle the appropriate number on the rating scale.

Please note that this is not a test and there is no right or wrong answer to any of the items. Complete this inventory in one sitting and within 30 minutes. Avoid pondering too much about any of the items.

Item	Strongly Disagree	Disagree	Undecided	Agree	Strongly Agree
This person . . .					
1. Is not clear about life goals.	1	2	3	4	5
2. Feels proud of him/herself.	1	2	3	4	5
3. Is self-motivated.	1	2	3	4	5
4. Fails to control moods.	1	2	3	4	5
5. Accepts criticism from juniors.	1	2	3	4	5
6. Controls gratification of desires.	1	2	3	4	5
7. Returns the support received from others.	1	2	3	4	5
8. Respects others' feelings.	1	2	3	4	5
9. Trusts people until they prove unworthy.	1	2	3	4	5

Item	Strongly Disagree	Disagree	Undecided	Agree	Strongly Agree
10. Does not enjoy parties and gatherings.	1	2	3	4	5
11. Is warm and kind to others.	1	2	3	4	5
12. Confidently interacts with strangers at parties.	1	2	3	4	5
13. Is not sensitive to the rights of others.	1	2	3	4	5
14. Feels sorrow when he/she sees others are in distress.	1	2	3	4	5
15. Follows ethical and moral principles.	1	2	3	4	5
16. Looks for win-win solutions.	1	2	3	4	5
17. Avoids problems rather than confronting them.	1	2	3	4	5
18. Remains balanced when faced with difficulties.	1	2	3	4	5
19. Is unhappy.	1	2	3	4	5
20. Dreams about a positive future.	1	2	3	4	5
21. Freely expresses positive emotions to others.	1	2	3	4	5
22. Is aware of his/her feelings and emotions.	1	2	3	4	5
23. Is dissatisfied with his/her achievements in life.	1	2	3	4	5
24. Is not self-motivated to work.	1	2	3	4	5
25. Manages his/her anger and emotions well.	1	2	3	4	5
26. Becomes angry if a junior questions his/her views.	1	2	3	4	5
27. Fails to resist temptations.	1	2	3	4	5
28. Expresses gratitude to others for their support.	1	2	3	4	5

Item	Strongly Disagree	Disagree	Undecided	Agree	Strongly Agree
29. Feels superior to others.	1	2	3	4	5
30. Does not trust others until they prove worthy.	1	2	3	4	5
31. Enjoys attending social gatherings.	1	2	3	4	5
32. Is effective in his/her interaction with others.	1	2	3	4	5
33. Avoids mixing with strangers in gatherings.	1	2	3	4	5
34. Does not consider the needs of others.	1	2	3	4	5
35. Helps people when they are facing any problem.	1	2	3	4	5
36. Is hard-working and reliable.	1	2	3	4	5
37. Prefers to collaborate rather than compete.	1	2	3	4	5
38. Confronts difficult people without fear.	1	2	3	4	5
39. Copes with work stress effectively.	1	2	3	4	5
40. Maintains a friendly and positive mood.	1	2	3	4	5
41. Is optimistic.	1	2	3	4	5
42. Appreciates others for their strengths.	1	2	3	4	5
43. Is not aware of his/her weaknesses and limitations.	1	2	3	4	5
44. Feels ashamed of his/her achievements in life.	1	2	3	4	5
45. Is self-driven and needs no pressure from others.	1	2	3	4	5
46. Does not shout or scream at others when upset.	1	2	3	4	5
47. Is hurt easily.	1	2	3	4	5

Item	Strongly Disagree	Disagree	Undecided	Agree	Strongly Agree
48. Acts in an impulsive manner without thinking.	1	2	3	4	5
49. Fails to return the favors to others.	1	2	3	4	5
50. Is sensitive to people and their feelings.	1	2	3	4	5
51. Is suspicious of the intentions of others.	1	2	3	4	5
52. Likes interacting with groups of people.	1	2	3	4	5
53. Makes friends easily.	1	2	3	4	5
54. Fails to capture attention in groups.	1	2	3	4	5
55. Worries about the impact of his/her actions on others.	1	2	3	4	5
56. Feels sad about the suffering of others.	1	2	3	4	5
57. Avoids acting against his/her conscience.	1	2	3	4	5
58. Converts competition into collaboration.	1	2	3	4	5
59. Confronts problems rather than avoiding them.	1	2	3	4	5
60. Copes with problems that are not in his/her control.	1	2	3	4	5
61. Is frequently in a negative mood.	1	2	3	4	5
62. Converts problems and threats into opportunities.	1	2	3	4	5
63. Feels jealous about the achievements of others.	1	2	3	4	5

3D-ECI Score Prediction and Interpretation Sheet

3D-ECI Factors	Predicted Score	Actual Score (Self)	Actual Score (Others)*
1. *Maintain self-esteem and motivation:* Ability to maintain positive self-esteem, self-motivation, and self-awareness			
2. *Manage impulses and emotions:* Ability to manage one's emotions, impulses, and ego			
3. *Maintain relationships:* Ability to maintain healthy interpersonal relationships through trust, sensitivity to others, and by maintaining reciprocity			
4. *Manage social situations:* Ability to manage social situations effectively by taking active interest, demonstrating confidence, and showing friendly behavior toward others			
5. *Maintain compassion and conscientiousness:* Ability to be compassionate, considerate, and conscientious			
6. *Manage challenges and threats:* Ability to manage stress, threats, and challenges in life through confrontation, collaboration, or coping			
7. *Maintain positivity:* Ability to remain positive to oneself and others by focusing on positive thoughts, maintaining positive attitude, and expressing positive feelings			

*Actual Scores (Others) is applicable only if the "other" version of the inventory was used

3D-ECI Scoring Sheet

Instructions: Transfer your raw scores from each item to the scoring table on the next page. *While transferring scores to the shaded cells in the table, you must reverse the scores as indicated*:

     1 = 5; 2 = 4; 3 = 3; 4 = 2; 5 = 1

    Next calculate add the individual scores to obtain a total score for each of the twenty-one subscales and calculate the scores on the three dimensions.

Item No	Score	Item No	Score	Item No	Score	Sub-scale No	Total Scores on Subscales	Total Scores on Factors	Total Score on Dimensions
1		22		43		1A	Self awareness ___	Maintain self esteem and motivation (M1)= ___	Dealing with self ((M1+M2)/2) =
2		23		44		1B	Self esteem ___		
3		24		45		1C	Self motivation ___		
4		25		46		2A	Emotional control ___	Manage impulses and emotions (M2)= ___	
5		26		47		2B	Ego control ___		
6		27		48		2C	Impulse control ___		
7		28		49		3A	Interpersonal reciprocity ___	Maintain relationships (M3)= ___	Dealing with others ((M3+M4)/2) =
8		29		50		3B	Interpersonal Sensitivity ___		
9		30		51		3C	Interpersonal trust ___		
10		31		52		4A	Social interest ___	Manage social situations (M4)= ___	
11		32		53		4B	Social interaction ___		
12		33		54		4C	Social confidence ___		
13		34		55		5A	Considerateness ___	Maintain compassion and conscientiousness (M5)= ___	Dealing with life ((M5+M6+M7)/3) =
14		35		56		5B	Compassion ___		
15		36		57		5C	Conscientiousness ___		
16		37		58		6A	Collaboration ___	Manage challenges and threats (M6)= ___	
17		38		59		6B	Confrontation ___		
18		39		60		6C	Coping ___		
19		40		61		7A	Positive mood ___	Maintain positivity (M7)= ___	
20		41		62		7B	Positive thoughts ___		
21		42		63		7C	Positive expressions ___		

3D–ECI Profile Graph

Scores	M1 Maintain self esteem and motivation	M2 Manage impulses and emotions	M3 Maintain relationships	M4 Manage social situations	M5 Maintain compassion and conscientiousness	M6 Manage challenges and threats(M6)	M7 Maintain positivity
45							
43							
41							
39							
37							
35							
33							
31							
29							
27							
25							
23							
21							
19							
17							
15							
13							
11							
9							

Classroom Instructor Skills Survey

Jean Barbazette

Summary

Classroom trainers can only improve their skills if they have an appropriate model for instruction, are able to assess their own skills, gain feedback from others, and create and follow an improvement plan. The Classroom Instructor Skills Survey allows instructors to assess their own skills. This survey benchmarks essential behaviors for classroom instructors. It can also be used to assess an instructor's skills. An improvement plan is provided that helps the instructor make use of the survey results.

Instructors who conduct training in a classroom setting will benefit most from taking this survey, which is not intended for those who conduct training on the job. Instructors can measure their current training techniques and practices against certain benchmarks. Instructors' scores are collected in the form of a bar chart. A performance plan is included so those taking the survey can work on areas for improvement.

Training departments can use the survey to profile an entire department's strengths and weaknesses. A department development plan can be created that is aimed at eliminating widespread deficiencies.

Each skill area is presented as a checklist so that each respondent can easily rate him- or herself in that area. The checklists can also be used by classroom observers, who would provide feedback and suggestions for improvement.

The ten classroom instructor skills surveyed are:

1. Uses adult learning techniques

2. Gives feedback evaluation to learners

3. Uses lecture

4. Uses discussion techniques

5. Uses case studies, exercises, games, and simulations

6. Conducts demonstrations

7. Uses role play

8. Uses audiovisuals as a learning tool

9. Administers tests

10. Handles problem learners assertively

Description of the Survey

One hundred instructor behaviors, techniques, or practices are grouped into ten skill areas for assessment. Respondents use a scale from 0 to 10 to rate how often they currently use each behavior in the course of a normal training session. Frequency descriptions range from never (0) to always (10). Thus, a total of 100 points can be earned for *each* of the ten skill areas. Total scores for each skill are transferred to a bar chart so relative strengths and weaknesses can be seen prior to creating an individual development plan.

Having a development plan encourages respondents to identify strengths that can be used to mentor others. Deficiencies are sorted into those that require feedback and coaching versus those that require further training. If an instructor has already acquired a skill, feedback and coaching can serve as reminders to use that skill more often. If a skill is lacking, training is needed to improve in that area.

Administration of the Survey

Prior to handing out the survey, review the ten skill categories with respondents. Select only those categories that are used in an instructor's environment. For example, technical trainers would not use role play. If the behaviors are to be used as standards of performance, gain consensus on definitions for the quality measures. For example, gain agreement on what constitutes "desired performance" or "appropriate summary" or "efficiently performed." Depending on the use of the survey, instructors can be asked to complete it alone or in a mini-workshop setting.

After handing out the survey, review the directions with the respondents. For each skill category selected, they are to answer the question: "*How often* do you currently *use* this skill?" They then assign a number between 0 and 10 to describe how often they use each behavior. Remind them not to think too long about any one item, as initial reactions are usually the best.

The time to complete a survey with all ten skill areas is 20 to 30 minutes. Allow an additional 20 to 30 minutes for scoring, charting scores, and creating development plans. When the survey is administered in a group setting, additional discussion time with a peer or supervisor is suggested. Some possible discussion questions are given in the performance plan.

The Theory Behind the Survey

This is a self-reporting assessment. The respondent is asked to recall how *often* or how frequently he or she uses a behavior, technique, or practice in the classroom. The respondents are not asked how well they perform, but how well an instructor performs is presumably determined by the frequent completion of the behaviors listed. For example, when rating the "Uses Lecture" skill, the respondent rates whether he or she uses a participation technique every 15 minutes. If an instructor uses a participation technique every 15 minutes throughout a lecture, retention is likely to increase, and therefore the instructor is rated higher than an instructor who does not use the technique.

The ten behaviors in each skill area have been developed over twenty years of train-the-trainer experience and by instructing more than 100,000 trainers in classroom instruction techniques.

Predicting Scores

Respondents can be asked to predict which of the ten skill areas will be rated the highest for them or are their strengths. Predictions can also be made about which areas need the greatest improvement.

Predictions are likely to be more accurate if an instructor is experienced. Of course, because this is a self-reporting survey, predictions may show a conscious or unconscious bias.

Scoring Process

The competency level for each skill ranges from 0 to 100. To arrive at a numerical score, each of the ten behaviors was given a range of ten points. Respondents total the numbers assigned to each behavior to determine a score for that skill. They repeat this process for each of the ten skills and then use the score sheet to create a bar chart of the ten skills.

Interpreting Scores

Once each respondent has created a bar chart of his or her ten skills, relative strengths and weaknesses can be identified visually. Respondents can now develop performance plans. Based on the items that are rated high, the respondent can list strengths that can be used to mentor other instructors. Lower scores can be separated into two types of deficiencies:

1. Deficiencies that can be corrected by coaching because the instructor has already acquired a skill, but needs feedback and suggestions and a reminder to use that skill more often.

2. Deficiencies that can be corrected by training, because the instructor has never acquired that skill.

To determine what can be done to raise a score, the respondent can look at the individual behaviors within the skill that he or she rated with a lower score.

Posting Scores

If the survey is conducted with a group, individual scores can be posted. Scores from each respondent can be collected by skill. For example, if a department of eight instructors completed the survey, a profile of their scores for "Uses Lecture" can be completed. This will allow the group to identify common strengths and weaknesses. Mentors and coaches can be identified within the group to help low-scoring respondents work on deficiencies, or group training may be required for a specific skill.

It may also be appropriate for pairs to discuss their performance plans and ask for feedback on the validity of their self-reports from others who have observed them instruct. Questions for discussion are included in the performance plan.

Suggested Uses

Several uses are appropriate for the survey:

- *Self-Evaluation.* Instructors can identify relative strengths and weaknesses and develop performance plans for personal improvement. Those new to classroom instruction who have not received formal training may not have enough experience to accurately interpret their results without assistance.

- *Training Department Self-Evaluation.* A group of instructors in a given department can evaluate themselves to create a picture of common needs and then plan group development.

- *Training Department Other Evaluation.* Supervisors or peers can evaluate an instructor's performance using the survey skills as checklists during an observation of a training session.

- *Curriculum Development.* The behaviors can be used as the basis for a train-the-trainer curriculum.

- *Other Uses.* If the survey is used to select new employees as instructors, it should not be the only determining factor. If the survey is used to develop standards of performance for instructors and then to appraise performance as part of an annual performance appraisal process, other factors should be included also.

Reliability, Validity

The validity of the survey has not been formally established. As with all self-reporting surveys, bias and perception play a role in determining scores. This tendency is somewhat minimized if the respondents rate *how often* they use a behavior, rather than *how well* they perform.

Jean Barbazette *is president of The Training Clinic, a training consulting firm she founded in 1977. The firm specializes in train-the-trainer, new employee orientation, and enhancing the quality of training and instruction for major national and international clients. Jean holds a master's degree in education from Stanford University. Published works include* Successful New Employee Orientation, *now in a third edition;* The Trainer's Support Handbook; Instant Case Studies; The Trainer's Journey to Competence: Tools, Assessments, and Models; Training Needs Assessment; The Art of Great Training Delivery; *and* Managing the Training Function for Bottom-Line Results.

Classroom Instructor Skills Survey

Jean Barbazette

Instructions: Assign a number between 0 and 10 to indicate how often you use each behavior described below. Don't think too long about any one item. Trust your first reaction. The following scale will give you an idea of the range from 0 to 10.

0 = rarely; 2 = seldom; 4 = sometimes; 6 = often; 8 = with great regularity; 10 = almost always

1. Use Adult Learning Techniques

_____ 1. Encourage learners to determine their own learning experiences.

_____ 2. Ask learners to relate their past experiences to learn something new.

_____ 3. Help learners identify the benefits and tangible rewards of training.

_____ 4. Avoid wasting learners' time.

_____ 5. Use teaching techniques that include learner participation at least 50 percent of class time.

_____ 6. Help learners identify that they have a need to learn.

_____ 7. Recognize that adults use their knowledge from years of experience as a filter for new information and don't change readily.

_____ 8. Give practical answers for today's problems.

_____ 9. Provide for physical comfort with refreshments and breaks in a relaxed atmosphere.

_____ 10. Use practical problem-solving techniques.

_____ **Total points for this skill**

2. Give Feedback Evaluation to Learners

_____ 1. Describe what the learner is doing rather than place a value on it or make a judgment.

_____ 2. Stick to immediate issues. Avoid "always" and "never."

_____ 3. Select a few issues for feedback. Do not overload (no more than three issues).

0 = rarely; 2 = seldom; 4 = sometimes; 6 = often; 8 = with great regularity; 10 = almost always

_____ 4. Am specific rather than general in describing learner behavior.

_____ 5. Clearly focus on learner behavior rather than attitude.

_____ 6. Direct feedback toward behavior the learner can do something about. Avoid comparative statements.

_____ 7. Give information when usable (well-timed), neither too early nor too late.

_____ 8. Give feedback when it is asked for rather than impose it.

_____ 9. Identify whether the learner is capable of the desired performance.

_____ 10. Use paraphrasing to ensure clear communication and understanding.

_____ **Total points for this skill**

3. Use Lecture

_____ 1. Begin with climate-setting activity to encourage learning.

_____ 2. Provide clear and correct information.

_____ 3. Organize ideas so they are easy to follow.

_____ 4. Use handouts and visuals to enhance learning.

_____ 5. Provide enough examples and a variety of examples.

_____ 6. Address questions well.

_____ 7. Use a participation technique every 15 minutes.

_____ 8. Manage instructional time efficiently.

_____ 9. Practice appropriate platform techniques: gestures, eye contact, movement, avoids distracting words (ah, um, ya' know), vary speaking rate, pitch, and volume.

_____ 10. End with an appropriate summary or call to action.

_____ **Total points for this skill**

0 = rarely; 2 = seldom; 4 = sometimes; 6 = often; 8 = with great regularity;
10 = almost always

4. Use Discussion Techniques

_____ 1. Include each member of the group (draw out if needed); call people by name.

_____ 2. Remain impartial unless asked for an opinion.

_____ 3. Ask questions; do not make statements.

_____ 4. Question generalizations and encourage specific examples. Probe for deeper meanings until a question is answered.

_____ 5. Ask members of the group to relate specific examples of a general idea.

_____ 6. Direct the discussion by barring irrelevant details and redirect the discussion if necessary.

_____ 7. Call for a summary of one point before going to the next.

_____ 8. Have members of the group discuss with each other, not just with you.

_____ 9. Delegate members of the group to find more information if needed.

_____ 10. Clarify for better understanding; define terms so all have a common understanding.

_____ **Total points for this skill**

5. Use Case Studies, Exercises, Games, and Simulations

_____ 1. Identify the objectives of the activity.

_____ 2. Set up the activity by describing the objectives and the role of participants.

_____ 3. Give clear directions.

_____ 4. Efficiently and appropriately group participants.

_____ 5. Ask participants to complete the learning activity without overdirecting.

_____ 6. Encourage participants to share and interpret their reactions to the activity by asking appropriate open and closed questions.

_____ 7. Continue to probe for reactions until all viewpoints have been expressed.

_____ 8. Request that participants identify the concepts learned from the activity.

0 = rarely; 2 = seldom; 4 = sometimes; 6 = often; 8 = with great regularity; 10 = almost always

_____ 9. Help the participants apply the concepts to their own settings.

_____ 10. Handle unexpected learning appropriately.

_____ **Total points for this skill**

6. Conduct Demonstrations

_____ 1. Identify the objective of any demonstration and share it with the learners.

_____ 2. Assess the risk of any demonstration for the target population and take steps to handle the risk.

_____ 3. Demonstrate the task by showing what to do and tell why it is done that way.

_____ 4. Conduct a second demonstration of the task while the learners tell what is done and why it is done that way.

_____ 5. Correct the learner or reinstruct if necessary.

_____ 6. Require the learners to demonstrate the task.

_____ 7. Give feedback to the learners during the demonstration.

_____ 8. Ask the learners to summarize the demonstrated functions.

_____ 9. Supervise continued learner practice until a skill is learned.

_____ 10. Evaluate performance and assess skill after sufficient practice.

_____ **Total points for this skill**

7. Use Role Play

_____ 1. Identify a clear objective for role plays.

_____ 2. Set up a role play by sharing the objectives, selecting participants, and preparing the role players.

_____ 3. Structure role plays to be done in groups of three to avoid embarrassing learners in front of the entire group.

_____ 4. Instruct observers and provide a checklist of points to look for.

_____ 5. Ask participants to play the scene, without overdirecting.

0 = rarely; 2 = seldom; 4 = sometimes; 6 = often; 8 = with great regularity; 10 = almost always

_____ 6. Give directions to limit feedback to specific issues.

_____ 7. Ask participants to share and interpret reactions.

_____ 8. Ask participants to reverse roles.

_____ 9. Request that participants identify concepts developed through the role play.

_____ 10. Help participants apply what was learned to their own situations.

_____ **Total points for this skill**

8. Use Audiovisuals as a Learning Tool

_____ 1. Select appropriate audiovisuals to fit the learning objectives.

_____ 2. Limit copy to eight lines so visuals and writing are easy to read.

_____ 3. Use pictures/clip art in visuals to enhance retention.

_____ 4. Use colored visuals to enhance retention.

_____ 5. Write legibly on an easel pad. Spell words correctly.

_____ 6. Arrange the classroom so all participants can see the screen or hear the recording.

_____ 7. Avoid blocking participants' view of the visual.

_____ 8. Turn off the projector when the visual is not in use.

_____ 9. Operate mechanical equipment with ease.

_____ 10. Troubleshoot minor mechanical problems effectively.

_____ **Total points for this skill**

9. Administer Tests

_____ 1. Limit test content to material already taught.

_____ 2. Distribute materials efficiently and at the appropriate time.

_____ 3. Give clear directions.

_____ 4. Answer questions appropriately and clearly without providing unwarranted assistance.

0 = rarely; 2 = seldom; 4 = sometimes; 6 = often; 8 = with great regularity; 10 = almost always

_____ 5. If a test is given on the job, give feedback appropriately as steps are completed.

_____ 6. Monitor participants by moving around the room and give time remaining warnings at appropriate intervals.

_____ 7. Collect materials at the appropriate time.

_____ 8. Establish clear criteria for accuracy of test answers.

_____ 9. Correct and return tests in a timely manner.

_____ 10. Provide feedback to learners about incorrect answers.

_____ **Total points for this skill**

10. Handle Problem Learners Assertively

_____ 1. Recognize when problems are related to the content of training or the process of instruction.

_____ 2. Correctly identify the probable cause of problem behavior that is not related to a training issue.

_____ 3. Selectively ignore minor problems that will end by themselves.

_____ 4. Anticipate possible problems by becoming familiar with the content, target population, and classroom environment.

_____ 5. Take steps to prevent possible problems.

_____ 6. Use a small group activity to redirect the energy of a problem learner.

_____ 7. Incorporate questions appropriately to involve a passive learner.

_____ 8. Confront problem learners in private using a feedback model: observe, describe, agree on a resolution.

_____ 9. Confront problem learners in class using a disciplinary technique only after other methods fail.

_____ 10. Assess the results: the problem ends or continues (so start over).

_____ **Total points for this skill**

Classroom Instructor Skills Survey Scoring Sheet

Scores											
	100										
	90										
	80										
	70										
	60										
	50										
	40										
	30										
	20										
	10										
	0										
	Skills	1. Adult learner	2. Feedback	3. Lecture	4. Discussion	5. Case study	6. Demonstration	7. Role play	8. Audiovisual	9. Admin tests	10. Problem learners

Classroom Instructor Performance Plan

Instructor:

Date:

1. List strong skills from the scoring sheet:

2. Identify skills that need to be trained or retrained to perform current duties:

   Identify resources and/or dates for training:

3. Identify skills that require coaching and feedback:

   Select dates for observation and feedback:

4. Decide what else the manager can do to support this instructor:

   Highlight strengths for mentoring other instructors.

Institutional Climate Survey

K.S. Gupta

Summary

For the last century, business has been the driving force of our society, leading to extraordinary economic growth and opportunity. The leaders of educational institutions have the necessary knowledge and skills to make their institutions into effective businesses too. The Institutional Climate Survey is a way to assess an institution's current climate and find weak areas so leaders can operate their institution more successfully in the current global economy.

Due to extensive globalization, many changes have taken place in society and business today. Business schools have a crucial role to play through the way their institutions are managed and the way faculty and staff contribute to society as a whole, with the objective of ensuring the best possible level of education so that students are ready to contribute to organizations of the future.

Since the mid-1990s, the demand for business education has surged worldwide. In response to that demand, and because of the relatively low cost of entry into the business education sector, many new business programs—even entire business schools—have been established around the world. Assuming the world economy continues to expand, the demand for business education will continue to grow, especially in the developing world (Connolly, 2003; Mintzberg, 2004; Pfeifer & Fong, 2002, 2003).

The present global environment provides a great opportunity for business schools, particularly those located in high-growth economies such as India. But there are also a number of challenges, particularly for those located in mature economies such as the UK.

In order to meet these challenges, business schools must differentiate themselves from one another. Schools can strengthen their competitive positions by globalizing or by offering innovative programs. Schools that successfully leverage their investments can reach a larger number of students more effectively.

Job Satisfaction

Job satisfaction has received considerable attention by researchers and managers alike (Gautam, Mandal, & Dalal, 2006). Job satisfaction surveys provide important information about employees (Roznowski & Hulin, 1992).

Research suggests that job satisfaction and job performance are positively correlated (Bowran & Todd, 1999). Job satisfaction leads to higher employee commitment and high commitment leads to overall organizational success (Feinstein, 2000). Job satisfaction also leads to increased growth, effectiveness, and efficiency and reduces employees' desire to leave the organization (Mosadeghard, 2000).

Hagedorn (1994) found that, for faculty at different stages of career development, salary, total work hours, and co-workers' support affected job satisfaction. Bender and Heywood (2006) concluded that increased freedom and flexibility of academicians resulted in significantly greater job satisfaction. Other studies have shown that salary, social status, advancement, ability utilization, administration-employee relationships, creativity, and security were the main factors that determine job satisfaction among education sector employees (Sonmezer & Eryaman, 2008).

Lack of advancement opportunities, poor work environment, lack of encouragement, and lack of recognition may lead to stress, which ultimately causes dissatisfaction, burnout, and increased turnover rates (Ahmadi & Alireza, 2007). Job satisfaction is inversely related to burnout and intent to leave the organization (Penn, Ramono, & Foat, 1988). Job satisfaction is increased when income is greater than predicted income in the education sector (Bender & Heywood, 2006).

Due to intense competition in the education sector and the desire to reach a satisfactory return on investment as quickly as possible, there has been increased pressure to ensure job satisfaction among faculty in educational institutions because, for the past five years, in particular, faculty turnover rates have been alarmingly high in the management education area.

The Institutional Climate Survey presented here provides a framework to measure the job satisfaction of employees in educational institutes to help management understand what must be improved.

Framework for the Survey

Based on a literature search and discussions with experienced faculty and management in several business schools, the parameters in Figure 1 were used to develop an inventory to measure the environment of schools.

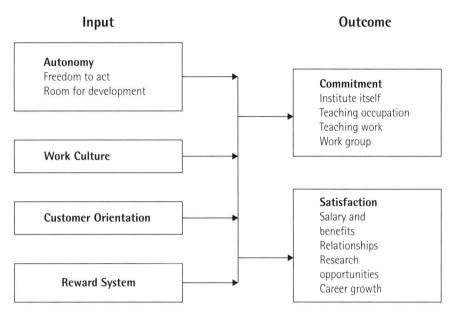

Figure 1. Framework of Institutional Climate Survey

Development of the Survey

The research design used a descriptive-correlative survey method, and data were collected through a questionnaire that was developed by the author. The original survey consisted of fifty-two items. However, after conducting a factor analysis with a rotating matrix, items were selected that had a score of .5 and higher. The final survey contains forty-four items and uses a 5-point Likert scale with responses varying from 1 (very dissatisfied) to 5 (very satisfied).

Reliability

The instrument was tested for reliability by conducting a pilot test with eighteen faculty members who were not included in the sample. Reliability was estimated by calculating the Cronbach alpha, resulting in a reliability of .93 for the overall instrument.

Description of the Survey

The various parameters of the survey are described below.

- *Autonomy.* For faculty, autonomy means freedom to act in terms of teaching methodology and taking action as needed, as well as support for self-development, such as conference participation.

- *Work Culture.* Faculty values equality, transparent policies, and professional fulfillment at the workplace. This type of culture also provides them with the power to influence others.

- *Customer Orientation.* In a school, students are the main customers. The faculty is required to maintain the students' interest in self-development, provide guidance for their career choices, and mentor them when needed.

- *Reward System.* Faculty satisfaction with the appraisal system and reviews of progress means that they feel they are rewarded properly.

- *Commitment.* The commitment of faculty can be measured based of four professional constituents: the institute itself, the teaching profession, teaching work itself, and the work group.

  - *Commitment to the institute* itself can be seen from the point of view of job stability, whether the institute was the person's first employment choice, and whether one is happy to serve the institute.

  - *Teaching Profession.* Satisfaction from the choice of occupation depends on both social recognition and teaching load. Higher self-esteem comes from the feeling that teaching is a respected occupation.

  - *Teaching Work.* This item measures whether the environment is enjoyable and conducive for teaching. It also considers the amount of flexibility the institute gives instructors on the job.

  - *Work Group.* The group faculty members work with is another important parameter for satisfaction. Knowledgeable, trustworthy, helpful, and polite faculty mean a respectful and happy work group.

- *Satisfaction.* Salary and benefits contribute the greater part of faculty satisfaction.

- *Relationships.* The belief that one is treated fairly is important. The leadership styles of senior management and fellow associates also contribute to a satisfactory environment.

- *Research.* Research plays a role in bringing out new concepts and applications. Better research support for individual faculty and support for organizing conferences provide increased satisfaction.

- *Career Growth.* Faculty satisfaction also depends on opportunities and support for career growth.

Who Should Use This Survey

Management can use this survey to determine the satisfaction levels of the faculty and the parameters on which they should improve.

Researchers can use this survey to conduct comparative studies to determine the level of satisfaction on different parameters in different institutions.

Consultants can use the survey to find the level of satisfaction and suggest improvements. After changes are made, the survey can be re-administered to determine the effectiveness of interventions used. Researchers and consultants can also use this instrument to find best practices for improving any institutional climate.

Administration of the Survey

The survey should be administered by a consultant and the responses collected within a prescribed time limit for the most accurate responses. The survey takes about 15 minutes to complete.

Scoring and Interpretation

The four input and two outcome variables were shown in the framework in Figure 1. There are two sub-parameters of autonomy and four sub-parameters of each outcome variable. Average scores of all items within each parameter should be calculated.

A score of more than 3 in an area is considered good and above 4 is excellent. Below 3 is considered poor and definitely requires immediate attention to improve the institutional climate.

References

Ahmadi, K., & Alireza, K. (2007). Stress and job satisfaction among Air Force military pilots. *Journal of Social Sciences, 3*(3), 159–163.

Bender, K.A., & Heywood, J.S. (2006). Job satisfaction of highly educated. *Scottish Journal of Political Economy, 53*(2), 253–279.

Bowran, J., & Todd, K. (1999). Job stressor and job satisfaction in a major metropolitan public EMS service. *Pre-Hospital and Disaster Medicine, 14*(4), 236–239.

Castillo, J.X., & Cano, J. (2004). Factors explaining job satisfaction among faculty; *Journal of Agricultural Education, 45*(3), 65–74.

Gautam, M., Mandal, K., & Dalal, R.S. (2006). Job satisfaction of faculty members of veterinary sciences: An analysis. *Livestock Research for Rural Development, 18*(7).

Hagedorn, L.S. (1994). Retirement proximity's role in the prediction of satisfaction in academe. *Research in Higher Education, 35*(6), 711–728.

Mosadeghard, A.M. (2008). A study of the relationship between job satisfaction, organizational commitment, and turnover intention among hospital employees. *Health Services Management Research, 21*, 211–217.

Penn, M., Romano, J.L., & Foat, D. (1988). The relationship between job satisfaction and burnout: A study of human service professionals. *Administration in Mental Health, 15*(3), 157–163.

Rosnowski, M., & Hulin, C. (1992). The scientific merit of valid measures of general constructs with special reference to job satisfaction and job withdrawal. In C.J. Cranny, P.C. Smith, & E.F. Stone (Eds.), *Job satisfaction: How people feel about their jobs and how it affects their performance.* New York: Lexington Books.

Sonmezer, M.G., & Eryaman, M.Y. (2008). A comparative analysis of job satisfaction level of public and private school. *Journal of Theory and Practice in Education, 4*(2), 189–212.

K.S. Gupta *is the director, School of Business and Management, Jaipur National University, Jaipur, India. He holds a doctorate in management with an MBA in HR and marketing and a master's in applied electronics. He has been a professor in business schools for the past five years after thirty-four years in aeronautical industries. As a consultant and trainer, he has conducted more than four hundred training programs for more than one hundred organizations. He has published more than fifty research papers on empowerment, leadership, knowledge management, supply chain management, empowerment of children, business models, and inventory development for quantitative measurement of behavioral aspects.*

Institutional Climate Survey

K.S. Gupta

Name:

Position:

Organization:

Department:

Instructions: Please rate the following statements as they apply to this institution, using the following scale:

Strongly Disagree   1   2   3   4   5   Strongly Agree

In general, this institute's environment:

1. Is knowledgeable.	1	2	3	4	5
2. Is trustworthy.	1	2	3	4	5
3. Is helpful.	1	2	3	4	5
4. Is polite.	1	2	3	4	5
5. Has students' best interests in mind.	1	2	3	4	5
6. Mentors students to overcome personal problems.	1	2	3	4	5
7. Helps students make better career choices.	1	2	3	4	5
8. Is enjoyable for teaching.	1	2	3	4	5
9. Is helpful in developing better relationships.	1	2	3	4	5
10. Is supportive in developing my ability to communicate with others.	1	2	3	4	5

This institute provides:

11. Maximum flexibility in the job.	1	2	3	4	5
12. Maximum stability.	1	2	3	4	5
13. Support for career growth.	1	2	3	4	5

Strongly Disagree   1   2   3   4   5   Strongly Agree

		1	2	3	4	5
14.	Social recognition.	1	2	3	4	5
15.	A basis for higher self-esteem.	1	2	3	4	5
16.	Maximum freedom in terms of teaching method.	1	2	3	4	5
17.	Maximum freedom to act.	1	2	3	4	5
18.	Maximum equality.	1	2	3	4	5
19.	Transparent policies.	1	2	3	4	5
20.	Excellent promotional prospects.	1	2	3	4	5
21.	Power to influence others.	1	2	3	4	5
22.	Opportunity for career growth.	1	2	3	4	5
23.	Research support.	1	2	3	4	5
24.	Professional fulfillment.					
25.	Autonomy in faculty work.	1	2	3	4	5

I am satisfied with:

		1	2	3	4	5
26.	My compensation.	1	2	3	4	5
27.	The amount of time I spend at work.	1	2	3	4	5
28.	My benefits.	1	2	3	4	5
29.	Support for conference participation.	1	2	3	4	5
30.	Amount of vacation time.	1	2	3	4	5
31.	Opportunities for self-development.	1	2	3	4	5
32.	My teaching load.	1	2	3	4	5
33.	The appraisal system.	1	2	3	4	5
34.	My progress review.	1	2	3	4	5
35.	Research support.	1	2	3	4	5
36.	Fair dealing.	1	2	3	4	5
37.	Leadership style of senior management.	1	2	3	4	5

Strongly Disagree	1	2	3	4	5	Strongly Agree

	1	2	3	4	5
38. Support for self-development		1	2	3	4	5
39. My associates.		1	2	3	4	5
40. Support for organizing conferences.		1	2	3	4	5

Overall:

41. My current institute is my first choice for employment.	1	2	3	4	5
42. I am happy with the service I receive from my institute.	1	2	3	4	5
43. I think that faculty like working in this institute.	1	2	3	4	5
44. I feel that teaching is the best occupation.	1	2	3	4	5

Institutional Climate Survey Scoring Sheet

Instructions: Put your scores for each item in the box in which the item number appears. Add your scores in each box together, and divide by the number of items in each category for your average score for each dimension of Autonomy and each dimension of Commitment. You will be able to see where your institutional climate could be improved for your satisfaction.

Variable Autonomy	Items	Variable Commitment	Items
Freedom to Act	16, 17, 25	Institute Itself	12, 41, 42, 43
Freedom for Development	10, 29, 31, 38	Teaching Occupation	14, 15, 44
		Teaching Work	8, 11, 32
		Work Group Satisfaction	1, 2, 3, 4
Work Culture	18, 19, 21, 24	Salary and benefits	26, 27, 28, 30
Customer Orientation	5, 6, 7	Relationships	9, 36, 37, 39
Reward System	33, 34	Research Opportunities	23, 35, 40
		Career Growth	13, 20, 22

Introduction
to the Articles and Discussion Resources Section

The Articles and Discussion Resources Section is a collection of materials useful to every facilitator. The theories, background information, models, and methods will challenge facilitators' thinking, enrich their professional development, and assist their internal and external clients with productive change. These articles may be used as a basis for lecturettes, as handouts in training sessions, or as background reading material. This section will provide you with a variety of useful ideas, theoretical opinions, teachable models, practical strategies, and proven intervention methods. The articles will add richness and depth to your training and consulting knowledge and skills. They will challenge you to think differently, explore new concepts, and experiment with new interventions. The articles will continue to add a fresh perspective to your work.

The 2012 Pfeiffer Annual: Training features twelve articles, including six that focus on this year's theme of Learning in the Moment.

The following categories are represented:

Individual Development: Personal Growth

> **One-Minute Learning Through Reflective Practice, by Homer H. Johnson and Anne H. Reilly

Communication: Coaching and Encouraging

> **Questioning the Teachable Moment, by Brittany Ashby

Communication: Technology

> †**Opportunities and Risks of Incorporating User-Created Content in an Organizational Training Strategy, by Christine Hipple and Zane L. Berge

---

**Learning in the Moment Topics
†Cutting-Edge Topics

Problem Solving: Models, Methods, and Techniques

Building Bridges Between Psychology and Conflict Resolution: Implications for Mediator Learning, by Kenneth Cloke

Problem Solving: Change and Change Agents

How to Avoid Change Management Workshops That Fail, by Rick Maurer

Groups and Teams: Techniques to Use with Groups

Mistakes That Trainers Make—And How to Avoid Them, by Deborah Spring Laurel

Consulting/Training: Strategies and Techniques

†**Adopting a Learning Continuum: The Urgency to Reinvent Training Organizations, by Gary G. Wise

Strategies and Technologies for Posting Training Presentations Online, by Tom Bunzel

Facilitating: Theories and Models

Online Learning 101: Using a Framework to Consider and Select e-Learning Tools, by Susan Landay

Facilitating: Techniques and Strategies

**Using Playbooks: A Unique Strategy in Technical Oversight of Highly Hazardous Operations, by James L. Gary and Michele L. Summers

Facilitating in the Virtual Classroom: How to Compensate for the Lack of Body Language, by Darlene B. Christopher

Facilitating: Evaluation

**The Story of the Kirkpatrick Four Levels: Evaluating in the Moment, by Don Kirkpatrick with Elaine Biech

As with previous *Annuals*, this volume covers a wide variety of topics. The range of articles presented encourages thought-provoking discussion about the present and future of HRD. We have done our best to categorize the articles for easy reference; however, many of the articles encompass a range of topics, disciplines, and applications. If you do not find what you are looking for under one category, check a related category. In some cases we may place an article in the "Training" *Annual* that also has implications for "Consulting" and vice versa. As the field of HRD continues to grow and develop, there is more and more crossover between training and consulting. Explore all the contents of both volumes of the *Annual* in order to realize the full potential for learning and development that each offers.

One-Minute Learning Through Reflective Practice

Homer H. Johnson and Anne H. Reilly

Summary

While the evidence is quite convincing that managers and leaders have their primary managerial learning experience on the job, a related key question is how they can best maximize their on-the-job learning. This article describes a reflective technique that is designed to be used immediately after challenging work events. Labeled "One-Minute Reflective Learning" and using the four R's—Replay, Reevaluate, Rethink, and Rehearse—this simple technique can enhance learning on the job, often within one minute.

How and where do people learn the important skills and behaviors that allow them to be successful at work and in life? Much of the authors' past research has focused on the learning of leadership skills (Johnson, 2008, 2009), and the results in this area are very clear: leadership development comes through experiences, particularly challenging experiences, coupled with reflecting on and learning from these experiences. Moreover, evidence now suggests that successful leaders are those who learn best from these experiences and who focus on adapting their behavior to better meet the demands of further complex and challenging situations.

McCall and his associates at the Center for Creative Leadership (Lindsey, Holmes, & McCall, 1987; McCall, Lombardo, & Morrison, 1998) were among the first to systematically explore where and how leaders learn. In a series of studies, successful executives were asked to list their most significant leadership learning experiences in an effort to determine where and how these effective leaders learned to lead. The results were quite consistent: The two highest ranking types of significant learning experiences were "hardships" and "challenging experiences." "Hardships" included business failures, failure to obtain an expected promotion, and being fired. Interestingly enough, also included in this category were personal traumas such as divorce and a death in the family. The other highly ranked category, "challenging experiences," included items from building an operation from scratch, managing a turnaround operation, or being part of a task force to being given increased responsibility in terms of people or functions.

However, simply *to have* significant experiences is not enough. There must be a further step that encourages the leader *to learn* from the experiences. As an illustration, Ready (1994) asked leaders to identify their main learning experiences. Job assignments, projects, and task forces were ranked at the top—very similar to the "challenging experiences" described. Ready concluded that "to develop leadership capacity one must be presented with challenging opportunity and must be ready and capable of acting on it. The lessons gained from this opportunity will be leveraged considerably when the individual is offered honest, thoughtful, and timely feedback on his or her performance. In addition to opportunity and feedback, the person must have the time and capacity to reflect on this feedback, to internalize it, and to transfer the lessons learned to day-to-day behaviors" (p. 27). Note that Ready explicitly adds the steps of reflecting, internalizing, and transferring those lessons learned to future experiences.

Using a slightly different approach, Leslie and Velsor (1996) examined why executives derail. These researchers found that the most important factor for the success of their sample of successful executives was the leaders' ability to adapt and develop. Respondents described effective leaders as "growing" and "maturing over time" as the job or the organization expanded; they were also characterized as capable of "learning from mistakes" and "learning from direct feedback." In contrast, the leading cause of executive derailment (executives who were fired or demoted) among their sample of unsuccessful executives was their failure to adapt and change their management styles. Thus, while both successful and unsuccessful executives encountered plenty of difficult events, the unsuccessful executives were unable to learn from these challenging experiences.

These studies strongly suggest that one key component in the development of effective leaders is the opportunity to experience "stretch" job assignments and duties. But the second crucial component is that these leaders or potential leaders must be able to learn from these experiences. The difficult opportunities in themselves are not enough to foster leader development, as is evident from the number of leaders who were unable to learn from what they were doing and thus "derailed." Learning from these experiences seems to be equally critical for the development of leadership. Important questions include: How can we help leaders better learn from their experiences? What do leaders need to do to take charge of their own learning? This article describes one such learning opportunity: brief reflection about an event immediately after it occurs. Such focused reflection, which we have labeled "One-Minute Reflective Learning," can be a powerful learning technique for leaders and potential leaders.

One-Minute Learning: The Key Is Reflective Practice

While people will learn in a wide variety of settings and through a broad range of means, one of the most important learning moments is immediately after a challenging event occurs. For example, a salesperson has a difficult encounter with a customer. As she is walking out of the meeting, she starts thinking immediately about how she could have handled the encounter differently. Or a parent reprimanding a child will often immediately rethink how he or she could have better helped the child without scolding.

These types of brief, focused learning opportunities are the topic of this article. "Learning moments" are very powerful experiences. The triggering event is fresh, providing the chance to review what happened and how "next time" could be more successful. We propose this technique is analogous to what educators call "teachable moments," in which a parent or teacher helps a child reflect on a (usually unplanned) event. As we said, immediate reflection can be a powerful learning tool.

Over the years, an extensive literature has developed in multiple fields, including education and psychology (Dewey, 1938; Schön, 1983), on the importance of reflective learning. In the domain of management education, scholars and practitioners alike have advocated using reflective practice to help develop effective managers (Cunliffe, 2004), and Rhee (2003) notes that management students should be provided with ample opportunities for reflection and sense-making about their own skill development. As Hedberg notes, "When we reflect, we give the learning a space to be processed, understood, and more likely integrated into further thoughts and actions" (2008, p. 2).

Prior research has documented that reflective practice tools may be implemented in numerous ways, from lengthy written self-analyses to personal journals to professional portfolios. Indeed, one drawback of many reflective practice techniques is their length, as they may require reflection and regular written assessment over a long period of time. But many managers do not have the time—or the inclination—to participate in extended reflective practice. In this article we illustrate how an intentionally *brief* reflective practice exercise can facilitate managerial learning, as it provides an option for managers to reflect and learn instantly while on the job.

The Four R's of One-Minute Learning

To facilitate One-Minute Learning, we developed four steps (the four R's) that are very helpful in extracting learning immediately after the challenging event occurs. We believe these four steps, in sequence, are quite useful, but certainly managers may develop their own learning sequence. The important point remains the same: With one-minute reflective learning, the leader reflects on the experience immediately to learn from it, in particular to consider how he or she can effectively handle similar events in the future. The four R's represent our contribution to One-Minute Reflective Learning on the job.

1. *Replay*—What just happened? Seek to replay the sequence from start to finish *as objectively as possible*. No need to assign blame or decide who was most at fault in the difficult situation; this step calls simply for a review of the event.

2. *Reevaluate*—After the Replay, try to identify which specific elements seemed to be critical to the event outcome: Behavior? Questions? Evasions? Body language? What were the positives and negatives? What happened that influenced the outcome?

3. *Rethink*—With the benefit of Steps 1 and 2, Rethink what could have been done differently. Using the key elements identified in the Reevaluate step, consider how the outcome could have been changed. If it was negative, how might this experience have unfolded differently to produce a better outcome? If it was positive, how might some derivation of this behavior be used in the future, to generate more positive outcomes?

4. *Rehearse*—To reinforce the learning, create a mental model for the future. Mentally rehearse the enhanced sequence of events. Practice what could be said or done differently—including thinking of some different options.

While these four steps are quite general, they become more real as we see some examples of how people have used the four R's in their jobs.

The Four R's in Action

Let's look at three different illustrations of the four R's in action. These are actual examples described to us by managers who have used reflective One-Minute Learning in their on-the-job experiences.

Example 1

Jan was a new principal of an elementary school. In one of her first conferences, she met with a teacher who was having a problem with a disruptive student. The meeting did not go well. When Jan asked for an explanation, the teacher quickly became defensive and blamed the student (and other students) for the classroom problem.

When the meeting (at last) ended, Jan applied the four R's:

- Step 1 was to replay the meeting in her head. Here she thought about what she had said in the meeting, how the teacher responded, and how the conversation escalated into conflict.

- In Step 2, Jan reevaluated her behavior in the situation. In this step Jan concluded that she had started the meeting on the wrong foot. She had begun by putting the teacher in a defensive role: the teacher believed it was a discipline meeting, and the teacher felt required to defend her actions.

- In Step 3, Rethink, Jan thought about how she could have begun this meeting (and other meetings in the future) on a more constructive note. One idea she had was to be more clear initially about the purpose of the meeting. In this case, the focus should have been how to handle a chronically disruptive student, *not* on how to be a better teacher.

- In Step 4, Jan mentally rehearsed what she would say at the beginning of future meetings. She also considered how she could keep the meeting on a constructive track if a teacher started to become defensive.

- Bottom line—Jan became a better principal by applying the four R's.

Jan also carried her reflective learning further. The next day she talked with the teacher to share some of her (Jan's) thoughts about the meeting, and she promised the teacher that future meetings would start on a more constructive note. The teacher responded positively, thus reinforcing Jan's learned behavior.

Example 2

Billy was the shift manager of a one of the restaurants in a well-known national chain. One very busy lunch time he was called to a table by a customer who had several complaints about the food and service. Billy recognized the person as someone who had complained to him before. He was feeling a bit irritated, and the discussion ended by his telling the customer that if she didn't like the food or service she could take her business elsewhere. While walking back to the checkout counter, Billy began to Replay (Step 1) the event from the point at which he was stopped by the customer to the point when he told her to go somewhere else. In Reevaluate (Step 2), he realized that he was feeling very hassled and frustrated when the customer stopped him and seeing her added to his irritation. In Rethink (Step 3), he realized that when she stopped him, he should have just "chilled" (his term) and listened patiently to what she had to say, putting the other issues out of his mind temporarily. "Just focus on the customer at hand and try to put the other issues aside" was his learning here. But how to do that was a problem and so he Rehearsed (Step 4) ways in which he could "just chill" when dealing with a customer with a problem.

- Bottom line—Billy had a major learning insight in how to better deal with a customer with service complaints.

When people are asked to think of events that they have reflected on, they tend to cite events that had negative outcomes or events that did not go as planned. The two cases above are examples of this tendency; both were negative events cited by persons using the reflection process. In general, people tend to reflect less about successful events than they do about unsuccessful events. For the latter events, the questions seem to be: "What did I do wrong?" and "How can I do it better next time?" However, it may be beneficial to reflect on successful events also. We find that elementary and high school teachers often do this after finishing a successful tutoring session with a student. They ask when reflecting on the event what they specifically did in the session that enabled the student to better understand the material. They use the insights from the reflection to better tutor students in the future.

As the next example illustrates, reflection on positive events may also be useful in the management and leadership area.

Example 3

Being an assistant general manager at a major hotel involves, among other duties, going on a daily "walk through" to inspect the facilities. As Angie was inspecting the facility one morning, she chanced upon one of the maintenance employees. After they exchanged greetings, she asked him about his family and how the job was going. As they were about to part, he said that he had been meaning to talk to her about something that may be important and told her about a possible safety issue in the storage of some chemicals used for cleaning. She took notes on what he said and thanked him for the information as well as his concern for the safety of the hotel and the guests. As they parted, he said that he wanted to thank her also, and said that he enjoyed working for her.

As Angie left, she felt very good about the event. She thought it was a very valuable discussion and wondered what it was about the meeting that contributed to its success. She Replayed (Step 1) the event in her mind from beginning to end. In the Reevaluate (Step 2) stage, she thought about the parts of the episode that seemed to be helpful. She thought that her interest in the employee's family and his job probably helped open the discussion; because he saw that she was concerned with his world, he wanted to be helpful with her world. In the Rethink (Step 3) phase, she thought about ways in which she could better connect with the hotel employees, how she could make them feel part of the hotel family. And in the Rehearsal (Step 4) phase she went through a couple of scenarios of how she might use the brief encounters in the daily "walk-around" to better connect and exchange information with employees.

- Bottom line—Angie improved her management style through this quick reflection.

This case illustrates how one can take a very positive event and turn it into a one-minute learning experience. Angie's assumption here was that her ability to "connect" with the employee made him more willing to share some information about a potential safety hazard. The process may have to be adjusted slightly for the nature of the event; however, the general approach is applicable to most brief events.

Teaching the Four R's

One of the main advantages of the One-Minute Reflective Learning/Four R's Model is its ease of teaching and use. Remembering all four R's and what they stand for is not mandatory. What is important is the focus on reflective learning: the need to recall a challenging experience in a focused, systematic way, with the goal of changing behavior to improve the outcome "next time."

The following is a basic format that can be used to teach One-Minute Reflective Learning in a classroom or training session.

1. Begin by explaining what reflective learning is all about and the research supporting it as a powerful learning tool.

2. Explain the focus on brevity: the One-Minute Reflective Learning process.

3. Review in some detail the four R's technique, using the explanation above.

4. Provide some examples of how to use the four R's. The three examples given earlier may be used, or participants may wish to contribute their own experiences. We have found that, with some prompting, participants can recall many interesting examples of "learning moments" on their jobs, even if they did not use some form of the four R's. The important point is that, whether they realized it at the time or not, they used reflective learning.

5. Ask each person to recall a recent event and deconstruct it using the four R's. If time and space permit, ask the participants to briefly write about the event, going through all four steps. Writing forces the participants to think through the process.

6. Seek volunteers to share their reflective learning experiences with the group. Again, using the four R's is not mandatory; what is important is using reflection to enhance learning.

7. Finally, debrief and summarize. Which of the four steps is easiest? Which is hardest? Are there additional steps that could be added to the reflective learning process?

A side note: We have found that an interesting modification to this process is to discuss the four R's in the group context. The wide range of topics that arise will provide a springboard for more in-depth discussion. For example, some managers may focus on process issues such as conflict resolution in their reflective learning, while others focus on more task-oriented problems. Diversity in age, work experience, and ethnic or socioeconomic background will offer a rich source of different points of view about reflective learning. As an illustration, we have experienced several lively debates between Generation X/Y managers and older Baby Boomers about organizational issues involving competition, ambition, motivation, and work/family priorities.

Conclusion

Overall, we have found One-Minute Reflective Learning to be a useful training tool for managers seeking to enhance their leadership skills in an on-the-job setting. It is a good example of how learning can be fostered almost anywhere—on an elevator, between meetings, driving to work. The technique is simple, easily adaptable to different situations, and above all, brief, which is an important factor in today's fast-paced business environment.

References

Cunliffe, A.L. (2004). On becoming a critically reflexive practitioner. *Journal of Management Education, 28*(4), 407–426.

Dewey, J. (1938). *Experience and education*. London and New York: Macmillan.

Hedberg, P.R. (2008, April 15). Learning through reflective classroom practice: Applications to educate the reflective manager. *Journal of Management Education* [Online], doi: 10.1177/1052562908316714.

Johnson, H.H. (2008). Helping leaders learn to lead. In E. Biech (Ed.), *The 2008 Pfeiffer annual: Training* (pp. 135–142). San Francisco: Pfeiffer.

Johnson, H.H. (2009). How leaders think: Developing effective leaders. In Biech, E. (Ed.), *The 2009 Pfeiffer annual: Training* (pp. 269–284). San Francisco: Pfeiffer.

Leslie, J., & Velsor, E. (1996). *A look at derailment today: North America and Europe.* Greensboro, NC: Center for Creative Leadership.

Lindsey, E.H., Holmes, V., & McCall, H.M., Jr. (1987). *Key events in executive lives.* Greensboro, NC: Center for Creative Leadership.

McCall, M.W., Jr., Lombardo, M.M., & Morrison, A.N. (1998). *Lessons from experience.* Lexington, MA: Lexington Books.

Ready, D. (1994). *Champions of change.* Lexington, MA: International Consortium for Executive Development Research.

Rhee, K.S. (2003). Self-directed learning: To be aware or not to be aware. *Journal of Management Education, 27*(5), 568–589.

Schön, D.A. (1983). *The reflective practitioner.* New York: Basic Books.

Homer H. Johnson, Ph.D., *is a professor in the School of Business Administration at Loyola University, Chicago, where he teaches courses in leadership and strategy. He is the author of numerous books and articles, and is the case editor of the* Organization Development Practitioner. *His most recent book (with Linda Stroh) is* Basic Essentials of Effective Consulting, *which was published by LEA in 2006.*

Anne H. Reilly, Ph.D., *teaches courses in organizational change and development, organizational behavior, and international management at Loyola University, Chicago, where she is a professor of management. Dr. Reilly has published many articles in both academic and practitioner journals. She is now applying the management theories she teaches in her current position as assistant provost and director of faculty administration.*

Questioning the Teachable Moment

Brittany Ashby

Summary

In today's world, employees can access information any time, anywhere. They can learn online, find answers to common questions in knowledge databases, view job aids at the touch of a button, or take classes offered by thousands of organizations right in their own communities. However, many of these methods focus on directly giving information rather than helping employees develop the problem-solving and critical-thinking skills they need to truly benefit from their newly acquired knowledge.

By using techniques that have been around for centuries, trainers may be able to not only give employees the information they need, but also teach them to think through the process. The Socratic Method does just that. By asking a series of logic-based questions, trainers, managers, and consultants can provide "just-in-time" learning that sticks.

"Just-in-time" learning appears repeatedly in the literature and jargon of trainers, consultants, and human resource professionals across the globe. While it is generally understood that the idea is to impart information where needed, when needed, there are a wide variety of ways in which this is accomplished. For some, "just in time" equates to online learning or accessing an internal knowledge database. For a few, it may include providing lecture-type training in the moment. As learning professionals, we need to take advantage of all of these techniques. However, sometimes we must return to our roots and reclaim techniques that many of us have encountered somewhere along the way, but may not think to use when the moment arises.

I am referring to teachable moments or situations when you can provide employees with the tools they need to learn the process, find the answer, and do the job without having to *give* them the answer or send them to an electronic resource. These are techniques that help build problem-solving and critical-thinking skills and make the information highly accessible to all types of people. One such technique is the Socratic Method. Asking questions is not necessarily natural for many people; however, with a little forethought, questions can be used very effectively to not only disburse information, but also to help people cultivate the critical-thinking skills they need to be successful.

The following case study describes a scenario that presents opportunities for "just-in-time" learning and the use of the Socratic Method.

Scenario

A veteran customer service employee has been a fabulous employee for over ten years now. She shows up to work, gracefully assists clients both on the phone and in-person, and meets deadlines. However, recently she has struggled to master the new process for making account updates in the electronic database. You hear her finish a call and see her open the system. She immediately starts the process incorrectly. What do you do? How can you help this employee learn and retain the process?

For this situation, the employee could easily be referred back to online resources for quick, easy answers. However, these resources seldom inspire critical-thinking skills or provide the in-depth knowledge that would be ideal for this employee. The Socratic Method described in the remainder of this article is probably not new to most readers, but many people forget to use it.

Socratic Method

Early Greek philosophers such as Plato and Socrates, for whom the method is named, are credited with using a series of logic-based questions to guide learners to answers using their own thought processes. Today's law schools frequently use the method to encourage law students to think critically, but no law degree is necessary to use this technique effectively.

Using the Socratic Method means asking a series of inductive questions that lead the learner to the answer (and a new way of thinking) in small, easily understood steps. The questioner must be comfortable asking questions and thinking logically to engage the mind of the learner. If the questioner feels awkward asking questions or is not prepared to use the process, the process can come across as condescending and overbearing, but when a competent and respectful questioner gently prods the learner, intellectual growth results.

In the scenario presented here, the situation lends itself well to using the Socratic Method. Let's assume that the trainer is familiar with the process and that the account updating process works logically. Let's look at how the method might be used.

First, the questioner needs to be sure that the employee is prepared to learn the process. If the person is distracted by another call or task, the questioning may only fluster her. The following may be a good way to begin the conversation: "Hi, Chris. I was just helping Robin over here and noticed that you had started an update in the new system. Would you mind if I asked a few questions to see whether I can help you better learn the new process?"

Once the employee has agreed, the trainer can initiate learning with questions, which should be tailored to the employee's specific needs. The trainer should ask questions that lead the person to rely on his or her independent thinking and avoid questions with answers that serve only to highlight the employee's ignorance rather than guide the employee toward the correct answer.

Questioner: Why do we update the system after our customer service calls?

Employee: So that there is a record of what we talked about.

Questioner: Why do we need a record of what we talked about?

Employee: So that if there is a question in the future of what was said and what was decided we have a record.

Questioner: Good. Who might need to look for that information later?

Employee: Another employee might need it if the customer calls again. An auditor might look at it during an audit or you might look at it as my manager.

Questioner: Anyone else who might look at it?

Employee: It probably could be looked at in reports that we use to determine whether we have done all of our due diligence.

Questioner: Correct. What information do we need to have to determine whether we have done our jobs correctly?

Employee: Well, we need to know who the person is, who talked to him or her, when, what was discussed, what options were offered, and what decisions were made. We would also need to know whether follow-up was done based on those decisions.

Questioner: Good. From where in the database does the report pull that information?

Employee: Well, I am not really sure.

Questioner: Ok, if you look at the screen right here, do you see that information?

> *Employee:*   Well, the name is on the client info page. My name is on the top because I am logged on as me. The date and time automatically pop up when I tell it to log history. Then I put in the history report, what we talked about, what I offered, and what was decided.
>
> *Questioner:*   What about the follow-up information?
>
> *Employee:*   Oh, that used to just populate in the old system.
>
> *Questioner:*   Do you see it anywhere here?
>
> *Employee*:   Yes, there is a "schedule follow-up" button at the bottom of the page that I need to click on in order to make sure the follow-up letter goes out. That is the part I forgot. Thank you!

While this example is fairly simple, the process remains the same. You can see that the question about follow-up information does not elicit the desired answer. Thus, the questioner approach the question in a different manner. If a questioner finds that a line of questioning yields answers that stray too far afield, it is acceptable to stop and rephrase questions. However, pausing too often may befuddle the learner, so take a moment to ensure that the questions are logical rather than using the first question that comes to mind.

Benefits

What are the benefits of the Socratic Method? Good adult education finds ways to build on the existing knowledge of learners. By asking questions, the trainer automatically requires learners to draw from knowledge they already have. If the questions are asked in a logical order, existing knowledge connects to new concepts. These connections grow organically from the question-and-answer process rather than from forcing fleeting artificial connections. Because the questioner and the employee are also directly interacting, the process builds a more personal relationship between manager and employee, which allows the learner to better relate to new ideas.

Drawbacks

What can seem like an interrogation can intimidate some learners. It is important to communicate that you are simply guiding the person through the learning process so that he or she will gain a thorough understanding and that you are not questioning anyone's intelligence. Questions can easily become too directive or condescending, so posing questions that logically guide the learner through the process is critical.

Conclusion

Using questions for learning may feel threatening to some learners, but it is not a difficult process. Taking a few minutes to think of questions that can help a person through a process or concept builds not only knowledge, but problem-solving and critical-thinking abilities as well. The next time you are tempted to lecture an employee or send him or her to the web for more "just-in-time" learning, see whether a few questions might elicit better retention and comprehension.

Brittany Ashby *is a principal consultant with Align, a consulting firm in Cheyenne, Wyoming. With a background in training, human performance, and facilitation, she brings a wealth of knowledge to her clients. She has a passion for working with nonprofit organizations and her résumé includes employment in the University of Northern Colorado Development Office and at the prestigious El Pomar Foundation in Colorado. Brittany holds a master of science degree in adult education from the University of Wyoming.*

Opportunities and Risks of Incorporating User-Created Content in an Organizational Training Strategy

Christine Hipple and Zane L. Berge

Summary

The ability for employees to use social media to create, distribute, and retrieve information and knowledge, independent of organizational direction provides many opportunities to enhance most organizations' training and development offerings. The risks of adverse consequences such as privacy violations and exposure of proprietary information pose genuine threats, however. This article examines the potential benefits and risks of incorporating user-created content in an organization's training strategy, provides a brief description of how several organizations are harnessing this type of learning resource while mitigating risks, and gives recommendations for organizations to consider when exploring how to integrate this type of content into their overall training strategies.

For decades, organizations have been investing in training programs to equip employees with the skills and knowledge they need to be productive. While methods of delivering training and supporting learners have evolved over the years, the basic goal remains the same. In a workplace populated largely by knowledge workers, the key to effective performance is usually immediate access to current, often rapidly changing, information and expertise.

In traditional formal organizational training functions, teams of instructional designers and trainers design programs with the input of subject-matter experts and deliver training through instructor-led or computer-based learning programs that are tracked and managed by learning management systems (LMS). A great deal of emphasis has been placed on using a learning management system, which can point employees

The 2012 Pfeiffer Annual: Training.

to the courses deemed necessary for their job roles, to track participation and to certify that a specific level of proficiency has been attained. One of the greatest challenges faced in organizational training is the difficulty in transferring knowledge and skills learned in training to the workplace. Berk (2009) notes that "measurement data typically indicates that 60 percent or more of training is never applied on the job" (p. 37).

Informal Learning in Organizations

While many organizations focus their energies on formal training, Cross (2009) and others have estimated that 70 to 90 percent of all corporate learning is informal. Cross states:

> "Learning is formal when someone other than the learner sets curriculum. Typically, it's an event on a schedule, and completion is generally recognized with a symbol, such as a grade, gold star, certificate, or check mark in a learning management system. By contrast, informal learners usually set their own learning objectives. They learn when they feel a need to know. The proof of their learning is their ability to do something they could not do before. Informal learning often is a pastiche of small chunks of observing how others do things, asking questions, trial and error, sharing stories with others, and casual conversation." (2009, p. 16)

With this in mind, some organizations are now seeking to maximize informal learning opportunities for their employees. This growing emphasis on informal learning may resonate with employees more than traditional, formal training does; the ability for employees themselves to create content and direct their own learning should help motivate employees to learn. Pink (2009) describes three core factors that appear to motivate all human behavior: autonomy, mastery, and purpose. Informal learning should appeal to all of these motivators, because employees have greater control over what, when, and how they learn. Training strategies that take advantage of these motivating aspects of informal learning are likely to lead to greater participation and engagement.

With the increased use of social media as a communication and learning tool, organizations are increasingly including content generated by users in their training strategies, both in formal training programs and as part of informal learning.

Social Media

Social media have significantly changed the methods individuals use to communicate with one another in daily life. Social networking sites such as Facebook and MySpace allow members to keep up with a vast network of friends simultaneously, sharing photos, videos, and current information. YouTube provides video-sharing capabilities to anyone with a video camera. With Twitter, one person can broadcast very brief snippets of information instantaneously to thousands of others. Blogs and wikis allow experts to capture and distribute facts and opinions to anyone who can locate and access them. Members of younger generations (Gen Y and Millennials) have grown up using these tools, and they expect the instant connection that they have experienced growing up to continue in the workplace. The ability for employees to use social media and social networks to create, share, and store learning content themselves brings opportunities for fast, cost-effective learning that meets employees' needs for autonomy and appeals to varied learning styles. At the same time, this user-created content can present the organization with some potential risks, such as corporate liability, poor quality of information, and reduced productivity that must be anticipated and mitigated. Risk factors are more thoroughly addressed later in this article.

Social media have been used extensively by many businesses, especially in marketing. One notable example, described by Craig (2010), is Ford Motor's launch of the Ford Fiesta. In place of traditional marketing, Ford empowered one hundred "agents" to drive the car for six months and then use social media to share their experiences with the car. Not only did this social networking create an interest in the car, but the feedback helped Ford with product development. This process opened the company to the public and set the stage for use of social media as a user-generated marketing tool.

Training industry analyst Bersin (2010) summarizes the penetration of some types of social media tools that support the integration of informal learning into mainstream corporate learning:

> "Virtual training is now mainstream. In 2009, 59 percent of organizations used virtual classrooms as a mainstream delivery method—up 45 percent from two years earlier. . . Our research shows that in 2009:

> - Seventeen percent of all organizations had some form of knowledge management platform.
> - Thirty-two percent had some form of self-publishing rapid e-learning platform.
> - Eighteen percent had some form of learning content management system.
> - Twenty-four percent used communities of practice.
> - Fourteen percent used blogs and wikis. (p. 14)

Opportunities for User-Generated Content in Formal Training

Combined with Formal Training Programs

The prospects for using social media to enable user-generated content as a part of an organization's formal training programs are considerable. One of the simplest options is to combine user-created content with formally presented instructor-led or web-based training (WBT) courses. Wilkins (2009) states that "embedding social media within WBT courses reintroduces . . . social exchanges without sacrificing the cost savings or WBT's time-of-need 'replay' capability" (p. 29). Instructors and instructional designers could add the ability for course participants to use organization-sponsored networks to make connections with other participants (before, during, and after the session), add their own links and perspectives, and rate components of the course for other prospective participants to view. If a formal social networking platform is used, the content of these discussions could become searchable and become an element in evaluating the experience for impact.

Knowledge Management

With an expected increase in retirement of knowledge workers and greater mobility of younger workers, many organizations struggle to develop and maintain knowledge management systems that can provide quick access to the organization's accumulated knowledge. Fuller (2007) explains how social networking can provide the means to collect tacit knowledge and transform it into explicit form so it can be accessed by others, expanded, and put to wider use. Tools range from an organized set of public folders to customized knowledge management software. The key to utility of these programs is a means to vet the information with subject-matter experts and to ensure that information can be accessed as quickly as possible by employees seeking information.

Opportunities for User–Generated Content in Informal Learning
Communities of Practice

Communities of practice are an integral part of informal learning. As described by Rosenheck (2010), a community of practice "provides a context for people to reflect, reinforce, and extend their knowledge by discussing it with each other. . . . Technology is not necessary for communities of practice to exist; they form when people with common interests and goals talk informally in the hallway and ask each other questions and share insights. However, technology—especially Web 2.0 technologies such as forums, wikis, virtual meetings, blogs and microblogs—can extend the reach, increase the number of possible connections, enable finding the right person or information and track the effectiveness of communities of practice" (p. 20). Employees with questions on products or procedures could query the database of user-created content and retrieve an answer just at the time it's needed.

Once a community is in place, systematic social network analysis can help organizations learn more about who is actively engaged in social learning, discover and nurture talent that could otherwise be hidden, and uncover the types of information workers need. Sherman (2010) describes how social graphing can show who is connected, what information is flowing through the network, who contributes new information, who accesses it, and who endorses it. Participation in networks has been shown to correlate with improved performance in engineers and consultants (Cross, 2004). Individuals with more ties inside and outside their organizations were shown to have access to greater quality and quantity of information, supporting enhanced job performance.

There are other benefits to user-generated learning. Self-directed employees participating in online learning communities will be able to articulate their own learning needs and create and execute their own learning plans, finding guidance and expertise from experts along the way. As the need for autonomy and purpose are met on the way to achieving mastery, Pink and others would predict that motivation would increase and turnover decrease as employees participate more fully in their own development. Also, because this type of learning occurs in the workplace rather than in the classroom, new knowledge and skills can be more directly and immediately applied on the job, increasing learning transfer.

Cognitive Apprenticeship

The concept of cognitive apprenticeship, based on the work by Collins and Brown more than twenty years ago, has been described by Rosenheck (2010). A cognitive apprenticeship occurs when someone with mastery of a particular subject teaches an apprentice, with an emphasis on bringing tacit processes out into the open. This learning cycle is highly suited for knowledge workers, who proliferate in the current workforce. User-created videos posted on YouTube or a corporate site could provide models of skills and behaviors. Learners could locate an ad-hoc coach by perusing a database of experienced mentors, who could provide coaching through web meetings or online forums. The flexibility provided by corporate-sponsored social media could provide scaffolding to support employee learning, creating varying levels of structure and support for workers as they become more proficient. Discussion groups and wikis could allow learners to reinforce learning through sharing experiences and ways to apply new knowledge and skills on the job.

Learning Maps

Incorporating social media into a training strategy can provide greater flexibility than a rigid curriculum can. Rosenheck (2010) describes similar initiatives at Cricket Communications and the U.S. Social Security Administration, two organizations that have utilized online tools to create learning maps that suggest alternate learning methods for skills associated with job roles. Employees can choose from traditional courses and informal means such as mentoring or instant messaging with more experienced co-workers, while the tracking technology integrated into the learning map tool serves to record learning progress.

Potential Risks

Opening up the organization's learning platform for user-created content is not without risks. Simonson (2009) outlines some of the most critical risks for organizations to assess before incorporating social media into their learning strategies. First, employers may be held liable for employee postings that violate privacy or could be construed as defamation or harassment. In one case, a hospital was found guilty of privacy violations when an employee divulged personal medical information about a patient on Facebook, even though the employee made the post outside the job. When employees have more open access to proprietary information, the organization is more open to leakage through Internet security breaches or employee sabotage. The damage that could be done by a disgruntled or careless employee could seriously hurt an organization's image and reputation.

Derven (2009) describes additional risks. One of these is that user-generated content may not be of high quality, either in content and design. Employees without complete knowledge of subject matter could post inaccurate or incomplete information that others follow, with dire consequences. Even accurate information presented poorly could be misleading or cause confusion. Learners could waste considerable time sifting through poorly written or inconsistently organized posts. Similarly, if information and resources are difficult to locate, employees could either waste time trying to find what they need or give up in frustration. Finally, some organizations may fear that employees will spend so much time using social media at work in the pursuit of sharing information that job duties will suffer.

Recommendations

Risk Assessment

Before embarking on an initiative to incorporate user-generated content into a learning strategy, organizations should assess their readiness for creating social networks and supporting user-created content. Derven (2009) outlines some factors that can lead to a successful initiative. Organizations with geographically dispersed employees who need to share knowledge quickly and require cross-functional collaboration are most likely to benefit. Adoption may be easier if social networking is already being used for other functions or a significant proportion of the workforce is already deeply involved in social networking personally. Cultures that value innovation and experimentation and encourage employee engagement will be most likely to work through the risks to sustain a vibrant social network. Wilkins (2009) recommends that organizations start implementing at a level that matches their tolerance for risk. Embedding social media into existing programs is most likely a lower risk than developing and supporting decentralized learning communities.

Learning Strategy

A learning strategy that clearly articulates how social networking fits into the overall enterprise strategy is essential. Emelo (2010) predicts that, without such a strategy, social networking will be used simply to connect socially and that any real learning would be accidental. Sherman (2010) suggests that a social learning strategy should "encourage social learning throughout the organization, measure outcomes that align with learning and business objectives, and support a culture of agile, continuous improvement" (p. 32). The strategy should encourage intentional social learning relationships through databases, search functions, and internal social networking platforms. It should help employees to find their best pathways to competence and point them to resources that are aligned with the organization's strategy, mission, and competencies.

Leadership

Learning communities, forums, and knowledge depositories should be moderated in a manner that is consistent with the learning strategy. Hurdle (2010) states that a learning forum needs "a coach, not a dictator, to ensure that employees have an effective means of expressing their concerns, successes, and frustrations, as well as obtaining advice from leaders. It is critical that leadership consistently read comments and engage in the discussions as participants, sharing their own professional stories, advice, and resources" (p. 76). Sherman (2010) advises that "social learning environments must be managed by people capable of serving as online community managers who monitor the health of the community and promote its best solutions" (p. 34). He also suggests that lessons on community management can be found in the marketing department, where social networking has already taken hold. A successful marketing community manager "encourages contributions from fans, creates campaigns to attract new members, serves as bidirectional conduits between fans and organizations, and reports on the health of the community to the organization" (Sherman, 2010, p. 35).

Business-Use Policy

In order to mitigate the risks, Simonson (2009) recommends that organizations develop internal social media business-use policies that clearly state that employees are "not allowed to use electronic communications . . . in ways that are contrary to the company's interest, are illegal, or violate antidiscrimination policies. The policy should also remind employees about protecting proprietary information and avoiding violation of privacy issues. Finally, they should be told that their electronic communications may be intercepted, analyzed, and archived by the company" (p. 11). This policy should include the consequences for violations, should be communicated to employees upon hire and through periodic reminders, and should be available for reference. Organizations must be prepared to monitor usage, follow their policies, and take the prescribed actions for violations.

Training should be provided to employees, not only on the business-use policy, but also on how to best contribute to and learn from a social network. Younger workers who have grown up with social networking may need less support in learning to use these technologies than older workers who may never have used them. Social-media-savvy employees could draft tutorials and job aids that are distributed via traditional means such as the organization's intranet or LMS as well as in the social network itself.

Technology

The technology used to support organizational social learning should be selected with the social learning strategy and business-use policy in mind. Berk (2009) suggests that companies "feed the learning measurement system from the HRIS and LMS in a way that the integrity of the source data is maintained . . . using standardized SML schema to extract data. Integrations require an up-front investment, but in the long run produce significant efficiency gains while mitigating risk of data integrity issues" (p. 38).

Databases that contain information about available experts and other resources should be secure and easy for newcomers to the organization to use to find either an immediate answer to a pressing question or a mentor to provide longer-term coaching. Derven (2009) describes the use of IBM's EXCaliber system and Blue Pages and how these corporate social networking platforms help to link learners and information around the globe. Photographs of users are displayed on pages they've visited, further personalizing the technology and encouraging further networking and exploration.

Evaluation

Just as with any other element of a learning strategy, social networking must be measured and evaluated. While traditional, formal learning programs may lend themselves to Kirkpatrick's four levels of evaluation (participant reaction, learning, behavior change, and organizational change), informal learning may be better measured by other means. The success case method described by Brinkerhoff (2003) may be a more effective evaluation tool. Using this method, the evaluator seeks out people (key informants) who have had the best and worst experiences with the initiative being studied. Collecting evidence and stories from these extremes provides valuable data about what aspects of the initiative are having the desired impact on the organization, as well as on what needs to be changed.

For more effective measurement, Berk (2009) suggests creation of customized dashboards that present data using a balanced approach. These scorecards would include financial data (budget and expenditures), operational data (completion numbers), performance data linking training to business results, and cultural data (manager support).

Summary

While it is unlikely that user-generated content will completely replace organizationally generated content in corporate learning, most organizations would benefit from incorporating user-generated content into their training strategies, both to support and enhance formal training and to provide a forum for informal learning. Pushed by the new generations of employees who are used to immediate and unlimited access to other people and information, and supported by the ability to generate cost-effective knowledge quickly, the use of social media and social learning networks will continue to attract the attention of corporate training professionals. While organizations must carefully assess the potential risks inherent in using social media as part of the overall training strategy and implement actions to mitigate them, the capacity to help employees learn and perform more effectively should not be overlooked.

References

Berk, J. (2009). Emerging issues in measurement. *Chief Learning Officer, 8*(11), 34–39.

Bersin, J. (2010). Managing through the tipping point. *Chief Learning Officer, 9*(2), 14.

Brinkerhoff, R. (2003). *The success case method.* San Francisco: Berrett-Koehler.

Craig, S. (2010). Trust me. No, really. How organizations, people, and the social web are reinventing trust. *econtent, 33*(2), 24–29.

Cross, J. (2009). Informal learning 2.0: Sustaining the corporation in the network era. *Chief Learning Officer, 8*(8), 16.

Cross, R., & Cummings, J.N. (2004). Tie and network correlates of individual performance in knowledge intensive work. *Academy of Management Journal, 47*(6), 928–937.

Derven, M. (2009). Social networking: Force for development? *T + D, 63*(7), 59–63.

Emelo, R. (2010). Increasing productivity with social learning. *Industrial and Commercial Training, 42*(4), 203–210.

Fuller, A., Unwin, L., Felstead, A., Jewson, N., & Kakavelakis, K. (2007). Creating and using knowledge: An analysis of the differentiated nature of workplace learning environments. *British Educational Research Journal, 33*(5), 743–759.

Hurdle, L. (2010). Adult learning principles to consider when using web 2.0. *T + D, 64*(7), 76–77.

Pink, D. (2009). *Drive: The surprising truth about what motivates us*. New York: Riverhead Books.

Rosenheck, M. (2010). Navigating the interactive workplace. *Chief Learning Officer, 9*(5), 18–21.

Sherman, B. (2010). The social LMS. *Chief Learning Officer, 9*(3), 32–35.

Simonson, K. (2009). Four ways to manage the risks of social media. *Baseline* (101), 11.

Wilkins, D. (2009) Learning 2.0 and workplace communities. *T + D, 63*(4), 28–30.

Christine Hipple *has more than twenty-five years of strategic human resource and training experience. Currently, she is the director of workforce development solutions for Avilar Technologies, providing talent management consultation services to clients in government, nonprofit, and corporate sectors. Previously, Christine held leadership and senior training practitioner roles in health care, academia, and government. Her portfolio includes competency-based pay-for-performance plans, mentoring programs, and competency-based leadership development and selection processes. She is past president of the Maryland ASTD chapter.*

Zane L. Berge, Ph.D., *is a professor and former director of the training systems graduate programs at the UMBC Campus, University of Maryland System. He teaches courses involving workplace training and distance education. Prior to UMBC, Dr. Berge was founder and director of the Center for Teaching and Technology, Georgetown University, Washington, D.C. Dr. Berge's publications include work as a primary author, editor, or presenter of ten books and more than two hundred book chapters, articles, conference presentations, and invited speeches worldwide.*

Building Bridges Between Psychology and Conflict Resolution
Implications for Mediator Learning
Kenneth Cloke

Summary

Many people are trained in conflict-resolution skills. This article examines better ways to learn these skills through a combination of psychology and mediation.

Over the last three decades, hundreds of thousands of people around the world have been trained in community, divorce, family, commercial, organizational, and workplace mediation, as well as in allied conflict resolution skills such as collaborative negotiation, group facilitation, public dialogue, restorative justice, victim-offender mediation, ombudsmanship, collaborative law, consensus decision making, creative problem solving, prejudice reduction and bias awareness, conflict resolution systems design, and dozens of associated practices.

Among the most important and powerful of these skills are a number of core ideas and interventions that originate in psychology, particularly in what is commonly known as "brief therapy," where the border separating conflict resolution from psychological intervention has become indistinct, in many places blurred beyond recognition. Examples of the positive consequences of blurring this line can be found in recent discoveries in neurophysiology, "emotional intelligence," and solution-focused approaches to conflict resolution.

While it is, of course, both necessary and vital that we recognize the key differences between the professionals in the fields of psychology and conflict resolution, it is *more* necessary and vital that we recognize their essential similarities, collaborate in developing creative new techniques, and invite them to learn as much as they can from each other.

Beyond this, it is increasingly important for us to *consciously* generate a fertile, collaborative space between them; discourage the tendency to jealously guard protected territory; and oppose efforts to create new forms of private property in techniques that reduce hostility and relieve suffering.

It is therefore critical that we think carefully and strategically about how best to translate a deeper understanding of the emotional and neurophysiological underpinnings of conflict and resolution processes into practical, hands-on mediation techniques; that we explore the evolving relationship between mediation and psychology, and other professions as well; and that we translate that understanding into improved ways of helping people become competent, successful mediators.

Among the urgent reasons for doing so are the rise of increasingly destructive global conflicts that *cannot* even be solved by a single nation, let alone by a single style, approach, profession, or technique; the persistence of intractable conflicts that require more advanced techniques; and the recent rise of innovative, transformational techniques that form only a small part of the curriculum of most mediation training.

Questions of Today

The present generation is being asked a profound set of questions that require immediate action based on complex, diverse, complementary, even contradictory answers. In my judgment, these questions include:

1. What is our responsibility as global citizens for solving the environmental, social, economic, and political conflicts that are taking place around us?

2. Is it possible to successfully apply conflict resolution principles to the inequalities, inequities, and dysfunctions that are continuing to fuel chronic social, economic, and political conflicts?

3. Can we find ways of working beyond national, religious, ethnic, and professional borders in order to strengthen our capacity for international collaboration and help save the planet?

4. Can we build bridges across diverse disciplines to integrate the unique understanding and skills that other professions have produced regarding conflict and resolution?

5. How can we use this knowledge to improve the ways we impact mediator learning to better achieve these goals?

Locating potential synergies between psychology and conflict resolution will allow us to take a few small steps toward answering these questions. And small steps, as we learn in mediation, are precisely what are needed to achieve meaningful results. Why should we consider the possibilities of ego defenses or solution-focused mediation? For the same reasons we consider the potential utility of a variety of interventions—because they allow us to understand conflict and enter it in unique and useful ways.

The logical chain that connects conflict resolution with psychology is simple yet inexorable and logically rigorous, and proceeds as follows:

1. It is possible for people to disagree with each other without experiencing conflict.

2. What distinguishes conflict from disagreement is the presence of what are commonly referred to as "negative" emotions, such as anger, fear, guilt, and shame.

3. Thus, *every* conflict, by definition, contains an indispensible emotional element.

4. Conflicts can only be reached and resolved in their emotional location by people who have acquired emotional processing skills, or what Daniel Goleman (1995) broadly describes as "emotional intelligence."

5. The discipline that is most familiar with these emotional dynamics is psychology.

6. Therefore, mediation can learn from psychology how to be more effective in resolving conflicts.

This logic alone should be sufficient to prompt a deeper assessment of psychological research and techniques. Yet, considering the problem from a deeper perspective, we all know that no clear line can be drawn that allows us to separate our emotions from our ideas, or our neurophysiology from our behaviors. Quite simply, we are all emotional beings and must discover our inner logic if we do not want to be trapped in or driven by our emotions.

Deeper still, when we distinguish, simplify, or isolate different aspects of a problem, we disregard their essential unity and, with it, countless opportunities to resolve critically important conflicts and disagreements, simply by approaching them with a predetermined, single-minded, *particular* point of view, no matter how profound or useful it may happen to be.

There is an equally simple, inexorable, and logically rigorous analysis based on a few simple philosophical assumptions that point us in a different direction. It goes like this: No two human beings are the same. No single human being is the same from one moment to the next. The interactions and relationships between human beings are complex, multi-determined, subtle, and unpredictable. Conflicts are even more complex, multi-determined, subtle, and unpredictable. Most conflicts take place beneath the surface, well below the superficial topics over which people are fighting, and frequently hidden from their conscious awareness.

Thus, each person's attitudes, intentions, intuitions, awareness, context, and capacity for empathetic and honest emotional communication have a significant impact on that person's experience of conflict and capacity for resolution. As a result, *no one* can know objectively or in advance how to resolve any particular conflict, as anything chaotic and rapidly changing cannot be successfully predicted or managed.

For this reason, it is impossible to teach anyone how to resolve a conflict. Instead, we need to develop people's skills, improve their awareness and self-confidence, and help them develop a broad range of diverse ideas and techniques that may or may not succeed, depending on inherently unpredictable conditions. Moreover, we have known since John Dewey that learning is accelerated when it is connected to doing. Yet we continue to train mediators based on a set of false assumptions.

An Approach to Mediator Training

As an illustration of why it is important to take a different approach to mediator learning, consider these questions, directed primarily to those who are already experienced mediators:

- What have you learned since you began mediating that you wish had been included in your training?

- What are the training values that seem to you to flow naturally from the mediation process?

- Were these values reflected in the way your training was actually conducted? If not, how might they have been reflected?

- How did you learn the *art* of mediation? Especially, how did you learn to be more intuitive, empathetic, openhearted, and wise?

- What skills would you like to be able to develop in the future? How might these be incorporated in the way mediation training is conducted?

Every mediator we asked has easily identified a number of important topics that were not covered in his or her training, but that were critical lessons discovered only after he or she started mediating. Here are some of the responses mediators gave regarding what they wished they had been taught:

- Ways of using "brief therapy" and similar psychologically based techniques in mediation.

- Detailed techniques for responding *uniquely* to each negative emotion, that is, fear, anger, shame, jealousy, pain, and grief.

- Coaching skills for working with individual parties in caucus.

- Methods for increasing emotional intelligence.

- Ways of discovering what people think or want subconsciously, and of bringing them into conscious awareness.

- Facilitation and public dialogue skills for working with groups.

- Consulting skills for working with organizations on systems design.

- Better ways of analyzing the narrative structure of conflict stories and a list of techniques for transforming them.

- Better techniques for option generating and "expanding the pie."

- Learning when to take risks and mediate "dangerously."

- Ways of becoming more aware of and responding to the "energies" and "vibrations" of conflict.

- How to develop, calibrate, and fine-tune intuition, wisdom, and insight.

- Techniques for surfacing, clarifying, and encouraging people to act based on shared values.

- Ways of gaining permission to work with people on a spiritual or heartfelt level.

- Methods for opening heart-to-heart conversations.

- Knowing how to strike the right balance between head and heart.

- Improved techniques for responding to negativity and resistance.

- How to maintain the right balance between control and chaos.

- Helping people reach deeper levels of resolution, including forgiveness and reconciliation.

- Ways of addressing the underlying systemic issues and chronic sources of conflict.

- How to transition into positive action, prevention, and systems design in organizational conflicts.

- Techniques for maintaining balance and equanimity and avoiding frustration and self-doubt when conflicts don't settle.

- Ways of addressing our own unresolved conflicts and making sure our emotions and judgments don't get in our way.

Many of these directly concern the interplay between psychology and conflict resolution, but what is especially interesting about these responses is that the way we *teach* mediation often does not conform to the core values and principles we *practice* in the mediation process, to what we know is successful in reaching people who are in conflict, to what stimulates our learning, or even to how we would most like to be taught.

Values and Actions

As described elsewhere, values are essentially priorities and integrity-based choices. They can be found both in what we do and in what we do not do, in what we grow accustomed to and in what we are willing to tolerate. They are openly and publicly expressed, acted on repeatedly, and upheld when they run counter to self-interest. In this way, they are *creators* of integrity and responsibility, builders of optimism and self-esteem, and definitions of who we are. They become manifest and alive through action, including the action of sincere declaration.

At a deeper level, we all communicate values by what we do and say, by how we behave, and by who we become when we are in conflict. While these values are often inchoate and difficult to articulate, beneath many commonly recognized mediation practices we can identify a set of values, even *meta-values*, that may represent our best practices as a profession. Our most fundamental values appear and become manifest to others when we:

- Show up and are present: physically, mentally, emotionally, and spiritually

- Listen empathetically to what lies hidden beneath words

- Tell the truth without blaming or judgment

- Are open-minded, open-hearted, and unattached to outcomes

- Search for positive, practical, satisfying outcomes

- Act collaboratively in relationships

- Display *unconditional* authenticity, integrity, and respect

- Draw on our deepest intuition

- Are on both parties' sides at the same time

- Encourage diverse, honest, heartfelt communication

- Always act in accordance with our core values and principles

- Are ready for anything at every moment

- Seek completion and closure

- Are able to let go, yet abandon no one

While not everyone will accept these values, merely articulating, debating, and engaging in dialogue over them, considering how to implement them, and deciding to commit and live by them will automatically give rise to a higher order of values—the value of *having* values. Practicing them over time—not solely in what we say or do, but how we say and do it—will initiate to the highest order of values—the value of *being* what we value.

By living our values, we become what we practice, integrating who we are with what we preach and do. This is the deeper message of mediation: that by continually and collaboratively searching for positive solutions to conflict, bringing them into conscious attention, living them as fully as possible, and developing the theories, practices, processes, and relationships that allow others to do the same, we enhance our relationships to the mediation process as a whole and build a collaborative community of reflective, emotionally intelligent practitioners.

Thus, to be fully realized, our values have to be reflected not merely in our practices, but in all aspects of our personal lives, including the ways we ourselves handle conflict, teach mediation, and interact with those who wish to learn it. Yet many mediators' lives are filled with intense adversarial conflicts, many mediation training is conducted in ways that do not conform to its core values, and many mediators interact with students in ways that undermine their ability to learn.

For example, when trainers do not acknowledge or respect differences among cultures, styles, and diverse approaches to conflict; when they try to promote one-size-fits-all models as applicable to all circumstances; when they downplay and ignore the role of emotion or heartfelt communication; when they do not pay attention to the diverse ways people learn, or even to the ways people are seated in the classroom; when they ignore the systemic sources of conflict; or when they fail to listen and learn from those they are teaching, we can say that the processes they are using are not congruent with the values they espouse. Here is a simple, concrete illustration.

How We Learn

Howard Gardner (1993) at Harvard University has famously described the diverse ways people learn using the idea of "multiple intelligences." The core of this theory is a recognition that people think and learn differently. Gardner believes there is not one form of cognition that cuts across all human thinking but that traditional notions of intelligence are misleading because I.Q. tests focus primarily or exclusively only on two areas of competence: logic and linguistics. Instead, Gardner (1993) believes there are at least eight areas of intelligence that account for the range of human potential:

1. *Linguistic intelligence,* the capacity to use the written or spoken language to express ourselves

2. *Logical-mathematical intelligence,* the ability to understand scientific principles or logic systems

3. *Spatial intelligence,* the ability to conceptualize spatial relationships

4. *Bodily kinesthetic intelligence,* the ability to use our whole body or parts of it to solve problems, make things, or express ideas and emotions through movement

5. *Musical intelligence,* the ability to "think" in music, be able to recognize and manipulate patterns

6. *Interpersonal intelligence,* the ability to understand other people and form and build strong, productive relationships

7. *Intrapersonal intelligence,* the ability to understand ourselves and know who we are, including our strengths and limitations

8. *Naturalist intelligence,* the ability to see and understand the interrelationship and interdependence of all living things and have a special sensitivity to the natural world

While each of us may quibble with this list and perhaps suggest alternative forms of intelligence, such as emotional, heart or spiritual, and political intelligence, it is clear that most mediations and conflict resolution training programs narrowly focus on linguistic and logical skills and ignore other forms of intelligence, intervention styles, and conflict-processing skills that might contribute significantly to success in mediation. Even the word "training" is problematic. There are, for example, fundamental differences between various approaches to teaching and learning, and these same differences can be found in the ways we seek to resolve conflict. We can distinguish, for example:

- *Lecture and Recitation*, which involve rote memorization and recall of facts and result in a transfer of information, yet often end in testing and forgetting

- *Education and Courses*, which involve exposure to ideas, specialized theories, and practical techniques that result in learning and understanding, yet often end in disputation and clashes of opinion over minutia

- *Training and Workshops*, which involve group discussion and result in improved technical skills, competency, and confidence, yet often end in mechanical repetition, inflexibility, and inability to handle problems not addressed in the training

- *Practice and Exercises*, which involve role plays and practical drills and result in increased self-confidence and some degree of flexibility, yet often end in improving skills without also improving the understanding needed to successfully implement them

- *Personal Development and Seminars*, which involve discovery, self-awareness, and self-actualization and result in authenticity, integrity, and personal transformation, yet often end in non-engagement with others

- *Meditation and Retreats*, which involve insight and concentration and result in wisdom, spiritual growth, and transcendence, yet often end in nothing changing or being accomplished and a lack of interest in improving others

These diverse forms of learning invisibly shift our focus, activity, and forms of interaction from an orientation toward memorizing to one of knowing, understanding, doing, and being. As we transition to deeper levels of capability in our practice, understanding, and commitment to conflict resolution, we require learning methods that allow us to develop more collaborative, democratic, self-aware, and diversely competent skills as mediators.

While every learning process has a value and each has times and circumstances that justify and make it successful, those that improve our ability to work through the *emotional*, psychological, and heart-based underpinnings of conflict—especially our own—create the greatest leverage in terms of the development of values, integrity, and overall capacity building.

Mediation Training

Approaching the problem of mediation competency, learning, and training design from this point of view suggests a number of interesting questions we can begin asking prospective mediators in order to improve their psychological awareness, develop their emotional intelligence, and facilitate the design of more advanced training programs. For example:

- What are the most significant transformational learning experiences you have had?

- What made them significant or transformational for you?

- What did these experiences have in common that you might want to incorporate into a training experience?

- Why attend this training? What do you want to achieve?

- What are your larger goals and priorities? How might this training support them?

- What could block your ability to achieve these goals and priorities? How could these obstacles be anticipated and overcome?

- What specifically do you want to be taught? How did you learn *that*?

- What do you think will be the best way to teach what you want to learn?

- Who else should be trained? Why those people? Who should not be trained? Why not?

- Who would be the ideal trainer? Why? Who would not be an ideal trainer? Why?

- What values, ideas, and skills do you most want to learn?

- How might those values, ideas, and skills be built into the content and process of the training?

- How will the training actually result in changed behavior? How should you be supported in changing?

- How might others support you in changing?

- Will the training lead to improved systems, processes, and relationships? If so, in what way?

- How will you learn the *art* of what you want to do?

- Should the training encourage you to participate, think critically, and feel free to be yourself? How would that come about?

- How might your future needs and problems be anticipated in the content and process of the training?

- How will you know whether the training has been effective?

- Based on your answers to these questions, how should the training be designed and conducted?

The answers to these questions may help stimulate a number of potential growth areas in the field of conflict resolution, such as marital mediation between couples who would like to improve their relationships; applying conflict resolution systems design skills to a broad range of social, economic, and political issues; mediating the connections between families, community groups, workplaces, and organizations; integrating conflict resolution skills into team-building and project-management workshops; extending school mediations to encourage parents and teachers to work through their personal conflicts along with the students; working with a broad range of hospital and health care disputes that flow from the need to process grief, guilt, rage, and loss; and new ideas for resolving intractable international conflicts.

Part of the object of a truly *meditative* approach to education ought to be to encourage students to become responsible for their own learning and teachers to be responsible for finding the deepest, most profound, effective way of supporting them. One way of doing so, inspired by paradoxical approaches to therapy, is by asking students to complete the following questionnaire *before* their training, then discuss their answers:

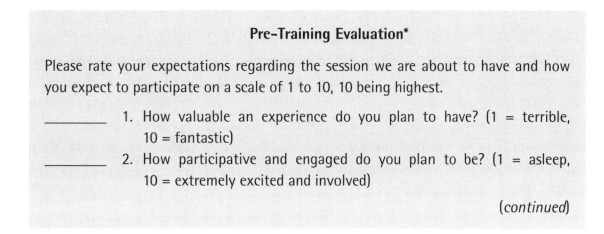

Pre-Training Evaluation*

Please rate your expectations regarding the session we are about to have and how you expect to participate on a scale of 1 to 10, 10 being highest.

_____ 1. How valuable an experience do you plan to have? (1 = terrible, 10 = fantastic)

_____ 2. How participative and engaged do you plan to be? (1 = asleep, 10 = extremely excited and involved)

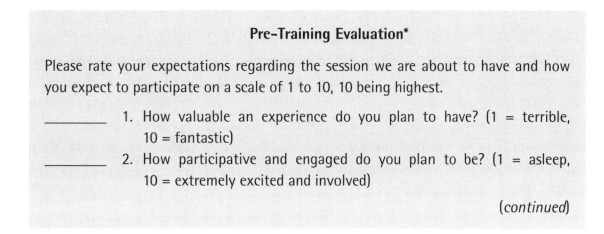*(continued)*

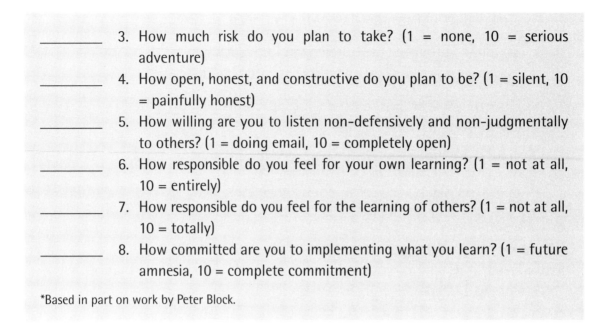

3. How much risk do you plan to take? (1 = none, 10 = serious adventure)

4. How open, honest, and constructive do you plan to be? (1 = silent, 10 = painfully honest)

5. How willing are you to listen non-defensively and non-judgmentally to others? (1 = doing email, 10 = completely open)

6. How responsible do you feel for your own learning? (1 = not at all, 10 = entirely)

7. How responsible do you feel for the learning of others? (1 = not at all, 10 = totally)

8. How committed are you to implementing what you learn? (1 = future amnesia, 10 = complete commitment)

*Based in part on work by Peter Block.

Applying these ideas to conflict resolution, we all know intuitively that mediators are not immune from conflicts and that we will become better dispute-resolvers by working through and resolving our own conflicts. It therefore makes sense for us to incorporate into the mediation training process the psychological components that will allow people to work directly on resolving their personal conflicts. At present, few mediation programs allow or encourage participants to do so.

Conclusion

In the end, we *are* the technique. As imperfect as we are, it is who we *are* that forms the path to resolution, and that same path invites us to become better human beings, simply in order to become better mediators. This realization returns mediation to its *human* origins and essence, as an exercise not solely in empathy and compassion, but in creative problem solving, emotional clarity, heartfelt wisdom, and social collaboration.

We hope these practices will encourage us to look more deeply and wisely at the world within, as well as the world without, and assist us in finding ways to translate our own suffering into methods and understandings that will lead to a better, less hostile and adversarial world.

References

Gardner, H. (1993). *Multiple intelligences: New horizons in theory and practice.* New York: Basic Books.

Goleman, D. (1995). *Emotional intelligence.* New York: Bantam.

Kenneth Cloke, J.D., Ph.D., LLM, *is a mediator, arbitrator, consultant, and trainer, specializing in resolving complex multi-party conflicts. He is author of* Mediation: Revenge and the Magic of Forgiveness; Mediating Dangerously; Thank God It's Monday!; Resolving Conflicts at Work; Resolving Personal and Organizational Conflict: Stories of Transformation and Forgiveness; The End of Management and the Rise of Organizational Democracy; *and other books. For more on mediating global conflicts, see his book,* Conflict Revolution: Mediating Evil, War, Injustice, and Terrorism—How Mediators Can Help Save the Planet.

Kenneth is president and co-founder of Mediators Without Borders.

How to Avoid Change Management Workshops That Fail

Rick Maurer

Summary

People are tired of change management. They think they've been there and done that. Unfortunately, they haven't. Seventy percent of changes in organizations still fail (Keller & Aiken, 2008). My work has focused on change (particularly resistance to change) since the early 1990s. I think I've learned (sometimes the hard way) why training fails and what makes sessions successful. The following article sums up my findings.

What to Avoid

Sheep Dip Training

My Uncle Red used to have a kennel of hunting dogs. Once or twice a year he would immerse each dog in sheep dip, a foul smelling concoction that killed tics and fleas and who knows what else. He dipped all the dogs—whether they needed it or not. Training is a lot like that. Organizations send everyone to these sessions hoping that when people need what they learned, they will remember it. (I am still waiting for the need for 9th grade algebra to appear.) When education is not linked to action, the retention rate is low. And education without application invites people to be docile learners. There is nothing to question or challenge because everything is hypothetical.

Sheep dip training fails to recognize who needs education and who doesn't. In some weird attempt to be fair, organizations send every manager to the same management training. It is a massive waste of time and talent.

Confusing Motivation with Education

Organizations wrongly assume that people need to be motivated when it comes to change. If they just change their attitudes, get with the program, and imagine they are building cathedrals, then all will be well.

Sometimes trainers are asked to pump people up—to motivate them. If people aren't motivated about a change, it is not a training problem, it's a leadership problem. When you accept those assignments, you become the handmaiden of ineffective leaders. This type of training insults the will and purpose of the employees who are forced to take part.

When people resist change, they are usually doing it for a good reason. Often the leaders have failed to make a compelling case, or people know that this will just be another "flavor of the month." In these instances, people are right to not be motivated. And that's where you can help. A better use of your time would be to "train" leaders. Find out why people aren't motivated and show leaders ways that they can turn apathy or anger into support.

Assuming That Leading and Managing Change Is Easy

Look at the popularity of *Who Moved My Cheese* (Johnson, 2002). It is perhaps the largest selling book on organizational change ever written. Its message is simple. People (or mice) need to get with the program or else they will die. That message leaves leaders off the hook. The leaders don't need to improve how they lead change; they only need mice who will do their bidding (to avoid death).

When people are involved, change is complex and often not linear. So neat one-two-three steps often lack the subtlety needed to move back a step or to the side, or dig deeper to find out what's bothering people.

Talking and Talking at Them

Mark Twain once wrote, "No sinner was ever converted after the first twenty minutes of a sermon." Long lectures, especially those heavy on slides, numb people to death. I have seen potentially helpful training start with hours of executives talking from slide decks. You could see energy seep from the room. By the end of the day, only those pumped on caffeine were still asking questions. The rest had tuned out.

Events R Us

Organizations sometimes think that the success of a change rests on planning a kickoff event that rivals Ringling Brothers in its theatrical hoopla. Events are great if they are used to engage people in planning. They risk becoming bad jokes when they are used to try to fill people's heads with details about the change. Training and development professionals can use this request as an opportunity to help plan an event that treats people like adults and engages them in the process.

What to Do

Link Education with a Specific Need to Know

When people feel that they need to know how to lead change, and are looking to you to help them, they don't need fancy stuff. They need—and desperately want—to know what they need to know. The education must be practical. Examples, self-assessments, 360-degree assessments, and realistic simulations and activities can help anchor learning. But all the learning must be in service of preparing these men and women to take on the massive task of leading change more effectively.

Create a Spring Training Camp

Professional baseball players attend spring training every year to practice what they already know how to do. The practice sessions are demanding and target specific moves. They don't just play games; they spend hours working on particular plays. They are coached. They watch game films. They talk strategy. They try out a new batting stance or work on adding a new pitch to their repertoires. It is hard work.

Organizations need to give people a place to practice before sending them on the field before large crowds.

Base the Education on a Sound Foundation

I have seen organizations hand out books during training. That can be good, of course, but sometimes these books recommend quite different courses of action. If the ideas in these books became the subject of intense debate on the best way for this organization to go, I would say "Bravo." But they are passed out like party favors and often aren't even discussed seriously during classes.

Decide what approach works for your organization. For example, I use an approach I developed as a basis for almost all of my consulting and training. I may supplement my material, but I never waver from what I believe to be a sound way to lead change. People learn enough so that they can question my approach—and that's a good thing. If they ask you and themselves, "Will that really work here?" or "What about this situation?" you know that they are chewing on the materials and trying to find something that will work for them.

Offering too many theories and models results in a "pick and choose" menu that lacks the logical coherence a single model provides. There are a number of good approaches to change; pick one that works in your type of organization and in your unique culture, and then stick with it. Teach it. Give people an opportunity to practice applying it. Make it the lens through which the organization talks about change. It will do you little good to teach John Kotter to executives, Jim Collins to managers, and William Bridges to everyone else. You will just create confusion. Pick one approach. Period. Every time you are tempted to add in a personality theory or some nifty game, ask, "Does this support people learning about this approach to change?" If not, skip it.

Conclusion

Change is tough, but educating people doesn't have to be. Think engagement. As you plan a training event (or other educational process), ask, "Will this engage people in ways that will increase their knowledge and capacity to lead change well in our organization?"

References

Johnson, S. (2002). *Who moved my cheese?* New York: Vermilion.

Keller, S., & Aiken, C. (2008). *The inconvenient truth about change management.* New York: McKinsey & Company.

Rick Maurer *is author of* Beyond the Wall of Resistance: Why 70% of Changes Still Fail and What You Can Do About It *(Bard Press, 2010). Ideas in this article are adapted from this book.*

Mistakes That Trainers Make—And How to Avoid Them

Deborah Spring Laurel

Summary

The purpose of this article is to help both new and seasoned trainers avoid common mistakes when designing and facilitating training programs. Suggestions are offered to ensure that trainers train the right people at the right learning level with the right amount of information and the right learning activities and that they use relevant and participative learning activities that engage the participants and ensure a vibrant and validating learning experience.

Suggestions are also offered so that everything possible is done to set up an effective learning experience, maintain a comfortable learning environment, enhance trainer credibility, and generate participant respect and trust.

Adhering to these suggestions should help both new and seasoned trainers avoid common pitfalls that limit the success of their training design and delivery.

Avoiding Content Selection Mistakes

Five mistakes that new and seasoned trainers should avoid when they select the content for their training programs are described below.

Mistake 1. Not Conducting a Training Needs Assessment

It is important for a trainer to know who the participants will be, why they will be attending, and what they are supposed to know or be able to do when they leave the training session. Otherwise, the trainer may end up providing the wrong training to the wrong people, wasting everyone's time.

Mistake 2. Not Identifying the Desired Level of Learning

The fallback instructional method for trainers tends to be lecture, which can only provide knowledge. Trainers need to know what the participants should be able to do when they leave. Based on that information, the trainer can decide whether the desired level of learning is comprehension, application, analysis, evaluation, or creation and select the appropriate learning activities to achieve that level.

Mistake 3. Cramming Too Much Information into One Training Session

Learners can absorb only so much at one time, so it's ineffective to try to fit too much content into a single session. Also, the desire to deliver abundant information tends to result in a long lecture, which will probably not accomplish the desired level of learning or meet the needs of every learning style.

Focus on the critical information and provide reference materials to support the remaining information. This way there will be sufficient time to check for participant comprehension and give them an opportunity to apply what they have learned.

Mistake 4. Putting Times on Agendas

Trainers need the flexibility to take more or less time when they need it, depending on the group. If the times are written next to the agenda items, some participants will start to worry when the session is not where the agenda says it should be. Trainers should save the participants from needless concern and themselves from unnecessary aggravation. The times should only be on the trainer's agenda.

Mistake 5. Placing All Training Information on PowerPoint Slides

Training information belongs in the participants' manuals or handouts. PowerPoint should only be used to augment the training, not deliver the training. PowerPoint slides should contain only a few points or pictures per slide that emphasize or summarize important content.

Following these suggestions should help to ensure that trainers train the right people at the right learning level with the right amount of information and the right learning activities.

Avoiding Mistakes When Choosing Learning Activities

Part of the fun in designing and facilitating training programs is selecting which learning activities to incorporate. There is a wide range and variety of activities from which to choose. However, both new and seasoned trainers make seven common mistakes that should be avoided.

Mistake 1. Assuming the Trainer Knows More Than the Participants

Trainers don't want to waste time or bore participants silly teaching them what they already know. So a trainer should ask questions first. If participant know the answers, the trainer can move on to the next topic area. Remember this mantra: Ask participants first. Tell them the information only if no one can answer questions on the material. It is important to recognize and honor the collective expertise in the room.

Mistake 2. Not Meeting the Needs of Different Learning Styles

Trainers tend to train people either the way they like to learn or the way that was modeled for them in school. Using just one training approach will limit the trainer's effectiveness and the ability of all participants to learn. It doesn't matter what learning style model you prefer. Just keep in mind that people learn differently and enrich the learning activities to meet a wide range of learning needs. At the very least, enhance the activities so that the oral, visual, and kinesthetic learners are set up for success.

Mistake 3. Scheduling Lots of Activities That Have No Real Bearing on the Training Content

In order to lighten up training and make it enjoyable, it can be very tempting to add icebreakers and activities simply for fun. That is a fine approach if you have been hired to entertain, not build skills. However, if the participants must gain new information or practice new skills, there are lots of interactive and enjoyable learning activities that will get the job done.

Mistake 4. Assuming That Dry or Technical Information Needs to Be Taught in a Dry or Technical Manner

A number of participant-centered learning activities ensure that the necessary learning occurs. Take the key points and place them into a questionnaire for group discussion. Pair up participants to complete an information sheet by finding key points in rules or regulations. Provide a case study to analyze. Choose activities that put the focus and responsibility for learning on the participants. That will bring the content alive and make both the content and the learning process engaging and interesting.

Mistake 5. Not Modeling What the Participants Are Expected to Do

When giving an assignment, make sure that you not only give clear and complete instructions, but also walk the participants through a brief example of what you want the participants to do.

If you don't model the assignment, it is difficult to guarantee either an effective learning experience or a successful outcome. Instead, you are likely to be unhappy with some of the results, and that will further frustrate participants.

Mistake 6. Not Debriefing Learning Activities

Group activities take time, so it is understandable if you would rather skip debriefing in order to move the lesson along. However, often the best learning occurs during the debriefing. Debriefing requires participants to consciously reflect on their experience, develop their own theories, and articulate what they have learned. As each group reports on its activity, the other groups benefit from the ideas and outcomes. This also gives you an opportunity to refocus the participants when necessary, add additional information, and provide a final summation.

Mistake 7. Giving a Lecture After Lunch

It probably goes without saying that post-lunch activities need to be highly interactive to keep the participants awake and focused. Despite this truism, many trainers still proceed to lecture because that is where they are in their lesson plan. Don't be afraid to be flexible. Before the lecture, add in a quick activity that will check for comprehension of the morning's content. Ideally, this activity should also get the participants up and moving. There are lots of effective kinesthetic learning activities that are quick and easy to set up, such as a relay race, pop-ups, a scavenger hunt, or a gallery walk.

Following these suggestions should help to ensure that you use relevant and participative learning activities that engage participants and provide a vibrant and validating learning experience.

Avoiding Facilitation Mistakes

A good training plan, good content, and good learning activities do not automatically ensure a good training experience. The trainer is ultimately responsible for establishing and maintaining an effective learning environment. This begins with training room and training process logistics.

Mistake 1. Not Preparing the Room

Check all audiovisual equipment and hook-ups before the session, to make sure everything is in operating order. Cover or tape down extension cords so that no one trips over them. Have a backup plan in case there is a problem with equipment or software.

Mistake 2. Not Checking to See Whether Everyone Can Hear and See During the Session

Always circle the room before a session begins to make sure that all participants will be seated where they can see you and any audiovisuals without obstruction. Move tables and chairs to make adjustments. At the beginning of the session, ask participants to let you know if they can't hear you or other participants. Also ask them whether their seats give them a clear view and, if not, have them move.

Mistake 3. Not Giving Breaks

Brain studies have found that people's brains become overloaded after about 50 minutes. You will reap two major benefits if you give participants a 10-minute break every 50 minutes. First, the participants will stay more alert and focused. Second, there will be more beginning and endings to the lesson, which is when participants are most ripe for learning.

Mistake 4. Moving Closer to Participants Who Speak Too Softly

Although it is counterintuitive, you need to move away from soft-spoken people. This will encourage participants to speak more loudly so that you (and the rest of the group) can hear them. If you move closer, you will be the only person able to hear what the participant says. In that event, you will need to repeat what was said so the group can hear it. This is a great way for trainers to lose their voices.

Mistake 5. Talking Too Much

Limit a lecture to 10 minutes, which will keep it a "lecturette." Then check for participant comprehension by asking or opening up for questions, showing relevant pictures, or assigning a learning activity wherein the participants have to apply what they have learned so far.

Following these suggestions should help to ensure that you set up an effective learning experience and maintain a comfortable learning environment.

Avoiding Mistakes That Affect Trainer Credibility and Respect

Trainers make seven mistakes that adversely affect their credibility and effectiveness. If trainers want participants to respect and trust them, they should follow these suggestions.

Mistake 1. Assuming the Trainer Is Supposed to Have All the Answers

Just because trainers are standing in front of the group does not mean that they need to be experts on the subject. Even if you are an expert, you can still be stumped by a question. If a participant asks a question that you can't answer, first ask the rest of the group if someone has an answer. If no one does, be honest, admit that you don't know the answer, and promise to find out and get back to the group. An anonymous quote says, "Knowledge is knowing where to find the answers." As long as you follow through on your promise, you will retain your credibility.

Mistake 2. Being Afraid to Admit to Making a Mistake

Trust is an essential element in any learning environment. The participants will be more likely to trust and like trainers if they are willing to admit when they are wrong. If you do it with humor rather than getting upset about it, the participants will laugh with you, not at you. Your credibility with participants will actually increase.

Mistake 3. Not Staying Aware of What Is Happening During Small-Group Activities

There is the tendency to assume that groups have understood the assigned task and are working well together. Unless you move around the room to listen in on the conversations, you really won't know whether the participants need assistance, whether they need additional clarification, or whether one participant is dominating the discussion. Just be unobtrusive so the participants don't become distracted.

Mistake 4. Not Waiting Long Enough for Participants to Answer a Question

Trainers are often uncomfortable with silence, so they tend to jump in to rephrase or answer a question much too soon. Participants need time to consider the question and frame their answers. Silently count to ten, or higher if the group is particularly thoughtful. Otherwise, participants will have the impression that you don't really expect them to answer and are merely asking rhetorical questions. If that happens, you will leave the training session wondering why participants stopped participating.

Mistake 5. Being Afraid to Correct Incorrect Answers to Questions

It is a given that participants will sometimes provide the wrong information in response to a question that a trainer asks. Of course you wouldn't say, "No, you're wrong," because that will embarrass the person and he or she may not volunteer to answer any more questions. Instead, take responsibility for possibly being unclear when you originally posed the question. Clarify and rephrase the question to coach the participant for a correct response. Bottom line: Don't ignore or gloss over an incorrect answer, because that will confuse everyone. Calmly and diplomatically get the discussion back on the right track.

Mistake 6. Not Managing Disruptive Participants

Trainers absolutely need to manage disruptive participants. Trainers create even more problems for themselves if they don't. Clearly, the learning experience for everyone else will be ruined. Equally important, the other participants will cease to respect you, become uncomfortable, and even feel unsafe because you have not established and maintained control over the training room.

Mistake 7. Not Handling Disruptive Participants with Respect

It doesn't matter how disruptive a participant may be. The minute trainers treat that person disrespectfully in front of the group, the entire group will turn against the trainer. Why? They will suddenly feel vulnerable. Instead, use humor, agree to disagree, ask the group whether they agree with the individual, and/or refer to the training room rules of conduct. If none of these approaches is effective, assign a task to the group and ask the disruptive individual to meet with you outside of the room.

How trainers present and handle themselves, the learning process, and the participants can positively or negatively impact the trainers' credibility and respect as a trainer. Following the suggestions in this article should help both new and seasoned trainers to avoid common training design and delivery mistakes that limit the success of their training programs.

Deborah Spring Laurel *has been a trainer and a consultant in workplace learning and performance improvement for over thirty years. She was adjunct faculty in executive management at the University of Wisconsin-Madison for thirty years. The principal of Laurel and Associates, Ltd., Deborah has a master's degree from the University of Wisconsin-Madison. She is a past president of the South Central Wisconsin Chapter of ASTD and facilitates train-the-trainer programs nationally and internationally.*

Adopting a Learning Continuum
The Urgency to Reinvent Training Organizations

Gary G. Wise

Summary

Recent cross-industry trends include flattening budgets, decreasing human resource allocations, downsizing, and reductions in force. Training organizations are not immune to these trends and very often are among the first business areas to feel the pinch.

These reductions are particularly troubling for training organizations that are already under-staffed and stressed, with limited resources, and for whom virtually every demand has priority status. We can easily point to tough economic times as a key driver; however, tough times are not the cause but the catalyst. Tough times stimulate a "value inspection" across an organization to identify who does and who does not contribute to the bottom line. Since investment goes where positive return is generated, the training organization of the future must demonstrate expanded skills and competencies. The time for reinvention is now.

Passing Muster on a Value Inspection

This article addresses a common outcome when the training organization faces a value inspection and, surprisingly, what consistently contributes to this strain on our training resources—*the results we deliver.* Why would training organizations, which are tasked as most capable to drive improved workforce performance [and value] through enhancing knowledge and skills, be one of the first to lose budget allocations? The answer comes in the form of a two-pronged indictment that traditional training leaders do not want to hear.

1. Traditional training approaches do not consistently *demonstrate tangible business value* as an outcome.

2. Long-term training efforts do precious little to *sustain capability*.

Are these statements too strong? Or not strong enough? Either way, I anticipate protest from my peers. Before casting judgment, however, keep in mind that I have been in the learning industry for over thirty years and am forced to look into that same corporate training mirror. Quite frankly, I do not like what I see, and as a long-term member of the offending party, I can only add that it is past time for a little change. Having recently been on the receiving end of a reduction in force, I am more convinced than ever that now is the time for a *reinvention* of the role of corporate training. For some learning professionals, this reinvention will indeed seem like a disruption—or worse—a threat. For others, it represents an exciting time to reinvent what we do and expand into a role as value-generating members of the organization.

Reread the two-pronged indictment—just the italicized phrases. Truly, if we are serious about creating *tangible business value* and *sustained capability*, we have an expanded responsibility to support the workforce in which these two outcomes are manifest. Unfortunately, "where these outcomes are manifest" is not aligned with where we currently spend a majority of our time and resources (see Figure 1). The velocity of business demands our presence *downstream in the work context*. Learning moments of need have converged with the urgency for high-quality performance

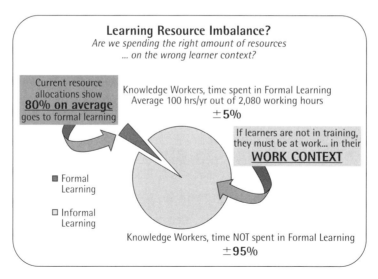

Figure 1. Learning Resource Imbalance
Source: Josh Bersin, "The Future of the Business of Learning," July 23, 2009

and effectively changed the rules of engagement for learning organizations. The broad scope of our role is forcing us to be as proficient with informal learning methods and technologies as we are with designing, developing, and delivering traditional, linear, formal learning solutions.

In July 2009, during a half-day webinar on "The Future of the Business of Learning," panelist Josh Bersin, of Bersin & Associates, shared his firm's research that revealed *the average amount of time spent annually in formal learning [a.k.a. training] was around 5 percent*. Obviously, this number will vary depending on the industry and mandatory training and/or compliance requirements. I developed Figure 1 to illustrate the disparity of time available to learn in our traditional *formal* venues compared with those opportunities where *informal* learning is available—represented by the 95 percent slice of the pie. The key point is the fact that the 95 percent is where the workers are engaged in productive endeavors—their *work context*. They are downstream from the classroom and/or online training venues and are actively at work on the job, where they execute their assigned tasks and generate tangible value for the organization.

The second research finding Josh shared was even more condemning, and it further validates the momentum behind the indictment. *On average, up to 80 percent of training resources are allocated to the 5 percent slice of the pie*. If business value is generated in the 95 percent slice of this pie—if flawless execution of work tasks occur in the 95 percent slice, if urgency to perform and business risk and liability are greatest in the 95 percent slice, if sustained capability is manifest in the 95 percent slice—why are training organizations clinging to—and funding—a paradigm that is stuck in the 5 percent slice? Bersin's research begs us to look into the mirror and assess what we see in order to honestly answer the question: *"Are we spending the right resources in the wrong learning context?"*

Implications of Moving Downstream

Bersin's research does *not* nullify all the successful training we do in the 5 percent slice. However, clearly the scope of our responsibility just became significantly larger. Seems to me like a perfect time for reinventing what we do as learning organizations. With trends and economic times being what they are, the traditional approach to training is no longer sustainable. Reinvention involves *change*, and we all know what manner of chaos comes with change, especially when we start introducing new Learning 2.0 methodologies and leveraging unfamiliar Web 2.0 technologies; not to mention the related competencies to integrate and optimize both into expanded design, development, and delivery protocols. It also means that long-held traditions and existing paradigms are fair game for eradication, and this scares training traditionalists to the core.

With every training organization being somewhat unique in terms of existing roles and skill sets, the answers to the questions of what are the *right resources* and what is the *optimum balance between formal and informal learning context* will be equally as unique. I think the larger question we have is: *"Do we have the right skill sets and the right competencies in place to move downstream and into the work context?"* The decision to move downstream can no longer be avoided, nor can it be taken lightly. One of the first implications to be addressed, therefore, is assessing your readiness to make the move. This will require taking an inventory of existing roles and competencies and comparing them against potential future roles learning organizations will likely include. Table 1 provides a collection of projected future roles, competencies, and required outcomes to consider in your assessment.

As you can see from Table 1, some familiar skills and competencies are already within reach. Others may be a stretch to accomplish or may be completely non-existent. Again, depending on the demands of your industry and the cultural commitment to

Table 1. Future Roles, Competencies, and Outcomes

Role/Capability	Skill/Competency	Accomplishment/Outcome
Capability Lead/ Performance Consultant	Business acumen	Business relevancy in client interactions
	Performance consulting/root cause analysis	Isolate solutions training can impact
	Discovery/questioning	Integrate learning solutions with attributes of the work context
	Business process analysis, process mapping	Segmenting training impact potential
	Effective communications, oral and written presentation	Learner-focused work context solutions
	Project management	Set expectations related to training impact
		Consulting integrated with solution development
Holistic Learning Designers and Developers	Expanded discovery/effective questioning	Holistic learning solutions that use both formal and informal learning assets that reflect learner's work context
	Alignment of instructional design methods with five moments of learning need	Learning assets available in right amount and in a work context–friendly format
	Rich-media capture/creation/insertion	"View to learn" vs. "read to learn"
	Integration/editing of video/rich-media	Single point of update: "Create once; use many times"
	Object design methods for re-use and/or repurpose	Interactive, compelling, engaging learning experiences
	Collaboration and SME engagement	
	Simulation/job emulation activity design	

Role/Capability	Skill/Competency	Accomplishment/Outcome
Facilitators, Coaches, Mentors, and Learning Counselors	Synchronous virtual learning facilitation	Remote learners engaged in virtual events
	Advanced group facilitation skills	Downstream reinforcement from manager coaching support
	Coaching/mentoring	
	Balanced feedback	Point-of-work feedback
	Learning needs assessment	Individual development plans
	Development planning	
Learning Technology Integrator	Learning technology capability awareness	Access to learning assets is seamless, frictionless, and ubiquitous
	Ability to define learning technology business requirements	Development of accurate Use Case Scenarios for vendor evaluation and selection
	Establish and maintain positive relationship with IT resources	IS partnership
	Visualize/anticipate the future applications that may benefit from technology	Learning technology roadmap with near-term (1 to 2 years) to long-term (3+) requirements
	Innovative/creative	
	Effective communications	Transparency—less jargon/techno-speak
Collaborator, Social Learning Integrator	Managing successful communities	Peer-to-peer access to shared knowledge
	Integrate Web 2.0 tools into learning solutions	Engaging, targeted, collaborative environments
	Community/blog moderation	Social learning routinized for learners through integration with daily workflows
	Virtual facilitation and engagement	Rapid access to—and sharing of—knowledge
Knowledge Broker	Effective questioning	Relevant knowledge bases and best practice integration into learning flow
	Interviewing skills	Harvest downstream best practice and end-user innovation
	Community of practice/blog/wiki management, administration, maintenance, and moderation	Acquisition of performer support relevance and end-user feedback
		Active, engaging communities are used as part of normal workflow/routine
Evaluator	Effective questioning	Tangible demonstration of business impact
	Business acumen	Routinized Level 3 and 4 evaluation
	Identification of business-relevant key performance indicators	Actionable business metrics
	Data gathering, analysis, reporting	

organizational learning within senior leadership, the mix of necessary competencies will vary. Regardless, skills and competencies have expanded, and the importance of moving your training staff to a state of readiness cannot be underestimated.

Moving Downstream to Address Learning as an Ecosystem

When we consider the task of supporting learners in their work context, we are addressing a broader, robust, inclusive, or, if you prefer, *holistic ecosystem*. To effectively define this ecosystem, we will establish some ground rules. Unlike the controlled, structured environment of formal learning events, we find little control and even less structure in the work context. Further, we have to consider that not every learner is going to have the same needs, at the same time, and at the same point in the workflow. One can safely make the assumption that familiar, linear design models are not applicable. Some training organizations are already shifting to design methodologies that objectize content and are introducing Web 2.0 technologies (such as electronic performance support systems) into the learning mix to accommodate the "just-in-time" nature of unique learning demands. To address this uniqueness, I recommmend using a framework developed by Dr. Conrad Gottfreson in collaboration with Bob Mosher called Learning Moments of Need (see Figure 2).

As hard as I have tried to dream up a sixth need, it seems that everything falls into one of the categories in the model. These "moments" have become a guiding framework for all of my learning design work.

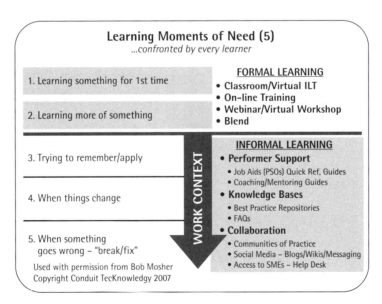

Figure 2. Learning Moments of Need
Used with permission of Bob Mosher. Copyright Conduit TecKnowledgy 2007

It is safe to say that we have mastered the first two moments of need and address them effectively in controlled, premeditated learning environments from instructor-led classroom sessions, in self-paced asynchronous courses, and in virtual webinars and workshops. Keep in mind that these first two moments also represent that 5 percent slice illustrated in Figure 1. But training support is less likely to be present in the work context, away from the formal learning venues and in the uncontrolled chaos of the work context. The learners continue to have moments of need; however, they are more targeted and more aligned with actual work tasks. They find themselves trying to *recall* what they learned in the formal venues (Moment 3); they find themselves confronted with immediate needs to adapt to new processes or work protocols when things have *changed* (Moment 4); or they are under the gun to react with good decisions and high-quality performance when things *fail or something goes wrong* (Moment 5). All three take place in the work context. All three carry urgency and business risk in addition to the demands of rapid, accurate response or performance execution. Clearly, the stakes just go higher and the needs of the learner are different in the post-training, downstream environment.

Design methodologies based on a linear model can be limiting when addressing Moments 3 through 5, but they do not necessarily have to be. This is where the concept of *treating learning like an ecosystem* shows promise. We cannot look myopically at the learning asset we produce without consideration of the *work context*. In addition, we have to consider the technology that can facilitate access to/from those assets in the moment of need. During these moments we find the most unpredictability and individuality of needs. Linearity is no longer relevant.

Does this mean the popular design model of ADDIE (Analysis, Design, Development, Implementation, and Evaluation) is no longer valid? Not exactly. Linearity is still alive and well when you consider that the workflow itself has linear qualities. But the moments of learning are no longer linear. These surface at different times, for different individuals, at different points within the workflow. That does *not* mean ADDIE is as dead as some would have us think. ADDIE is still a valid model, but the application of the model may require a different spin.

In reality, it is not about the design model as much as about the way we provide access to the learning content. The true nature of "just-in-time" is compounded by other demands that must be met. To serve our learners in a *learning ecosystem*, our task has become more complicated, more inclusive, and decidedly more holistic, with an ultimate output that I define as follows:

> Seamless, frictionless, ubiquitous access by the right knowledge worker to the right learning assets, at his or her moment(s) of learning need, in a work context–friendly amount, in a readily consumable, compelling format, to/from the right devices.

Seamless implies that learners should not have to fight through numerous systems or interfaces or have to remember which repository holds the assets they require. *Frictionless* implies that the learners access learning assets with a minimum of effort, searching, or "clicks." *Ubiquitous* implies connectivity that supports access at any time and from anywhere. This definition of accessibility holds true for any of the five moments of need.

Work context–friendly amounts and *readily consumable formats* imply that the designer included some considerations of object size, task relevancy, task urgency, and usability. Throw in the need to accommodate "pull" by the learner or "push" by the content owner on demand and the *devices* (technologies) on both ends of that transaction become an important design consideration. That's why I suggest we treat this encompassing environment as a *learning ecosystem.* Our rules of engagement change when we head downstream.

Performer Support in the Work Context

Anyone who has endured endless hours of training related to an online application like SAP or PeopleSoft or [enter application name of your choice here] can identify with unreasonable expectations that, upon completion of the course, he or she will be fully functional using that application—not to mention several weeks later when the opportunity next arises. I've been through numerous organization-wide launches of enterprise systems and have learned that reliance on formal training to create a state of readiness in the end-user population is an unreasonable expectation. I use systems training as my example, but the same results hold true regardless of the content or topic if it not reinforced and *recall memory* is the only crutch. The primary reason training cannot ensure a successful implementation is based on the learners' inability to retain the knowledge we so expertly pump into their heads (see Figure 3).

Before learners even leave the classroom and return to their desks, a significant portion of the learning they gained is lost. Sleep on it over the weekend, and two-thirds of it is history. As you can see in the diagram in Figure 3, it does not get any better with time.

Informal learning is a perfect fit for providing the support performers need in their work context, hence the term "performer support." These learning assets are usually short, object-based, and task-oriented at step and/or sub-step level of granularity. If a process has twelve steps, the asset may include up to twelve performer support objects (PSOs). Performer support removes the burden from the learners use of recall and shifts it to their using reference knowledge instead. Learners no longer have to remember how to do something. They only need to remember what PSO to use when they are confronted with a need. What complicates our ability to design

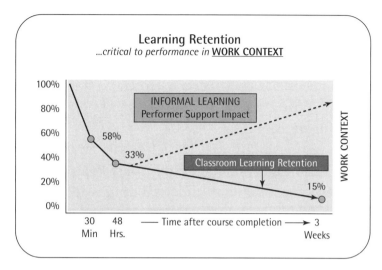

Figure 3. Learning Retention
Source: Research Institute of America. Used with permission from Bob Mosher.
Copyright Conduit TecKnowledgy 2007.

suitable PSOs is the individuality of potential learning moments. People don't remember the same things. The moment of need for one is often not the same as for another, so traditional design methodology falls short when we move downstream.

New "Design Think" Competencies

No design methodology used to construct linear learning solutions (used in the first two moments of need) can satisfy the demand for immediacy found in the work context; nor can it anticipate the diversity of need across an entire workforce. When we are in the work context, the moment of need becomes highly individualized, and one-size-fits-all designs do not meet the diversity of demand. Therefore, our discovery methods must expand beyond the traditional scope.

The environment we are now trying to support is characterized by chaos that we did not have to deal with in formal training venues. Certainly, we attempt to emulate some of that *realism* with simulations and role plays, but nothing compares to the *urgency* and *risk* afforded in the heat of battle with its potential for failure. Our success criteria of maintaining high Level 1 evaluation scores and meeting positive Level 2 assessment thresholds in the formal training environment are meaningless when we are downstream in the work context. Success in the formal learning world (the 5 percent slice) does not accurately predict performance outcomes in the work context (the 95 percent slice). The stakes are higher downstream and a potential shortfall is more serious. We measure execution in the work context with performance indicators like tangible business impact, risk, liability, and gain or loss.

None of those "success/failure metrics" are part of our 5 percent world; however, they are downstream when we want to point to our contributions as business value generators. Otherwise, we can only point to how "busy: we have been with the number of butts in seats, average Level 1 scores, volume of online courses consumed, and so forth. Those are not the metrics to crow about when senior leadership is making funding decisions.

To meet this new responsibility, our "design think" must expand and include a heightened sense of business acumen. Our discovery competencies should include asking pertinent questions about and understanding workflow. Our design methodology shifts from a linear model to one that allows us to serve needs across job roles and work functions. Task-level activities required of learners become drivers for those smaller design outputs we called PSOs.

We must adopt a *create once—use many times* regimen. We must design objects that are stand-alone to the extent that they are what is needed to get the learner through a specific task. The more complex the task, the greater the number of PSOs developed. This does not imply that traditional linear learning is outdated or no longer needed; quite to the contrary. We still need to storyboard, but we put reusable content objects (our PSOs) throughout and access them through embedded links to promote repetitive use and eliminate duplicate development efforts.

Back in the 5 percent slice, classroom events have changed, too, particularly in process-centric training efforts. For example, instead of blasting through an entire online business application from beginning to end, we break down the transactions into screens or task-level steps, and the learners work through each step using relevant PSOs in role-based scenarios. For example, if a linear module on a twelve-step transaction to accomplish an internal employee transfer using SAP now consists of a cluster of twelve PSOs. These PSOs are also available to users downstream when a moment of need arises. By using the same PSOs many times, we are accomplishing *a thread of continuity*.

In effect, we are training users how to access the PSOs they need to accomplish a task instead of putting the burden on them to remember how to complete the task. We dramatically reduce the emphasis on *"How do I do this?"* and shift it to *"Where do I go to find help to do this?"* Classroom training time typically goes down, and some organizations have experienced up to 50 percent reduction in formal training requirements on system-centric and other process/fact-heavy training. As an additional side benefit, calls to the Help Desk often go down by almost as much.

This methodology will enable other benefits, like the ability to maintain and modify content as workflows change due to in-house customizations or vendor upgrades, patches, or new releases. Developers have just one place to go to make changes—a PSO repository sitting in SharePoint or some other URL-addressable repository. An update to a single object satisfies the formal, linear learning world, and it handles the just-in-time, PSO-based informal world. If a new object is required, the developer only has to embed a new link into the formal learning flow. Certainly, there is additional development time to add new content and modify learning flows, but rework is reduced significantly.

Accomplishing Discovery in the Work Context

As we move downstream, three clusters of attributes have the potential to impact the learners in their work context: space, media, and systems. These attributes can also dramatically impact design, development, and delivery decisions related to any training solutions we create (see Figure 4).

Attributes of Space

The concept of *space* represents physical location and proximity to work and to workflow. Note in Figure 4 that attributes of *space* influence decisions related to media selection. Without clear knowledge of where the learner is physically located and conditions related to urgency and risk, making an informed decision about media can be hit or miss. Likewise, a combination of *space* and *media* attributes influences decisions related to *systems* selections. A mobile learner accessing streamed media has implications for bandwidth, network connectivity, and so on. Several key points should be satisfied before decisions are made related

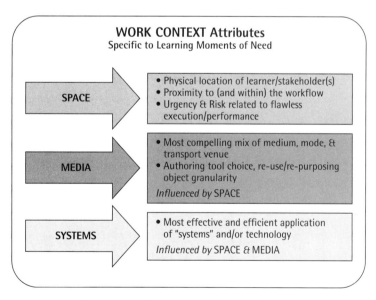

Figure 4. Work Context Attributes

to design, development, and delivery of the learning solution. Some of these are listed below:

Learning Stakeholder(s)

- Who are the primary learning stakeholders?

- What does their role/function produce in their work context? (*e.g., searching for tangible, measurable outcomes*)

- Who are the other stakeholders? (*e.g., manager, Help Desk, SME, mentors, etc.*)

Physical Location

- Where are the learners physically located at the moment(s) of learning need?

Work Flow

- Where are the learners within the context of their work flow or work process during their moment(s) of need? (*e.g., using online system at bedside, managing workers who work remotely, or engaged in training of a colleague as the resident SME, etc.*)

Urgency

- What is the level of urgency associated with high-quality execution at the moment of need? (*e.g., planning learning for ninety days in the future [low] or accessing a job aid "just-in-time" for a critical work flow task [high]*)

Risk

- What is at risk if execution falls short? (*e.g., business impact, death or injury, material waste, non-compliance liability, financial loss, etc.*)

Attributes of Media

The concept of *media* addresses the format (medium, modes, and/or venues) that contribute to a compelling transfer of information and/or knowledge. The attributes of *space* are key dependencies that influence the media options. *Media* selection may be a blend of several components that complement the physical space the learner occupies. Those blends may include any combination of the following:

Verbal

- Will the learning event include live/recorded delivery? If yes, describe interactivity (one-way or two-way) and whether/how Q&A will be handled.

Written

- Will content reside on hard-copy documents? (*e.g., Word, Excel, PPT, PDF, etc.*)

Visual

- What type of graphics are required to make the message compelling? (*e.g., photos, graphs, charts, video clips, animations, etc.*)

Rich Media

- Will video content be embedded in the learning asset?

- Will audio content be embedded in the learning asset?

- Will video or audio be accessed/streamed from media archives?

Web-Based

- Will content be accessed through online links? If yes, define links (internal intranet, Internet) and consider issue of access rights.

CD/DVD

- Will content reside on CD/DVD or other portable media?

Authoring Tool(s)

- What authoring/capture application(s) will be utilized?

Content Editing

- Will you need to be able to edit original files/material? (*Not every capture tool renders output that is easily edited outside of its native state.*)

Repurposing and Re-Use

- Does the content already exist in some other format? If so, can it be edited and/or reformatting to be reutilized all or in part?

- Will content created for this solution serve another purpose or a secondary audience? (*Potential for re-use may determine initial capture methods.*)

Granularity

- What is the optimal size of learning content objects? (*A learning object is a "chunk" of learning that holds learning value on a stand-alone basis, e.g., a 15-minute e-learning module, 30-second video clip, 3-minute podcast, or other formats.*)

Attributes of Blended Systems

We now have two layers of dependency defined—*space* and *media*—and we know details regarding the learner's work context. Both of these attribute influence the *systems* technology required. Without these two dependencies being identified, our selection of the correct technology for the solution is compromised. Technology cannot be treated as a one-size-fits-all proposition. Obviously, additional peripheral criteria must be considered when building a holistic technology solution. Consider the following:

End-User Devices

- What technology is in the hands of, or is accessible to, learners in their moments of need? (*e.g., individually assigned computer, shared workstation, DVD player, smart phone, etc.*)

Internet Connectivity

- Is access to the Internet required to serve the learning moment(s)?

- If so, what bandwidth requirements must be available (*in the aggregate*) to accommodate anticipated content transfer rates?

- Are all users on the network or are non-employees participating using their own computers? If non-employees are participating, how many? Will they need to view video?

Access to Content

- Will the system "push" the content to the learners or will the learners download or "pull" the content on demand?

- Are there access rights/restrictions to consider?

- Who will be accountable for content management and currency?

Content Repositories

- Given the nature of the content, where will it be archived?

- How will it be retrieved? (*e.g., facilitated virtually, downloaded by learners, streamed on-demand, etc.*)

- Will the content be searchable? (*This implies presence of a taxonomy and criteria around selection of metadata, keywords, tags.*)

Tracking

- Will consumption of the learning asset require a record of completion?

- If so, describe acceptable recording format (*e.g., training history in the LMS, printed certificate, etc.*)

Evaluation

- Will learning asset consumption require evaluation or testing? If so, describe the format. (*e.g., hard-copy instrument or online access*)

- Will the impact render a tangible result or not?

- Define key performance indicator(s) expected if successful. What evidence will be realized if successful? What does success look like?

- What is a reasonable expectation for time-to-impact? (*e.g., Should evaluation be captured immediately or after "X" months post-event, or another time frame?*)

Help/Escalation

- Who does the learner turn to if help is needed? (*e.g., Help Desk, content owner, subject-matter expert, etc.*)

- Will there be a knowledge base and/or a community of practice? If so, how do learners gain access?

- Who are the SMEs, under what conditions are they accessible, and how do learners access them?

- Do resources like the Help Desk and/or SMEs need to have training on PSO content in addition to access to PSOs?

- What tracking methodology will be used to measure usage volumes, content usability, relevance, and/or user ratings?

Defining the Learning Continuum

Now that we have described the potential work context attributes that impact design, development, and delivery decisions, we have to re-focus on the learners and the actual journey they take to competency. What better way to describe a journey than with a continuum, right? Humor me for a few more minutes. Not only does a continuum work, but it serves as an essential design architecture that facilitates *critical design iterations* that do not exist in traditional linear design efforts. Refer to Figure 5 for this part of the discussion.

The Learning Continuum is a design model based on three distinct phases: *Prepare, Deploy, Reinforce.* Going back to our "ecosystem" concept, the first two

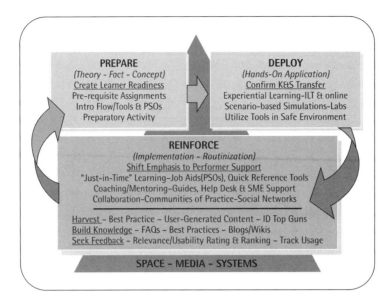

Figure 5. PDR Learning Continuum

phases, *prepare* and *deploy*, represent the 5 percent slice of the pie or, if you prefer, the formal learning components. The third phase, and I stress it as the most critical, represents the 95 percent slice through informal learning *reinforcement* activities. Let's outline the specifics in each phase.

Prepare—Primary Outcome Is Creating Learner Readiness

We can compare the *prepare* phase of the Learning Continuum to a common learning technique we already know as "pre-work." Interestingly, the actual "pre-work" activity may have absolutely nothing to do with learning. In a previous life, I taught a popular sales training curriculum where the *prepare* activity involved the sales reps selecting potential customers from their account base and completing an analysis worksheet in advance of coming to class. That exercise was a *preparatory activity* that readied them for moving into the next level of learning in a live classroom event (the *deploy* phase).

Potentially, the *prepare* phase can be nothing more than an advanced agenda that *introduces the learning flow* and expectations of the next phase of learning. This introduction could be more complex by revealing *tools or job aids (PSOs)* that can be used at the next level of learning. Closer to tradition, this phase is where prerequisite online course work or pre-reading assignments necessary for the next phase are completed.

Regardless of the *prepare* activity, this phase presents an opportunity to raise the level of readiness in the learner to the extent that those same efforts are no longer required during the formal classroom event. If *prepare* activities are effective, we reduce unproductive activity time in the classroom.

Deploy—Primary Outcome Is to Ensure Transfer of Knowledge and/or Skills

We can now focus on providing a structured and safe environment in which to apply and practice activities that are relevant to the performance outcomes we seek. This phase is where we use role-based simulations integrated with the same PSOs that we introduced in the *prepare* phase—the same PSOs the learners rely on when they are back on the job. Do you remember that *thread of continuity* I mentioned earlier? Now you can see how it threads through all three phases of the continuum, providing consistency and familiarity that improves retention.

Reinforce—Primary Outcome Is to Promote Sustained Capability by Directly Supporting Performers in Their Work Context

This phase represents new ground to some training organizations. It represents the greatest potential to directly generate value for the organization through improving performance and productivity, avoiding loss, preventing business liability, and/ or anywhere that human performance outcomes drive tangible business impact. Participants in the *reinforce* phase include human resources other than the learner, such as managers/supervisors, Help Desk staff, and SMEs. If they are part of the learning reinforcement structure, what design decisions must also support these assets' needs. Note that the *collaboration* component shines the light on *social media* resources that can help to connect learners with each other and with SMEs when necessary.

The ball, however, is not entirely in the learner's court. The training organization has significant skin in this game. One key activity involves *harvesting* potential knowledge and learning assets from the knowledge worker population. A perfect example of this comes from my previous life in sales training, where we spent time in the field with top sales reps to evaluate what methods were behind their success. We captured best practices from numerous points in the selling process and studied the job aids and cheat sheets (future PSOs) they developed (user-generated content).

With the advent of Web 2.0 technologies, the ability to collaborate has become a matter of routine for learners. *Sharing best practices* and *contributing to knowledge bases* is rapidly becoming standard practice on the web. Are you enabling that to happen within your organization? If not, you may be missing an opportunity to build a relevant knowledge network.

Integrating the Learning Continuum into a Design Methodology

Earlier I mentioned that ADDIE was not dead yet and that a different "spin" made it a viable design methodology. The "spin" takes shape in an *iterative process.* Work context attributes differ as learners journey along the Learning Continuum. Consider the attribute of *space.* Where is the learner physically located when in the *prepare* phase? Could a different physical location be associated with the *deploy* phase? Certainly, the location is different when the learner is back at his or her work context in the *reinforce* phase. So let's assume there are three different localities involved. What does that change? A great deal can, and should, change. Refer to Table 2.

The PDR Learning Continuum Design Map in Table 2 is based on a learning solution crafted for a large pharmaceutical company to train a mobile sales force. This design map clearly demonstrates that the presence of a Learning Continuum is

Table 2. PDR Learning Continuum Design Map

Work Context Attributes	Prepare	Deploy	Reinforce
Space	**Space**	**Space**	**Space**
Stakeholders	Learner	Learner and Instructor	Learner, Help Desk
Physical Location	Mobile-In Car	Hotel, Corporate Office	Mobile @ Corporation
Proximity in Workflow	Between Visits	Scheduled ILT Event	Sales Activity
Urgency and Risk	Low/Minimal	Low/Minimal	High/Revenue Risk
Media	**Media**	**Media**	**Media**
Medium/Mode/Venue	Podcast-Workflow	Synch–Virtual	Synch and Asynchronous
Authoring Tool(s)	Audio, Visio	PowerPoint	SnagIt/Word PDF
Re-Use/Re-Purpose	Streaming Archive	Embedded PSOs	Download PSO
Object Granularity	15-Minute Podcast	Process-Step Chunks	PSO-Level Push and Pull
Systems	**Systems**	**Systems**	**Systems**
End-User Devices	MP3 Devices	Laptops	i-Phone/Laptops
Delivery Systems	Streaming Server	Virtual Classroom	Server Download
Network Access	Broadband Cell	Broadband/Wireless	Broadband Wi-Fi
Access to Content	Email Link	LMS ID and Password	Network ID and Password
Utilization and Tracking	Return Receipt	LMS and Test Tool	Relevance and Feedback

good to have when it comes to making instructional design, content development, and training asset delivery decisions. The primary point is that *the work context is driving the design process*. This point highlights why training organizations may have knowledge and skill gaps within their current staff roles.

The pharmaceutical company's work context offered a few key challenges. First, a key cultural obstacle (attribute), in the form of a business mandate, confronted the design team—*there would be no training during business hours*. Business hours were devoted to selling pharmaceuticals. Period. The learner population was 100 percent mobile and geographically spread all over the United States. All learners had laptops and smart phones. Average drive time between appointments was 35 to 40 minutes. After hours, a high population of learners stayed overnight in hotels and the rest were at home.

A few key components highlight the importance of designing on a learning continuum. Starting with *space*, note the change in stakeholders as the continuum phases progress. The learner is the only constant; however, the potential learning moments are anything but constant. The work context attribute of proximity in workflow (under *space*) is a perfect illustration. During the *prepare* phase, the learners are in their cars traveling to their next appointments. In *deploy*, they are outside of normal business hours and either in a hotel or at home when they participate in an instructor-led virtual classroom event. Finally, in the *reinforce* phase, the learners are downstream in their work context—in this example, sitting across the desk from an actual client trying to recall product information critical to making the sale. *This is a very key point*! Look across the continuum at *urgency and risk*. It was low/minimal for both *prepare* and *deploy* (the 5 percent slice of the pie). During *reinforce*, the stakes shoot up to "high" related to urgency (the 95 percent slice). Failure at this point comes with a price tag of an average sale of five or six figures lost. I'd like to point out here that most training organizations are not involved in supporting performance at this downstream point.

Review how the authoring tool mix changes as you work across the continuum. In *prepare*, we used audio podcasts (captured with Audacity) and a single-page graphic of a new product sales workflow (built in Visio). The actual training class, held virtually, used PowerPoint in the *deploy* phase. When in the field, the reps had downloadable access to screenshots captured in SnagIt and PDFs authored in Word. Here again, without knowing the attributes of the work context, how could design decisions related to authoring platform selections be made in an informed manner?

If you review the *systems* attributes, you also find variability that factors into design decisions. Does this mean instructional designers have to become experts on LMS systems, able to size network bandwidth requirements, become wiki-maniacs, and monitor in-house social networking sites? Perhaps not the instructional designers, but somebody has to do those things. The instructional designer should be fluent enough with these technologies to recognize the challenge or opportunity they present.

Selling the Learning Continuum Concept Within Your Organization

At first blush, it may seem like a lot of additional work to sell this concept. Additional steps are necessary to support the learner on a continuum, but those steps are necessary for training to drive value. I wager that is probably the most important sale to make to training directors, but a lot of other selling has to happen first. It has been my experience that the hardest business entity to persuade to embrace a Learning Continuum is the training organization. Imagine that. Why? One word: Change!

I have been most successful with this concept in the non-training business units. Why? One word: Change! Seriously. How can one word—the same word—mean two completely different things to business units in the same organization? Not too surprisingly, its a matter of perspective: the slice of the pie in which you work. Think about it. Training is dropping 80 percent or so of their dime on 5 percent of the ecosystem. The remaining business units are living in the work context where they are focused on one thing: generating, protecting, or maintaining tangible value for the business in the form of *sustained capability*.

If what the training organization proposes to a business unit is perceived as a change that will assist with creating a *sustained capability*, the business unit is going to welcome you. If you are selling training that takes productive workers off-task and then doesn't support them downstream, you are adding questionable value and are potentially a liability when the next reduction in force rolls around. The trend is growing for non-strategic work to move outside the organization to contracted resources. I would argue that a *fully integrated learning ecosystem is extremely strategic* because it can result in tangible outcomes.

I am convinced that now is the time to reinvent training. Start the process by holding the training organization up to the mirror. Do you see a reflection of readiness? If not, here is the best starting point: Assess your readiness, identify the gaps, fill them from inside or out. Take a critical look at your training mix. How much of it is non-strategic? Should you even be chasing that rabbit any longer?

Going back to what I said at the beginning of this article, about the velocity of business outpacing training's ability to keep up, it's not a myth. Our traditional approach to training is antiquated. The strategic parts of what we do should be retained and strengthened by integrating a Learning Continuum to enable learning *across an ecosystem*. The non-strategic parts may be fodder for outsourcing or jettisoning altogether.

- Radical? Absolutely.

- Disruptive? It had better be.

- Opportunity for reinvention? Only if you choose to look into the mirror.

References

Bersin, J. (2009, July 23). The future of the business of learning [webinar].

Gottfredson, C., & Mosher, B. (2008). Leveraging performer support. Learning 2008 training conference session.

Gary G. Wise *is a thirty-year veteran of cross-industry corporate learning roles, spanning road warrior sales trainer to senior leadership assignments. He has mellowed into a passionate visionary and an innovative architect of learning strategy that drives creation of sustained capability. He frequently speaks at national training conferences and serves on the HRD Graduate Program Advisory Board at Indiana State University. He is a graduate of the Terry College of Business at the University of Georgia.*

Strategies and Technologies for Posting Training Presentations Online

Tom Bunzel

Summary

The Internet has broadened the potential reach of training materials exponentially. But what is the best way to reach audiences for training and development online? To the extent that a presentation has already been developed and perhaps presented, the ability to have it "live online" adds significant value both for the presenter and the audience. Although technology is evolving and changing rapidly, there are still some basic strategies that can be implemented to make training presentations available after an event has concluded, or to supplement training activities.

Three basic scenarios are offered here for saving a presentation in digital format and posting it successfully online. These scenarios share one significant advantage—in addition to presenting the subject matter of the event, they *also include the audio (and in some cases the video) soundtrack that explains the material in detail to the audience.*

Most training presentations are created and presented in Microsoft PowerPoint, so the examples in the scenarios presented in this article will illustrate the way a slide show with narration can be saved and posted online. The three scenarios are:

- authorSTREAM, a web-hosting site specifically for PowerPoint presentations, hosting a presentation with *embedded* narration;

- Camtasia, a screen capture program capable of recording a live PowerPoint presentation with narration (and optional video of the presenter) and saving it in various digital video formats that are web-friendly; and

- GoToTraining, a web-conferencing solution created specifically for training professionals that lets you show PowerPoint during an online event and archive a digital video version for hosting online.

authorSTREAM

authorSTREAM has the capability of posting a presentation on YouTube and it has one big advantage—it actually uploads and converts the narration you put directly into PowerPoint.

Other sites such as SlideShare or YouTube have conversion issues. SlideShare requires a synchronized MP3 file for narration; YouTube requires a video file of the PowerPoint (which you can create using Camtasia, as described in the next section).

Narration in PowerPoint 2007 is available under the Slide Show tab of the Ribbon (see Figure 1). You no longer need to save the file as a PowerPoint 1997–2003 file for it to play in authorSTREAM.

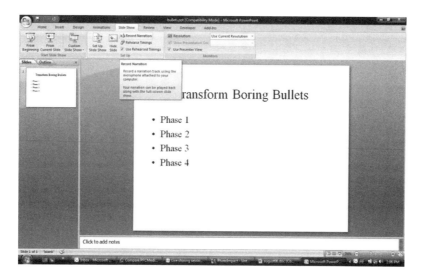

Figure 1. Narration Is Available

In order for the presentation to work in authorSTREAM, the sound must be embedded; therefore do NOT select the option to link sound files. They will become part of the actual presentation. (See Figure 2.)

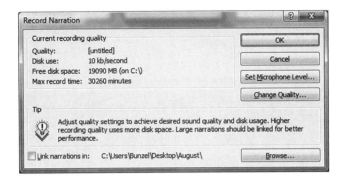

Figure 2. Options in authorSTREAM

With your narration options set (check your microphone levels first), click OK, and the presentation goes full screen at Slide 1 (see Figure 3). You (or another speaker or trainer) can now speak and narrate the slides, playing any animation and moving through the slides.

Figure 3. Presentation Goes Full Screen

When the slide show is complete and speakers have finished, click ESC to end the show and choose to save the timings. You can see the saved duration of the slides in Slide Sorter view.

Save the presentation in a PowerPoint slide show format (as shown n Figure 4) and it's ready to upload to the web.

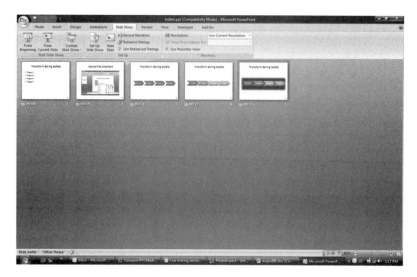

Figure 4. Save as Slide Show

To load the presentation on authorSTREAM, go to your account and simply click Upload a New Presentation, as shown in Figure 5.

Figure 5. Click Upload to a New Presentation

The next thing is to simply fill in the presentation details—title, description, and key words (for search engines), as shown in Figure 6. You can maintain up to twenty private presentations or make the show public.

Figure 6. Fill in the Presentation Details

Once the presentation is uploaded, check the confirmation screen (shown in Figure 7). You will also receive an email to confirm that the slide show is ready to view.

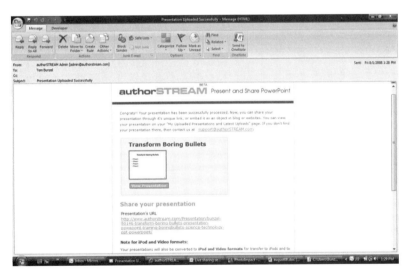

Figure 7. Confirmation Screen

Clicking the link brings up the presentation page; there you find a set of links to copy and paste for the URL to embed the show in a web page or to show the presentation as a thumbnail (see Figure 8).

Figure 8. Thumbnail View

After upload, you can preview the show directly in its page on authorSTREAM by clicking Play and Pause (see Figure 9).

Figure 9. Viewing on authorSTREAM

You can use the embed code or URL to post the slide show on other blogs and networks. There's also link to send it directly to a YouTube account as a video file. Figure 10 shows how the converted file appears on a YouTube page. It appears as just another video, but it's actually a training presentation with audio.

Figure 10. How It Looks on YouTube

The ability to use *embedded audio* in PowerPoint, rather than exporting an MP3 file and coordinating it or editing video in Camtasia, makes authorSTREAM an attractive hosting site for training content.

Create a Video with Camtasia

Besides serving as a fine video editor, Camtasia's main forte is the ability to capture a series of screens with narration (and video) for training. Recent versions of Camtasia have added quite a few bells and whistles, including pan and zoom key frames, audio effects and noise reduction, and an expanded set of output options.

In Camtasia, you have an expanded list of project settings that are available when the recording or project is complete. There is even an HD output setting. This uses the new H.264 codec (codec, which is short for coder-decoder, is simply a computer program capable of encoding or decoding a digital data stream or signal), which is about the best compression for excellent quality with compact file sizes. Five pre-sets use this codec (which you can change in the production output if you like): blog and web pre-sets were available before; now there are YouTube, HD, and Screencast.com pre-sets as well (see Figure 11).

Once you have tested some output pre-sets, the same quality of video can be repeated many times; you can also create custom project settings for output and save them to reuse in the future.

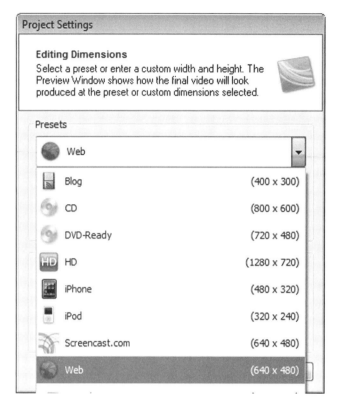

Figure 11. Available Pre-Sets

The main Camtasia Recorder interface has a full-screen selection button and the ability remember the previous screen size dimensions (see Figure 12).

Figure 12. Camtasia Recorder Interface

You can also use the Camtasia Recording feature directly within PowerPoint, as shown in Figure 13.

When you click Record, the slide show plays full screen (see Figure 14) and everything that occurs in a slide is recorded—including animation and video.

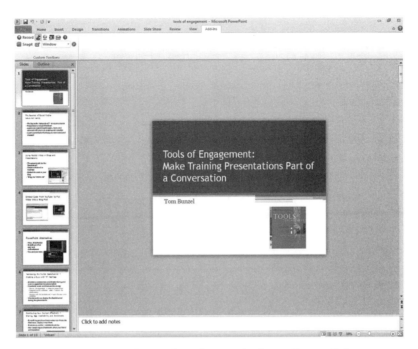

Figure 13. Accessing Camtasia from PowerPoint

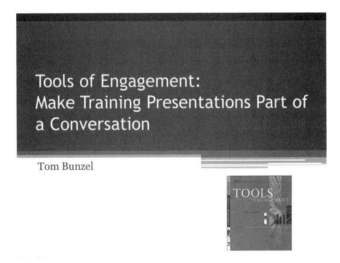

Figure 14. Full-Screen Slide Show

With a properly set up microphone, narration is also captured and there is an option to include a video window with the presenter, but this can distract from the slides and also obscure some information.

In the editor, there are up to three separate audio tracks, in addition to the PIP (picture in picture (narration)) audio track, as shown in Figure 15.

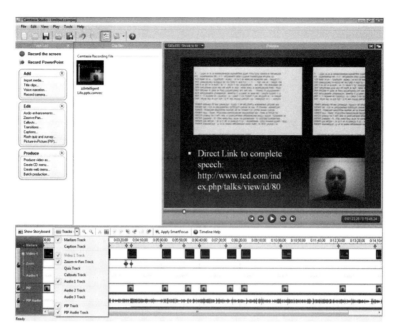

Figure 15. Choice of Audio Tracks

When you unlink any audio track (in Figure 16, the PIP track is unlinked), you can maneuver the audio, split it, and add new audio separate from the video sequence.

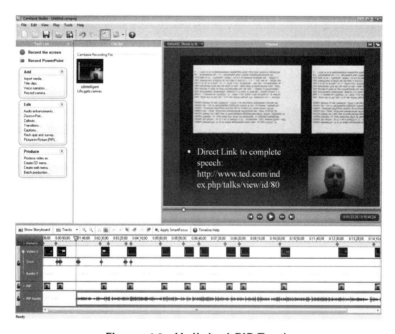

Figure 16. Unlinked PIP Track

Like many of the top video editors, Camtasia also has seven customizable hot keys, so that you can add a transition (T) or call out (C) simply by tapping the key on the keyboard.

There is now also the capability of editing (some but not all) QuickTime (MOV) or MP4 videos by adding the clips to the Clip Bin and then the Timeline.

For those desiring cooler effects, in addition to the previous pan and zoom capability, there is now a slider under Advanced options to tilt the zoomed portion of the video along the Y axis, as shown in Figure 17.

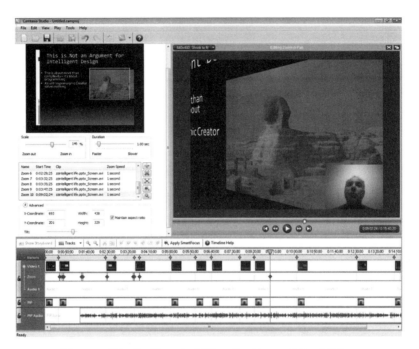

Figure 17. Option to Tilt a Portion of the Video

There is also a more precise ability to control transition duration, down to a tenth of a second (see Figure 18).

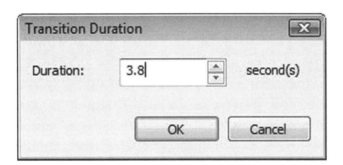

Figure 18. Controlling Duration

When editing is complete, click Produce–Produce Video As and use the Production wizard to choose output options that will result in a video that can be posted on YouTube, played directly in Media Player, or otherwise distributed to recreate the training presentation faithfully. (See Figure 19.)

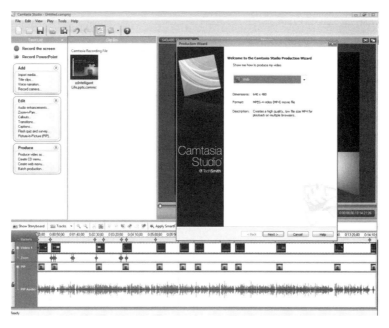

Figure 19. Choose an Output Option

Camtasia, with its video editing capabilities and full range of outputs, provides additional flexibility when you want to create a video of your presentation for web or other distribution.

Archive a Web Conference with GoToMeeting, GoToWebinar, and/or GoToTraining

A third scenario for distributing a presentation online is really a hybrid of a live online presentation and the result of recording it live and archiving it.

The Citrix Online tools, GoToMeeting, GoToWebinar, and GoToTraining, all let you present a PowerPoint slide show to an audience as part of a live online learning event and record the event for future replay and distribution.

The webinar or meeting process begins with inviting an audience and actually delivering the training event online. All three programs feature invitation capability along with registration processes that allow you to track attendees and to coordinate the event with social media.

During the event, a slide show can be shown to the audience on screen as the training takes place; other programs or graphics, annotation, and polling can also be delivered during the online event and everything is available on a console invisible to the audience that floats above the presenter's screen, as shown in Figure 20.

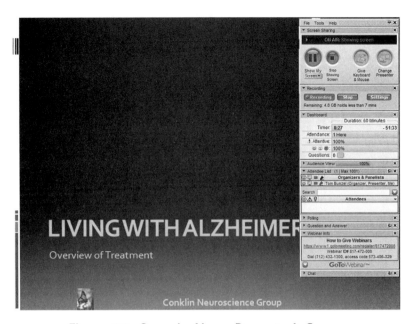

Figure 20. Console Above Presenter's Screen

You can monitor chat and audience moods and see how the presentation is playing in Audience View on the console, as shown in Figure 21.

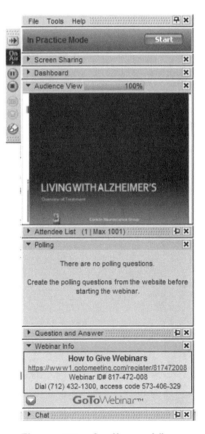

Figure 21. Audience View

The key to having a faithful recording of the event is to use the archive capability in any of the three tools. Set the recording options (see Figure 22) prior to the event to have the archive available locally or stored on the Citrix Online servers subsequent to the event.

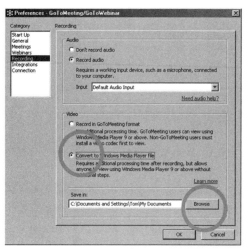

Figure 22. Recording Options

Recording should be started as the conference begins and confirmed throughout to make sure that everything, including the audio narration, is being captured. (See Figure 23.)

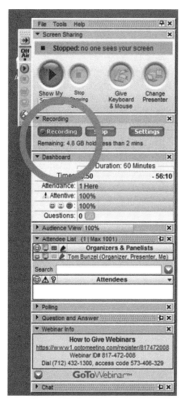

Figure 23. Confirm What's Being Recorded

The newest of the three programs, GoToTraining, is specifically designed for creating a training program of online content that can be redistributed later on as archived video.

While conventional web conferencing tools can support e-learning, organizations have discovered that the needs of organizational learning are very specific: to inter- act strategically in a way that will foster interactivity, build skills, and add value.

An online training platform must address this particular set of needs with a suite of tools designed to enhance the ability of educators to simulate an actual class- room. GoToTraining includes the following tools:

- *Customized registration to meet the needs of the program and the participants.* From an online administration center (see Figure 24), trainers can sched- ule new events with customized registration pages or copy existing events, as well as send invitations to participants.

Figure 24. Online Administration Center

- *A comprehensive catalog and calendar of events.* The centralized adminis- tration center (see Figure 25) provides a calendar of available events in catalog form, with tabs for upcoming training and archived (recorded) events.

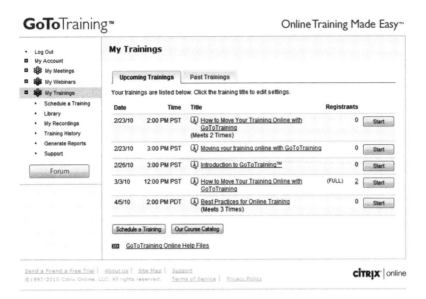

Figure 25. Upcoming Events

- *Content library.* The training staff can also maintain a library of content, including graphics, web pages, presentations, demo files, surveys, polling questions, training manuals and materials, reusable tests, and evaluations that can be (re)accessed for all of the organization's events. (See Figure 26.)

Figure 26. Content Library

The content library makes training materials, tests, and evaluations available for reuse/editing and allows trainers to upload and deliver dynamic content and analyze results.

- *Reporting.* GoToTraining has the ability to record, archive, and make classes available for review and attendance after the live event—with detailed reporting. In addition, database tools are able to analyze and adapt to the results of evaluations and tests to keep the training effective.

- *Communication tools.* Instructor-participant communication is assisted by a number of functions (chat, hand raising, presenter control, etc.), as shown in Figure 27.

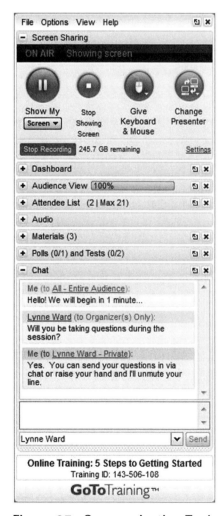

Figure 27. Communication Tools

- *Follow-up tools.* GoToTraining provides pre- and post-event assessments and follow-up activities to reinforce learned concepts and skills and ensure the transfer of training to the workplace or other venue of application.

- *Additional features:*

  - Self-service web pages and automated email reminders

  - Participant audio options for phone conferencing, including toll-free and VoIP

  - Configurable class sizes and the ability to perform pre-session tests and surveys

  - The ability to include Q&A from the audience if it was recorded at the conclusion of the event

  - Invitation of attendees "on the fly" during an event—especially if excitement has been generated

  - The ability to include a full range of subject-matter experts, regardless of physical location

When implementing a live online learning initiative to complement or augment existing modalities, it is vital that the training platform support a wide spectrum of capabilities. The ability to seamlessly plan, schedule events, deliver interactive and compelling content, analyze reports, and follow up with participants is a complete training process that will meet the needs of organization and the attendees.

These features make the final product, an archived video, a valuable piece of content to be distributed and shared appropriately to those who need to take the training, and for trainers to refer to when planning future events.

Conclusion

These three training scenarios, using the tools shown above, can empower training professionals to take advantage of social and other tools online to maintain a consistent flow of content in video format with their intended audiences, and enable their training events to reach many more eyeballs.

Tom Bunzel *specializes in knowing what presenters need and how to make technology work. He has appeared on Tech TV's Call for Help and has been a featured speaker at InfoComm and PowerPoint LIVE, as well as working as a "technology coach" for corporations, including Iomega, MTA Films, Nurses in Partnership, and the Neuroscience Education Institute. He has taught regularly at Learning Tree*

International, West LA College Extension, and privately around Southern California and does presentation and video consulting in Southern California.

Bunzel has written numerous books, including Tools of Engagement: Presenting and Training in a World of Social Media, Easy Using Office 2010, Master Visually Microsoft Office 2007, *and* Solving the PowerPoint Predicament: Using Digital Media for Effective Communication *and an e-book:* Do Your Own Ning Thing: A Step-By-Step Guide to Launching an Effective Social Network.

Online Learning 101
Using a Framework to Consider and Select e-Learning Tools

Susan Landay

Summary

Whatever you call it—web-based learning, computer-based learning, e-learning, online learning—it's here and now. For some, e-learning is an end in itself. For others, it's a supplement to live classroom experiences. For everyone, the question is not "Should I or shouldn't I?" but rather, "How can I do it affordably?" and "Where do I start?"

The plethora of e-learning tools and providers make it onerous to find a starting point or even know what questions to ask vendors. The following four-category framework (AGCL) has helped me and many others sort through the needs and options. These categories are:

- Authoring (course development and creating your content)

- Games and Add-on Tools (games and interactions to reinforce and/or teach)

- Conferencing (connectivity tools used for webinars and synchronous learning)

- Learning Management Systems (LMS) (systems to administer and track training)

To help you remember these four components of e-learning, perhaps this little mnemonic will help: **Any Goofball Can Learn!**

In this article, for each category of e-learning tools noted above, I'll explain what it is as well as:

1. The role it plays in enabling online experiences and

2. The criteria you might use to choose among the vendors.

Exhibits at the end of this article suggest a few reputable, cost-effective solutions for each. Note that the exhibit numbers tie to the acronym.

A couple of caveats: My selection of comments and suggestions is drawn from vendor websites, personal research, conversations at conferences, and LinkedIn discussions and is colored by my interest in focusing on solutions that are relatively low-cost, require minimal learning curves, and focus on lively and interactive tools—consistent with best practices in brain-based learning techniques.

Authoring/Course Development Tools

The authoring/course development tools are software programs that let you create your course content. The most readily available of these is PowerPoint. However, many trainers find PowerPoint limited. For instance, PowerPoint's interface is somewhat cumbersome when creating high-end animations that integrate text, images, audio, and video. Second, while PowerPoint is terrific for linear presentations, its interface is more difficult when creating "branching" presentations, whereby a user can dig down into any number of buttons or scenarios. Finally, since it's primarily a presentation software program, it contains a robust collection of slide templates; it does not, however, come loaded with a library of interactive game templates.

Criteria for Evaluation

If you want to move beyond PowerPoint for course development, following is a list of the criteria you might use to decide among the various options:

- PowerPoint interface:

  - Does the software work within PowerPoint by adding new toolbar items?

  - Does the software replace the need for PowerPoint?

  - Does the software create interactions that can be imported into PowerPoint, in case you'd like to use it for live training also?

- What file formats can be imported/exported? This is important if you want to load your content into a learning management system (which we'll define later) or some other program.

- Does the software reside on your desktop or online? This is an issue if you prefer to work offline.

- Are courses stored on desktop or online?

- How quickly can you learn the new program?

- How quickly can you create animations of images, text, etc.?

- What types of games and interactions come bundled with the software?

Games and Interactivities

This set of e-learning tools is not focused on creating entire courses, but rather on enabling you to quickly and easily load games and other "interactivities" into existing courses, PowerPoint presentations, a website, or webinar. If you prefer to stick with PowerPoint as your primary course development tool, these add-ons might help you add new dimensions of interactivity and game-play to your existing materials.

In general, these tools let you create and edit games then save them into a file format that is easy to integrate into a presentation, email to learners, post or link to on a website page, and embed links in authoring tools and LMSs.

Just to be clear, let me clarify what I mean by interactivity: an interactivity is any exercise in which the learner must interact with your content and do something with it—play a game, answer a question, sequence tasks, match answers, etc.

Criteria for Evaluation

The evaluation criteria for choosing among these software packages are fairly straightforward:

- How many different types of interactions are included in the package?

- What is the quality of the graphics?

- Do you prefer to create the games online or off?

- Will games be used for self-paced learning or in a guided webinar?

- Do you need to track results and integrate with a learning management system?

- How costly is it?

Live Connectivity/Web Conferencing Tools

Connectivity tools, also known as web conferencing tools, describe the ways you would bring remote learners together for a *synchronous* experience. If learners are attending a training *asynchronously*, that is, at different times, they might "meet" at an online URL, in which case a live connectivity tool is not required. If, however, you'd like to conduct a webinar or bring learners together in real time (*synchronously*), you will need a system that enables people to communicate by phone at the same time they are all viewing a common computer screen.

Criteria for Evaluation

There are quite a few vendors offering this capability right now, such as WebEx, GoToMeeting, and ConnectPRO. When deciding among the various vendors, consider these questions:

- How much chat/interaction is possible?

- How many people can it accommodate?

- Does the system have a muting ability?

- Do participants view *your* screen or a server screen?

- Do you need to be on the phone and online for the meeting to continue?

- Do you want participants to continue to interact with materials and each other when the meeting is over?

- Will a meeting room be required?

Learning Management Systems (LMSs)

The final component in the e-learning universe is referred to as a learning management system (LMS). Most simply, a *learning management system* is a software application for the administration, documentation, tracking, and reporting of training programs, classroom and online events, e-learning programs, and training content.

Wikipedia's definition is concise: "LMSs range from systems for managing training and educational records, to software for distributing courses over the Internet with features for online collaboration. Corporate training uses LMSs to automate record-keeping and employee registration. Student self-service (e.g., self-registration on instructor-led training), training workflow (e.g., user notification, manager approval, wait-list management), the provision of on-line learning (e.g., *Computer-Based*

Training, read and understand), online assessment, management of continuous professional education (CPE), *collaborative learning* (e.g., application sharing, discussion threads), and training resource management (e.g., instructors, facilities, equipment), are dimensions to learning management systems."

Criteria for Evaluation

LMS systems can become very costly and complex, but these few guidelines might help build your understanding. To differentiate among the many LMS providers, you'll want to consider any or all of the following:

- Ease of use

- Ease of content placement

- Ease of communication

- Ease of implementation

- Adequate progress tracking and activity tools

- Scalable to growing needs

  - Number of trainers

  - Number of learners it accommodates

  - Frequency of learning events

- Authoring/content creation—ability to control look and feel of content and/or load your own courses

- Integration of game tools

- Integration of conferencing tools

- e-Commerce—ability to sell courses

- Installation—hosted on vendors server versus on your own server

- Platform: stand-alone versus integration with company website

- Compliance with e-learning standards (e.g., SCORM)

- General sophistication of the system

  - Enables learner collaboration

  - Keeps learner profile data

  - Organizes reusable content

- Creation of test questions and test administration

- Ability to do pre-testing

- Management of certification status

- Support and service

Expect to pay a setup fee, as well as a per student cost. Investment in an LMS can be anywhere from $15,000 to $100,000+.

Closing Thoughts

As you use the "AGCL" framework to organize your thinking, you may see that some e-learning solutions cover multiple categories. In fact, many of the high-end solutions offer all-in-one capability, while many of the lower-end solutions address only one or two of these e-learning categories. If your budget is limited and you need to pick and choose features based on your specific priorities, the AGCL model should help you pinpoint your needs.

Susan Landay *is president of Trainers Warehouse (www.trainerswarehouse.com), a women-owned business that offers hundreds of effective and innovative products for trainers and educators across all industries. Trainers Warehouse develops exclusive new products and searches the world for the best tools to help trainers and teachers achieve their goals. Prior to joining Trainers Warehouse in 1997, Susan was a consultant and trainer in the field of negotiation and conflict resolution. She is a graduate of Yale University and The Kellogg Graduate School of Management at Northwestern University.*

Exhibit "A"—Authoring Tools

In listing vendors for course authoring tools, my goal was to find solutions that were reputable, cost-effective, easy-to-learn, and consistent with brain-based learning techniques. This is not to be taken as an exhaustive list. Also, the prices listed represent standard pricing at the time of writing; prices may be subject to change or discounts.

PowerPoint by Microsoft

Users can enhance the functionality of PowerPoint with the following:

- Presentation Pro

- Crystal Graphics

- eLearning Brothers Flash Templates

- Articulate Studio '09 by Articulate (see below)

- iSpring Presenter by iSpring Solutions (see below)

- Captivate and Presenter by Adobe (see below)

ProForm Rapid e-Learning Studio by Rapid Intake

A single-user desktop solution that enables designers of all ability levels to create professional-looking Flash-based (animated), interactive courses—without knowing Flash programming and without using PowerPoint. Under $1000.

Articulate Studio '09 by Articulate

A suite of e-learning authoring tools in one integrated package. "Presenter," "Quizmaker," "Engage," and "Video Encoder" let you quickly create e-learning courses from within PowerPoint, to develop interactive content, quizzes, assessments, and surveys. $1,000 to $1,500.

iSpring Presenter by iSpring Solutions

iSpring Presenter works as a PowerPoint add-in. It transforms PowerPoint into a high-end tool for creating engaging and interactive Flash-based e-learning courses that can be viewed on virtually any computer or platform. Under $500.

Captivate and Presenter by Adobe

These Adobe products let you quickly create, deliver, and maintain your e-learning content. You can easily add software demonstrations, interactive simulations, branching scenarios, and quizzes. With Adobe Presenter, just a few clicks in PowerPoint let you add narration, animations, interactivity, quizzes, and software simulations to create interactive multimedia e-learning experiences. $500 to $1,800, depending on the package. www.connectusers.com/forums/cucbb/view-topic.php?id=1213

CourseMill by Trivantis

CourseMill is an affordable, lower-end course-authoring tool and LMS for unlimited users. $15,000+.

Exhibit "G"—Game Tools

Here, I've divided product solutions into two sets:

- Interactivities you can post online or link to in a presentation; and
- Interactivities you can use in a webinar.

Interactivities You Can Post Online or Link to a Presentation

Raptivity by Harbinger

Award-winning Raptivity has a large number of interactivities, including learning games, simulations, videos, puzzles, animations, interactive diagrams, page-flipping books, and tons more, sold in a number of different "packs." $300 to $2,500, depending on package.

Interactivity Creator by Sealund

This inexpensive software solution lets you customize twelve different types of game questions and save them as Flash files. Under $300.

QuizPoint by LearningWare

Create and post online quizzes in two formats: TV Trivia Game and 60-Second Challenge. Under $1,000.

Thinking Worlds by Caspian Learning

Quickly create 3-D games and save them as Shockwave files (even though Flash doesn't do three dimensions). Under $1,500.

Quick Lessons by Quick Lessons LLC

This is a subscription-based online tool that lets you create online courses and integrate exercises and quizzes, using the built-in Character and Flash Game Templates. $100 to $150 per month.

BRAVO! by C3 SoftWorks!

Create and deliver custom-built game shows that learners can play online, on their own. Once the games are created online, trainers can manage and track results, by reporting to a robust learning management system or by emailing result to the end user and/or instructor. About $1,500.

e-Learning Flash Game Templates by eLearning Brothers

This suite of eight Flash game-show templates is a great development tool for people who own Adobe Flash software, but aren't necessarily experts in using it. About $700.

eActivity by ePath Learning

An online application that lets you build fifty-six custom e-learning Flash interactivities to be inserted in whatever platform you are using. No software needed because it works through the web. $49.00/month.

Interactivities You Can Conduct During a Webinar

AllPlay Web by LearningWare

This software lets you create games that can be used to make a live webinar more interactive and engaging. You create game-show type questions, then invite people to your webinar with GoToMeeting or WebEx. You'll host the game on your computer while attendees play at their own—working alone or in teams. One of the nice features here is that you can customize the look of the game with your own logo, etc. Under $1,500.

BRAVO and PING by C3 SoftWorks

This solution combines BRAVO's four TV-style game shows with some "virtual" response pads, so that all of your webinar attendees can stay engaged by "PINGing" in their answers. The game automatically collects the results so you can track results during and after the event. Use a connectivity/web conferencing tool, like GoToMeeting or WebEx, to launch these games. Under $1,500.

Exhibit "C"—Conferencing Tools

Most of these vendors offer thirty-day trials for free.

WebEx by Cisco

This service combines real-time desktop sharing with phone conferencing so everyone sees the same thing while you talk. It is among the most popular web conferencing tools out there. Cisco offers different packages with different features. $50 to $250/month, depending on number of participants

GoToMeeting by Citrix

This conferencing service offers great flexibility and many interactive features. Choose GoToMeeting, GoToWebinar, or GoToTraining. $49, $99, or $149/month

Acrobat Connect Pro by Adobe

This conferencing service can be purchased either through "specialist resellers" or online. Annual plans, monthly plans, and pay-per-use plans are available. $15 to $39 per month; or pay per month, per minute, per user.

Microsoft Office Live Meeting

This is an online conferencing system for which you pay a per user/per month fee, with a five-user minimum. Service is billed monthly with no one-time fees. Approximately $5 to $15 per month.

DimDim

A free service for up to twenty attendees, DimDim lets anyone host and attend live meetings, demos, and webinars using just a web browser. Paid subscriptions are $25/month or $90/month, which offer additional security and reporting features.

Exhibit "L"—LMS Vendors

Many LMS systems are quite costly. While I will list a few of the lower-cost systems here, many of the key LMS providers cannot quote pricing without first scoping the installation. Pricing varies based on features and usage.

Moodle

A free open source LMS system. Some say Moodle is quite cumbersome, but it is free! Some LMS vendors work off the Moodle platform and enhance it, giving users a low-cost solution but with better service, such as the two listed below. FREE

EasyCampus by Educadium

Based on Moodle, EasyCampus includes course templates and wizards; enrollment and reporting tools; social networking tools; payment services; etc. The professional version features unlimited courses, five hundred user accounts, and 2GB storage. $29/month.

Remote-Learner

Remote Learner advances the capabilities of Moodle and offers support. Starts at $795/year.

Odijoo

Odijoo lets you develop and post online Articulate courses for free (which you can conduct as facilitated or self-paced courses), and takes as its fee 10 percent of your revenue income.

Atlantic Link

A whole package of LMS and rapid e-learning software. Based in the UK, Atlantic Link has been in the U.S. since 2007. Its platform enables concurrent developing (two users can give feedback at once); lets you record and edit audio; and works with Captivate and Camtasia. A host of fun interactivities are built into the software. $3,300/year or buy for $2,700 + $6,000 + 18 percent update fee.

CourseMill by Trivantis

CourseMill is an affordable, adaptable LMS for unlimited users. $15,000+.

Making the Investment—Top LMS Vendors

Prices vary based on number of trainers, students, frequency of learning events, and organization type (business, education, or government). You should expect to pay a setup fee, as well as a per student cost. If you are looking into these solutions, Brandon Hall's LMS Knowledge Base may be well worth the investment. His research examines 108 systems and costs $995 for three-month access.

- Blackboard

- Learn.com

- Saba

- WebCT

- NetSpeed Learning

Using Playbooks
A Unique Strategy in Technical Oversight of Highly Hazardous Operations
James L. Gary and Michele L. Summers

Summary

Many operations that are extremely hazardous are executed every day, and it is common practice for owners to establish oversight programs to ensure these operations are being performed safely and within expected parameters. For oversight to be effective, those individuals performing it must be highly trained and consistent in the discharge of their duties. This article outlines a proven process, based on the concept of creating a "playbook," for delivering the desired results for oversight programs of highly hazardous operations. The playbook approach can be applied just as effectively to any project or program needing rigorous, consistent oversight.

In August 2008, the U.S. Army undertook the destruction of 1,269 tons of VX nerve agent at the Newport (Indiana) Chemical Disposal Facility (NECDF). Since VX is the deadliest toxic chemical warfare agent known to man, operational errors, mishaps, and other unplanned events during handling and destruction would be totally unacceptable. To protect site workers and the surrounding citizenry, a new and unique approach for defining and articulating "Technical Oversight" of operating preparedness, emergency response, and recovery from unplanned events was created.

Technical Oversight was the duty of independent representatives, certified by the U.S. Army as "government shift representatives" (GSRs), who served as the on-scene "eyes and ears" of the government site project manager (SPM). The GSR Certification

Program employed a rigorous six-phase process to prepare the GSRs for the assignment, including:

1. *Overview training* on how to conduct oversight duties;

2. *Technical process training*, which all NECDF plant operators, mechanics, and engineers also received;

3. *Required readings* of project specific plans, procedures, and reference documents;

4. *Critical systems demonstration* to communicate understanding of equipment locations and functions;

5. *Oversight effectiveness training* on conduct of operations topics; and

6. *Oral board examinations* to confirm readiness for oversight duties.

One key phase of the Oversight Effectiveness Training program incorporated creating and using a playbook to ensure uniformity of awareness and understanding between all GSRs as to required procedures during the destruction of the VX. For the Newport operation, playbook guidelines were individually prepared by the GSRs on all conduct of operations topics. To ensure consistency, the GSRs participated in roundtable sessions focused on discussing the details of each guideline. (As with a football playbook, having the entire team learn the plays [guidelines], practice them, and recognize them when called [or directed to execute], maximizes the chances that all team members will perform the right way and in exactly the same way every time.)

The Newport site used this disciplined approach to develop and execute an effective oversight program during the demonstrated safe destruction of all 1,269 tons of VX nerve agent. With these playbook guidelines serving as the cornerstone of the certification process, the program created a cadre of GSRs possessing the requisite skills and knowledge to successfully execute technical oversight of the VX destruction. This certification process was so successful, in fact, that it has been deemed a Best Practice by the U.S. Army (Haraburda, 2004).

The Need for Consistent Oversight

Highly hazardous operations fall into several categories, including chemical plants manufacturing reactive or explosive compounds, industrial construction involving huge and high lifts, transportation of flammable or acutely toxic materials, medical practices associated with potentially life-threatening procedures, and power plants utilizing nuclear reactors to produce energy.

All of these activities use procedures and practices requiring highly trained and skilled professionals and technicians. Yet, even the most highly trained and skilled professionals can make errors that could be extremely costly or result in termination of the activities or even the organization performing them. Most owners or senior executives responsible for such operations, therefore, establish independent oversight teams to monitor and report on the performance of the executing organization.

It is extremely important that these oversight teams have technical skills at least equal to, and preferably greater than, the organizations being monitored so that they will be able to quickly detect deviations from desired performance. It is also critical that oversight activities be consistent from individual to individual on the oversight team, which typically could include from four to more than twenty individuals, depending on the activity and organization undergoing oversight. These technical skills and uniformity are important because inconsistent oversight can damage the organization being monitored more than no oversight at all. Thus, it is critical that the oversight team be technically proficient and perform oversight consistently at all times.

To ensure that the oversight team performs at peak efficiency, all members must be trained and certified as professional oversight personnel, all trained in such a way as to make any team member virtually interchangeable with any other team member. It follows, therefore, that if owners and senior management are to be assured of consistent, high-quality oversight of their operations, an effective process of training and certification, including creating and using playbooks like the one employed at NECDF, must be put in place.

The Need for an Oversight Certification Process

The most effective oversight process is one that is targeted to deliver a team of technically competent and interchangeable individuals. That is, all members of the team must demonstrate technical knowledge and proficiency that meet minimum standards *and* be able to replace any other team member in any capacity, with no significant difference experienced by the organization for which oversight is being performed. These criteria are important because oversight team members must be able to engage the organization under their oversight on sound technical bases that are recognized and accepted quickly, with minimal disruption to the executing organization. Also, each oversight team member must comply with the agreed rules and processes of the organization undergoing oversight, without freelancing and/or developing standards independent of those already established. Failing to maintain this consistency can result in upsetting the organization under oversight to the point that it must delay or cease operations, or worse, proceed in an unsafe or environmentally unacceptable manner.

To achieve the goals delineated above requires a robust process that trains and certifies oversight personnel consistently, but which can be expedited (to save time and expense, for example). An expedited certification process is one that is very well defined, can be broken down into manageable components, and those components overlapped effectively. For example, while conducting classroom training, hands-on training can also be executed, allowing certification candidates to acquire advanced technical knowledge in the classroom while concurrently putting it in practice in the field. This fast-track feature was one of the elements of the NECDF certification process discussed earlier.

Structure of the Certification Process

The recommended certification process is composed of three phases: Qualification, Certification, and Authorization.

1. *Qualification.* Qualification activities improve knowledge and understanding of technical and background information associated with the
   principles and processes upon which the operation is based. Generally,
   qualification involves training in a classroom setting, reading assignments,
   participating in class lectures and discussions, studying history and lessons learned from similar operations, and satisfactorily completing tests
   and written examinations.

2. *Certification.* Certification requires candidates to demonstrate that they
   can apply the knowledge and principles obtained during qualification
   to the process and organization that are the objects of oversight. While
   qualification normally occurs in a classroom setting, certification activities
   are performed "in the field," or wherever project activities and operations
   actually take place. While oversight personnel do not normally operate
   equipment or execute actual operations tasks, during certification they are
   asked to physically locate various items or equipment and simulate their
   operation to an instructor or trainer. In this way, oversight candidates
   demonstrate that they completely understand what the executing organization is actually doing, or should be doing, when they observe a particular operation being performed.

3. *Authorization.* Authorization is the final phase of the process and is composed of situational testing of the candidate's knowledge to determine

whether he or she is capable of applying the skills acquired during the preceding two phases. Authorization is complete when the senior manager in charge signs off on the completion of the process, authorizing the candidate to assume the role of certified oversight team member.

Qualification

Qualification is composed of the following three phases: *oversight training, technical process training,* and *required reading.*

1. Oversight Training

During oversight training, the candidates are introduced to the process. Definitions and background on oversight are provided, along with ways it will be executed on a particular project. The training uses the oversight plan and procedures that have been developed based on what the owner considers to be the objectives of the program. This phase is crucial to begin forming a team that will be technically consistent and interchangeable.

At the completion of this phase, the candidates should have a good appreciation of what oversight is and the processes, protocols, and how the goals established by the owner will be accomplished. Because most highly hazardous operations involve activities and protocols, the need to develop a template for conduct of operations requirements is universally accepted. The following requirements, originally developed by the U.S. Department of Energy (DOE) for use at their facilities ("Guidelines," 2001), are used by many organizations and thus provide a common outline for oversight activities:

- Operations Organization and Administration
- Shift Routines and Operating Practices
- Control Area Activities
- Communications
- On-Shift Training
- Investigation of Abnormal Events
- Notifications
- Control of Equipment and System Status
- Lockouts and Tagouts

- Independent Verification

- Log-Keeping

- Operations Turnover

- Operations Aspects of Facility Chemistry and Unique Processes

- Required Reading

- Timely Orders to Operators

- Operations Procedures

- Operator Aid Postings

- Equipment and Piping Labeling

Often during this phase, case studies from other operations are reviewed for lessons learned that can be applied. For instance, the Union Carbide catastrophe in Bhopal, India, in 1984 (Eckerman, 2001; Kalelkar, 1988), which resulted in the deaths of approximately twenty thousand, illustrates a case in which successful oversight might have prevented the event. Candidates can also review cases from the U.S. Chemical Safety and Hazard Investigation Board ("Hazard," 2002) for lessons learned.

2. Technical Process Training

Following oversight training, candidates undergo rigorous technical orientation. In this phase, candidates participate in the same classroom training that is being presented to engineers, operators, and technicians of the executing organization to ensure that they all have the same degree of technical knowledge. This phase of training includes studying the design of the facilities and equipment, understanding the detailed steps involved in all processes, learning the sequence and justification for all steps in procedures to be used, and being introduced to emergency procedures for handling accidents. Detailed reviews of vendor and supplier manuals are also performed. Regular testing ensures that the candidates understand all the material covered. At the end of this phase, candidates should be as knowledgeable in the details of operating and maintaining the facility and responding to emergency situations as are the organization's engineers, operators, and technicians.

3. Required Reading

The final phase of qualification is required reading. Essentially a self-study program in which candidates are assigned a lengthy list of readings, this phase of training is finished when candidates provide documentation that all assigned readings have been completed. There are no formal meetings or classes covering these readings, but familiarity with their contents is important to successful completion of subsequent training phases. The readings are usually lengthy documents of a general rather than specific nature and referred to as high-level or plan-level documents. (In document hierarchy, plans are more general and developed first; thereafter procedures are prepared providing more specific details of the topics covered in the plans. Because there is often little or no time to study a procedure during the actual execution of an activity, procedures, unlike plans, must be known in detail.)

Certification

The second major area to be addressed is *certification*, which is composed of two phases: *critical systems demonstration* and *oversight effectiveness training*. During certification the concept of the *playbook* is introduced.

1. Critical Systems Demonstration

Because certification deals with demonstrating that knowledge acquired during qualification can be applied to actual field situations, candidates are required to demonstrate their familiarity with facility operations through a "walk and talk," during which candidates illustrate that they know how the process functions and can recognize whether or not members of the executing organization are carrying out their duties properly. Observed by a subject-matter expert who is already certified to operate the facility, candidates are asked to physically locate key systems and specific pieces of operating or safety equipment and verbally describe the major components of the system or equipment. Afterward, specific questions concerning function and performance of the system or equipment must be answered. For example, candidates may be directed to locate a particular pump and then respond to performance questions regarding pump capacity, discharge pressure, and other critical operating parameters. While not actually operating or manipulating equipment, candidates must demonstrate that they could perform the required functions if necessary, and would know, when observing someone else operating the equipment, whether it was being done safely and properly. Completion of the critical systems demonstration phase satisfies the requirement that a successful oversight team be highly trained and technically proficient.

2. Oversight Effectiveness Training

The second phase of the certification area, oversight effectiveness training, satisfies the second owner requirement: shift-to-shift consistency in execution of oversight activities. This is necessary to avoid inconsistent or conflicting feedback, which might result in inefficient or, even worse, unsafe operations. To achieve consistency, oversight personnel participate in a series of roundtable training and discussion sessions on the conduct of operations topics introduced during the oversight training phase.

Prior to a session, assigned oversight personnel draft guidelines for the conduct of operations topics. At the roundtable session, each draft guideline is presented to all oversight personnel and discussed. It is then placed into a reference book known as the "playbook," following the concept of a football playbook, which describes what each player will do when any given play is called.

The principle behind this playbook is the same. The whole team learns and practices each play (procedure), can recognize and immediately execute each play (procedure) when it's called (when directed to), which maximizes the chances that all team members will run the play (perform the procedure) the right way and exactly the same every time.

Based on further group feedback and comments, the proposed guidelines are either accepted and loaded into the playbook or pulled for revision and presented again at a later time. This process is continued until all guidelines are adopted by consensus and accepted for the playbook. Once the guidelines are in the playbook, all oversight personnel are committed to routinely follow the playbook in the execution of their oversight duties, thus ensuring consistency. (A more in-depth discussion of playbooks follows the section on the training and certification process.)

Authorization

The final major area, *authorization*, is also composed of two phases: an *oral board examination* and *management sign-off*.

1. Oral Board Examination

Now candidates sit for an oral board examination that covers all of the previously described phases of training, reading, and demonstrations. The board is composed of senior owner representatives, selected experienced oversight personnel, and experts from outside sources, such as similar operating sites.

A "test bank" of review questions is distributed to all candidates. Oversight candidates meet as a team and develop, review, and discuss acceptable answers to the questions. This activity helps to increase each candidate's knowledge, as well as to solidify oversight personnel into a team. In addition to technical questions, situational questions that explore the candidate's ability to apply his or her technical knowledge to specific situations are included. Responses to these types of questions predict how a candidate might react to conditions that are not routine.

Based upon two or three hours of individual examination and discussion, the oral board determines whether each candidate should be recommended to senior management for final approval and certification. If they are unsure, the board can recommend further study and oral board reevaluation at a later time.

2. Management Sign-Off

Once a favorable recommendation is received from the oral board, the candidate is scheduled to meet with the top manager of the organization responsible for the project. This final discussion between the manager and the candidate is meant to ensure that a good mutual understanding of the manager's vision, strategies, and goals exists and to provide the candidate an opportunity to ask questions or voice concerns. At this time, the candidate's performance in each of the phases of the certification process is usually also reviewed and discussed.

If the manager and candidate agree to proceed with final authorization, then the manager signs off on the official approval record and the candidate becomes a certified oversight team member.

Maintaining the Certification

Once certified, oversight team members are assigned to various areas and begin performing their oversight duties. Although they are still members of a larger oversight team, each person generally works alone and has little or no contact with other team members on a day-to-day basis. However, it is necessary to maintain technical expertise and to follow standards acquired during the formal certification process. The following is a list of commonly employed techniques for achieving retention:

- Preparing and sharing daily reports;
- Conducting routine weekly meetings;
- Completing assigned ongoing required readings;
- Reviewing applicable lessons learned from other oversight organizations;
- Periodically reviewing/updating the procedures and protocols;
- Reviewing feedback from the owner on the oversight being performed on the executing organization;

- Receiving new or refresher training by attending playbook sessions; and

- Annual recertification after review of individual performance and valida-
  tion of maintaining competency.

Playbook sessions are a particularly effective way to maintain certification.
During oversight, timely delivery of a playbook session will quickly add the topic(s)
covered to the body of knowledge needed to maintain certification.

Using Playbooks as the Key to Success

For the most part, the oversight certification process suggested here is similar to
other structured processes for training and certifying individuals for specialized
assignments. The unique element here is the playbook feature.

While most training and certification programs are passive for the participants,
playbooks provide a way for participants to assume a proactive leadership role.
Unlike training materials that are prepared in advance by engineering or procedural
technical writers and simply passed on for use, playbook guidelines are developed
from scratch by the participants.

Usually, some of the oversight personnel have past plant experience in shift
operating organizations. Others who might not have such experience may be familiar with industrial plant activities in general through having served in assignments
in engineering, construction, or startups. One of the strengths of the playbook
approach is that those with generalized experience can be "re-tooled" quickly into
members of an oversight team. Such a conversion draws on the person's general
experience, but also utilizes staff members more experienced in the actual activity.

For instance, for the Newport operation, the GSR team had a broad range of experience, and every member learned from and drew upon the best practices of the others. Because using Playbooks provided a systematic process for training individuals
for oversight roles, NECDF was able to retain staff from the engineering, construction, and startup phases of the project, instead of having to recruit new people. Thus,
the playbook program made the operation more time- and cost-effective and was
beneficial those already on the NECDF project and for the government leadership.

Because many of the GSRs had not had past experience creating a playbook,
they were provided general directions and were coached on how to proceed based
on the following information:

- Research of project documents;

- Review of handouts from other oversight training phases;

- Discussions with knowledgeable individuals at the site;

- Discussions/visits with key personnel at other similar sites;

- Personal experience; and

- Any other source deemed appropriate by the preparer.

Using this information, GSRs researched all project documents—plans, procedures, reports, permits, engineering studies, and publications—for background information applicable to the playbook guidelines. They also searched through handouts and instructional materials from other training they had completed for material to add to their final product. (It should be noted that GSRs were assigned topics that they did not necessarily fully understand, so it was a learning experience for them and they had to work harder than someone who was already a subject-matter expert (SME).)

After completing their research, the GSRs were encouraged to contact people knowledgeable on the topic, both those currently on-site and those at similar sites, to discuss their topics. Several other sites had completed or were currently conducting chemical demilitarization activities similar to what NECDF would be doing, so GSRs obtained first-hand input and increased their network of resources for future projects.

GSRs were also encouraged to bring their own experiences to bear on the preparation of their guidelines. While most had never worked in a chemical demilitarization facility before, they did have similar experiences at highly hazardous chemical plant operations, nuclear facilities, or military operations. (For example, lockout-tagout [LOTO] procedures at chemical and industrial plants were essentially the same as those used at NECDF, and shift turnovers and log-keeping principles were the same at both nuclear facilities and NECDF.)

Last, GSRs were asked to find other sources of information. They might use information from a conference or seminar on plant operating protocols, from a movie on industrial practices that lead to catastrophes, or conversations with highly experienced plant operating personnel.

Each playbook guideline was prepared following a prescribed template. The guidelines were composed of three sections: background information, desktop instructions, and guideline details.

1. *Background Information*—information on the topic, who prepared it, configuration control information, dates prepared, discussed, and revised, and references used. This satisfied the requirement for keeping the document up-to-date.

2. *Desktop Instructions*—a review and reference resource for GSRs in the field.

3. *Guideline Details*—used to bring the GSR up-to-date on the topic.

GSRs utilized the above to prepare their initial drafts, which they presented to the rest of the group. The emphasis was on "drafts." The final guidelines that made up the playbook were the result of input and consensus of the entire group using a roundtable process. This was also a way to build teamwork. A true consensus was achieved on every guideline, resulting in all GSRs taking ownership of every guide-line and committing to support and follow it. Because consistency of oversight activi-ties was crucial for the NECDF program, commitment was extremely important. It assured the systems contractor that issues would be dealt with in the same way every time and that there would be no changes that could cause them to lose focus.

After the playbook guidelines were accepted by all GSRs and became part of their resource documents, the playbook was often referred to while performing oversight duties. If the GSR needed a quick refresher or just wanted to review a topic in more detail, the playbook was the first resource he or she used. Indeed, the continual use of the playbook by all GSRs was a critical factor in the overall success of the NECDF project.

Conclusion

Many structured training and certification programs are available for preparing members of teams to execute a particular function. However, in traditional training programs, individuals often receive direction via previously outlined procedures or other directives and never really understand the need to accept and execute the functions uniformly and consistently. As a result, they have their own interpreta-tions of what the guidelines mean and act accordingly. Such independent action in the oversight of hazardous materials handling can be disastrous.

The unique training and certification program outlined here, creating and using a playbook, has been shown to produce outstanding results. The playbook approach has the benefit of building a team from a group of individuals, allowing them to take ownership of the guidelines by which they will execute their oversight duties, and establishing consistency in discharging those activities.

Through playbooks, participants come together as a collection of individuals and transform themselves into a "team" that consistently provides technically pro-ficient and effective feedback to leadership. The playbook program described here can be used at any highly hazardous operation, and it will be successful every time.

References

Eckerman, I. (2001). Chemical industry and public health: Bhopal as an example. *Master of Public Health*. Goteborg, Sweden: Nordic School of Public Health.

Guidelines for the conduct of operations at DOE facilities. (2001). (Order DOE 5480.19). Washington, DC: U.S. Department of Energy.

Haraburda, S.S., & Gary, J.L. (2004). Certification for government oversight of manufacturing. *Defense AT & L, 33*(4), DAU 180, 46–49.

Hazard investigation: Improving reactive hazard management. (2002). (Report 2001-01-H). Washington, DC: U.S. Chemical Safety and Hazard Investigation Board.

Kalelkar, A.S. (1988). Investigation of large-magnitude incidents: Bhopal as a case study. Presented at The Institution of Chemical Engineers Conference on Preventing Major Chemical Accidents, London, England.

James L. Gary, MBA, *is an experienced manager and consultant with forty years of leading commercial and government operations. He has extensive experience in coaching and mentoring executives and teaches organizational leadership at Purdue University. His specialty is demonstrating how achieving safety and environmental excellence results in improving overall organizational performance, particularly cost effectiveness. He has a B.S. in chemical engineering from Louisiana Tech University and earned his MBA from Loyola University of New Orleans.*

Michele L. Summers, *associate professor of organizational leadership and supervision (OLS) at Purdue University, has a B.S. in OLS and an M.S. in technology with a concentration in adult education. As assistant director of the College of Technology at Indianapolis/Lafayette, she works with outreach programs, education/industry partnerships, and improving workforce quality through leadership and technology training. In partnership with Subaru of Indiana Automotive, she is currently researching motivation in adult learners and development of leadership skills.*

Facilitating in the Virtual Classroom
How to Compensate for Lack of Body Language

Darlene B. Christopher

Summary

Increasingly, facilitators are training online participants in virtual classrooms . . . participants they can't see or make eye contact with. Facilitators who rely on their techniques for communicating and interacting with an in-person audience, without making any adjustments for an online audience will soon become frustrated, and frustrate their audiences as well.

One key challenge in a virtual classroom is that participants and trainers cannot "read" and interpret each other's body language as they do in a physical classroom. Just as content needs to be adjusted for a virtual classroom delivery, the trainer's facilitation technique needs to be adjusted to make up for the absence of body language.

Facilitators need to first adjust their spoken language, then use the interactive features in the virtual classroom to supplement that language.

Make Adjustments to Language

Facilitators who have taken presentation skills training or studied communications will be familiar with the research that shows that the impact of the speaker's message is based largely on how the message is conveyed, including body language, posture, and gestures, rather than the message itself. Borg (2008) found that 93 percent of communication is based on nonverbal behaviors.

Most facilitators have naturally mastered a style of communication in the classroom that is as much about "form" as it is about the message itself. They use eye contact, gestures, and physical movement to convey their messages. And for many, their first attempt at online facilitation makes them acutely aware of the extent to which they rely on visual cues and body language in the physical classroom—a fact they may not have even been aware of until they tried to facilitate online.

At first thought, a web cam displaying the facilitator on a portion of the screen visible to all participants appears to be the solution. However, even a high-quality web cam cannot fully overcome the physical separation between facilitator and participants. Furthermore, a web cam is typically one-way, which means the speaker cannot see participants.

Since participants cannot "read" the facilitator's body language as they do in a physical classroom, you need to adjust your word choice to make it more clear and purposeful. In a physical classroom, precise language may not be as important because participants watch for gestures and body language to fill in any gaps or even watch other participants to understand what the facilitator is saying or to understand what they are supposed to do. So in an online class without the visual cues you need to adjust your language to make it as clear and precise as possible. Whenever you want participants to take an action, such as respond to a question or turn to a page in the workbook, be specific and purposeful so that participants can follow along. When asking participants to respond, tell them how to respond as well—by typing in the chat area, by verbalizing out loud—and if it doesn't matter how they respond, tell them that as well. By adjusting what you say, you can prevent misunderstanding and frustration for participants.

Annotate While Speaking

In a physical classroom, facilitators may use a laser device or finger to point to a specific part of a projected slide. Or facilitators may make a big circle to indicate the cyclical nature of the steps displayed on a slide. Most virtual classroom platforms include a pointer device as well as annotation tools such as a highlighter and writing instruments. As you speak, be sure to use these annotation tools to emphasize key information on the screen. For example, as you display a slide, you can underline or circle key words while speaking, or use the pointer tool to point to a specific part of a graph or table or draw a circle around a cycle of steps for emphasis. Annotating the screen while speaking helps the audience know where to focus their attention, and it also approximates gesturing.

Some virtual facilitators like to stand up while speaking so they can gesture as if they had a physical audience in the room. Even though the participants can't see body language, they will hear it in the speaker's voice. Note that if you choose to stand, a second person will be needed to run the controls, forward the slides, and annotate the lesson.

Obtain Participant Feedback

Facilitators in physical classrooms rely heavily on participant body language such as nodding heads to indicate agreement or blank stares to indicate confusion. Because facilitators cannot see virtual participants, they also need to adjust their technique to compensate. Most virtual classrooms offer a variety of interactive features that the facilitator can use to obtain feedback from participants. However, simply having access to the feedback features is not enough. Facilitators must actively guide participants to use various features throughout a session.

Typical interactive features are listed in Table 1. You should become familiar with the chat, instant feedback, and polling features in order to make the best use of them to elicit the feedback from participants.

It's good to set the tone for an interactive session by familiarizing participants with how to give you feedback at the start of the session. Weave interactions into the first few minutes of your session by asking participants to type their locations into chat, respond to a poll about their backgrounds, and "raise" their hands if they can hear the audio clearly, for example.

Throughout the session, you can use the interactive features in a variety of ways to obtain feedback from participants. Examples of how to adapt techniques used in the physical classroom to a virtual classroom are listed in Table 2.

Ask, Then Pause

With in-person participants, body language is immediate, which means the facilitator is used to a certain pace. Facilitators must be aware that virtual classroom participants need more time to give feedback because they typically have to take a physical action, such as clicking on a part of the screen, typing, un-muting their

Table 1. Typical Interactive Features in a Virtual Classroom

Feature	Description
Chat	Allows participants to send text messages in real time to all participants, the facilitator, or each other, depending on the tool.
Instant Feedback	Allows participants to select an icon to raise a hand, agree, disagree, or provide other types of instant feedback.
Polls	Allow participants to respond to multiple-choice and true/false questions. Results can be displayed live or posted after all responses have been received.

Table 2.   Physical Classroom Facilitation Techniques Adapted to the Virtual Classroom

Physical Classroom	Virtual Classroom
Facilitator calls out a list of choices and asks participants to raise their hands when they hear the description of their experience level with the topic to be discussed (no experience, 1 to 2 years, 3 to 4 years, etc.)	Facilitator posts a poll with a question about experience level with the topic to be discussed and asks participants to mark the responses on the screen that correspond to their experience levels.
Facilitator makes a comment or statement, then relies on head nods or frowns to gauge agreement or disagreement.	Facilitator asks participants to use instant feedback features if they agree or disagree with a statement (feedback features vary by system, for example: checkmark for agree, X for disagree, etc.)
While explaining a difficult concept, facilitator scans audience and watches for nods or quizzical looks to judge comprehension.	Facilitator tells participants to use instant feedback features to indicate whether they understand and are ready to move on or not (feedback features vary by system, for example: smiley face = move on, sad face = confused, or thumbs up = move on, thumbs down = still has questions).
Facilitator watches participants to see when they look up to indicate they are done reading a document.	Facilitator tells participants to type "done" into the chat box when they are done reading a document.
Facilitator scans the room to look for participants with raised hands.	Facilitator checks the part of the screen where participants can click to "raise their hands."

phone, and so forth. There may also be slight delays on the screen after a participant takes action.

If you pose a question or ask participants to use a feature and the response is not immediate, the best technique is to pause. Once you've asked a question, your audience needs a few seconds to process the question and think of a response or review the poll response options to determine how they will respond. If respondents will be typing their responses, they will need even more time. Resist the urge to jump in and break the silence. Let participants fill the pause instead. The majority of the time you will be pleasantly surprised when your participants chime in with their ideas and thoughts.

The sound of silence while facilitating a virtual classroom session may be uncomfortable, but that silence is important and worth it. After posting a poll, typing a question in the chat box, or asking a question verbally, pause and give the audience time to respond. Some silence is ok; virtual classroom facilitation doesn't mean you have a license to conduct an unending monologue—that's pure "sage on the stage."

Rehearse Your Session

Getting used to facilitating when you need to adjust your language and use interactive features to make up for the lack of body language takes time. Rehearse in advance to get used to a new style of facilitation. Rehearsing with a mock online audience allows you to fine-tune your communication techniques and get used to the features of the virtual classroom. Ask your mock audience participants to give you feedback on their level of engagement and on your voice and use of annotation tools. If you cannot rehearse with others, use the recording feature in the virtual classroom. Then listen and watch the screen carefully to see how your communication techniques are working.

Conclusion

Bridging the distance between facilitator and participants online requires a variety of techniques to make up for the absence of body language. Facilitators who adjust their facilitation techniques to meet the needs of a virtual audience will be successful. By interacting with the online audience, using clear language, annotating the screen, and rehearsing new techniques, facilitators will be able to communicate clearly and effectively.

Reference

Borg, J. (2008). *Body language: Seven easy lessons to master the silent language*. Upper Saddle River, NJ: Pearson Education.

Darlene B. Christopher *is a learning officer at the World Bank Group in Washington, D.C. She has been designing and delivering online training programs for global audiences for over nine years. She has written numerous articles and is a frequent presenter at workplace learning conferences on the topic of virtual classrooms. She blogs regularly on this topic at www.webconferenceguru.com.*

The Story of the Kirkpatrick Four Levels™
Evaluating in the Moment

Don Kirkpatrick with Elaine Biech

Summary

The Kirkpatrick Model, or the Kirkpatrick Four Levels™ training evaluation model, is known throughout the training community as the steps required to measure training's effectiveness. The concept of four different levels of evaluation is an elegant but simple sequence that helps trainers understand the evaluation process. This article presents Don Kirkpatrick's story and introduces ideas for how evaluation can be "in the moment," too.

Don Kirkpatrick's Story

The four levels of evaluation was the topic of my 1954 Ph.D. dissertation from the University of Wisconsin; the levels were based on the research I had done between 1954 and 1959.

The amazing thing is that in 1959, five years after I had finished my dissertation, Bob Craig, editor of the *Training and Development Journal*, called and asked if I would write an article on "evaluation." He apparently heard from some ASTD member that I had done research on the subject. I told him I would write a series of four articles. He hesitated because no series had ever appeared in the *Journal*, but he finally agreed.

My articles on Reaction, Learning, Behavior, and Results were printed in the American Society for Training and Development's *Journal* more than fifty years ago. The articles immediately gained the attention of training professionals. Some called them the "four levels" while others named them the "Kirkpatrick Model" for evaluating training programs. I had not called them either one.

As I think back on Bob's decision to publish the series, I wonder whether they would have been published for the world to see if he had not asked. I had no thoughts then of writing an article or series of articles. I think the Lord had something to do with it because He knew it would have a tremendous effect on the way training programs would be evaluated all over the world and that trainers would help their organizations and even save their jobs by implementing the four levels.

As soon as the articles were published, the word spread like wildfire, and trainers began to write articles on each of the levels. It wasn't until 1993 that the first book was written when a friend, Jane Holcomb, suggested it. She said that interested trainers could not find copies of the original articles.

The first book was called simply, *Evaluating Training Programs: The Four Levels.* It contained not only descriptions and guidelines, but also case studies of sixteen organizations that had implemented one or more of the levels. The introduction to the book was written by Dave Basarab, describing how Motorola used the four levels. Motorola had implemented the model throughout the world and showed that the four levels were appropriate for all sizes and types of organizations.

In 2005 my son Jim and I wrote the book, *Transferring Learning to Behavior.* This book emphasized how to ensure that the learning would be applied on the job and how to evaluate the extent to which it happened.

Our third book, *Implementing the Four Levels* (2007), was designed to simplify the evaluation of the four levels by including examples, forms, and procedures from various organizations for evaluating each level. The most recent book on the subject is *Training on Trial,* written by my son Jim and his wife, Wendy, in 2010.

I recently asked members of the ASTD National LinkedIn discussion group if the four levels are out of date. I received more than forty responses that nearly unanimously stated "NO." The four levels work, most of them stated. The issue as I see it is that most training professionals are effective in evaluating Level 1 Reaction and Level 2 Learning, but they are not evaluating Level 3 Behavior and Level 4 Results. My son, Jim, and his wife, Wendy, are working with organizations around the world and demystifying Levels 3 and 4.

Evaluating In The Moment

So, how do you apply the Kirkpatrick Four Levels to today's demanding learning-in-the-moment mentality? What steps can you take that ensure you are measuring all four levels without spending all your time evaluating?

Level 1: Reaction

Level 1 measures participant satisfaction with the training and delivery. For example, how satisfied were participants about what they learned, how they learned, and how well prepared they are to implement what they learned? Level 1 evaluation may provide guidance about what to change. You can measure learning-in-the-moment in Level 1 without waiting until the end of the training. Instead, half-way through, create a T-grid on a flip chart. Place a plus on one side and a minus sign or a triangle (delta) representing change on the other. Ask participants to identify what is working and what needs to change. Asking for this feedback works well prior to a lunch break. Ask participants to give feedback on how they perceive the program, positively or negatively. This technique will also give you feedback on the level of engagement and how you can adjust the design to encourage learning.

You may also use index cards. Ask participants to rate the training so far on a 1 to 7 scale and include one reason why they gave it that rating. You will learn the most critical reactions to the training—both positive and negative. Fast? Yes. Evaluating in the moment? Yes. Effective? Yes.

In addition, Jim Kirkpatrick suggests that you examine all your evaluation forms to ensure that you are asking "learner-centered" questions, instead of the typical "trainer-centered" questions. For example, for a Likert scale item, use, "I will be able to apply what I learned" instead of "The material was relevant to my needs." This is something you can do in-the-moment to change the perspective for your learners. When asking open-ended questions, try "What are the three things you will implement when returning to the job?" or "What ultimate impact will you have once you apply what you learned?"

Level 2: Learning

Level 2 measures the extent to which learning has occurred. The measurement of knowledge, skill, or attitude change (KSAs) indicates what participants have absorbed and whether they know how to implement what they learned. Most training sessions include objectives that improve specific skills and increase knowledge. And some training sessions, such as diversity or team building, attempt to change attitudes.

How can you measure learning in the moment? You do not need to wait for participants to return to the workplace. Trainers can ask participants to evaluate their learning midway through and to develop questions for the trainer based on what they still don't know. You could pass out note cards and ask participants to identify a topic for which they require clarity thus far. Collect and sort the index cards over a break. Adjust your program to review or elaborate.

If measuring skills, you could set up assessment centers where participants could practice the skills and receive immediate feedback in-the-moment. You could also pair participants to practice on each other. An observer could be enlisted to provide feedback to each pair.

Level 3: Behavior

Measuring behavior in Level 3 determines whether the skills and knowledge are being implemented. Are participants applying what they learned and transferring what they learned to the job?

You can evaluate in-the-moment by encouraging supervisors to walk around and ask a few key questions of their employees shortly after training has been completed. Suggest questions such as:

- How are things going since you have been using the new system?

- What barriers are you facing?

- How can I help you apply this?

Encourage peer-to-peer accountability in much the same way. You could set up a "buddy" system and have partners meet weekly to review each other's work and to offer encouragement or suggestions to one another.

Evaluation-in-the-moment does not necessarily mean that you complete it instantly. It does mean that you may obtain data instantly. For example, you could conduct a focus group three months after training that weaves together the four levels to determine whether behaviors have changed. Basic questions may include:

- What are the main points from your training that you are now using on the job? (L2 and L3)

- How are things going with your new behaviors? (L3)

- What kind of early indications do you see that there is some positive impact? (L4)

- What do you wish you had learned three months ago but did not? (L1) How would that have changed your behavior in the past three months? (L3)

Level 4: Results

Level 4 measures the results of factors such as reduced turnover, improved quality, increased quantity or output, reduction of costs, increase in profits, increased sales, improved customer service, reduction in waste or errors, lower absenteeism, or fewer grievances. Measurements focus on the actual results on the business as participants successfully apply the program content.

You will use various data sources depending on what you are measuring. Evaluation in-the-moment may be tracked and displayed as the events occur; for example, contracts signed or sales closed could have a running total in real time.

As a trainer, you could also email supervisors of those who went through training and ask questions like these:

- What do you see your employees doing differently after training? (L3)

- What kind of initial impact have you seen? (L4) Please provide specifics.

- To what do you attribute the positive outcomes? (L4)

Conduct a "pulse check," that is, listen and watch for positive indications that all is on track for ultimate L4 targeted results. These pulse checks may take the form of reports from the field by customers, employees, and/or supervisors.

Closing

In this fast-paced world, we are all learning in the moment. The training community will need to stay abreast of the speed with which change, including acquiring knowledge and skills, is occurring and will need to tune into ways to evaluate the learning at all four levels in the Kirkpatrick Model.

Donald L. (Don) Kirkpatrick, Ph.D., *is professor emeritus at the University of Wisconsin and Honorary Chairman of Kirkpatrick Partners. He is the creator of the Kirkpatrick Four Levels*[TM] *Evaluation Model, the foremost training evaluation tool in the world. He is one of the most sought-after speakers in the workplace learning and performance field. Don is the author of seven books on training evaluation and HR topics, including the third edition of* Evaluating Training Programs: The Four Levels. *Don is a past president of the American Society for Training and Development (ASTD). He has been honored with the Lifetime Achievement in Workplace Learning and Performance award from ASTD and is a member of the HRD Hall of Fame of* Training *magazine.*

Contributors

Brittany Ashby
Align: Planning, Training, Consulting
  and Business Services
1401 Airport Parkway
Suite 300
Cheyenne, WY 82001
  (307) 772-9146
  fax: (307) 778-3943
  email: bashby@TheAlignTeam.org

Jean Barbazette
The Training Clinic
645 Seabreeze Drive
Seal Beach, CA 90740
  (562) 430-2484 or (800) 937-4698
  email: jean@thetrainingclinic.com
  website: www.thetrainingclinic.com

Brenda Barker, Ed.D.
Project Director
Tennessee Initiative for Perinatal
  Quality Care
1125 MRB 4/LH
Nashville, TN 37232-0656
  (615) 343- 8536
  email: Brenda.barker@tipqc.org

Zane L. Berge, Ph.D.
UMBC
1000 Hilltop Circle
Baltimore, MD 21250
  (410) 455-2306
  email: berge@umbc.edu

Robert Alan Black, Ph.D., CSP
Cre8ng People, Places &
  Possibilities
P.O. Box 5805
Athens, GA 30604
  (706) 353-3387
  email: alan@cre8ng.com
  website: www.cre8ng.com

Guido R. Britez
SUNERGOS
Venezuela 891 c/ Sgto. Gauto
Asuncion, Paraguay (South America)
  (595) (21) 213-991
  fax: (595) (21) 213-991
  email: contacto1@sunergos.com.py
  website: www.sunergos.com.py

Tom Bunzel
2180 South Beverly Glen Boulevard,
  #115
Los Angeles, CA 90025
  (310) 286-0969
  email: tbunzel@earthlink.net
  website: www.professorppt.com
  tbunzel.blogspot.com

Darlene B. Christopher
World Bank Group
1818 Pennsylvania Avenue NW
Washington, DC 20433
  (202) 473-6651
  email: Dchristopher1@worldbank.org

Kenneth Cloke
President, Mediators Beyond Borders
2411 18th Street
Santa Monica, CA 90405
   (310) 399-4426
   email: kenclokembb@gmail.com
   website: www.kennethcloke.com or
   www.mediatorsbeyondborders.org

Sharon Dera
8948 Random Road
Fort Worth, TX 76179
   (817) 236-7594
   email: sdera@charter.net
   website: www.proficiencegroup.com

Philip Donnison, Ph.D.
Philip Donnison Occupational
   Psychology Ltd.
4 Michaelson Road
Kendal, Cumbria, LA9 5JQ
United Kingdom
   phone and fax: +44 (0) 1539 721881
   mobile: +44 (0) 7771 602664
   email: phil.donnison@me.com

Noam Ebner
Tachlit Mediation and Negotiation
   Training
Winkler-Ebner Law Offices
36 Keren Hayesod Street
Jerusalem
Israel
   +972-523-786996
   email: NoamEbner@Creighton.edu.

Yael Efron
Tachlit Mediation and Negotiation
   Training
Shilat, 73188
Israel
   +972-523-557898
   email: yaele.law@gmail.com.

James L. Gary, MBA
SAIC
Tooele Chemical Agent Disposal
   Facility
11620 Stark Road
Stockton, UT 84071
   (435) 833-7752
   email: jim.gary@conus.army.mil or
   jlgary@urs.com

Dennis E. Gilbert
Appreciative Strategies, LLC
P.O. Box 164
Montoursville, PA 17754
   (570) 433-8286
   fax: (570) 371-4754
   email: dennis@
   appreciativestrategies.com

Dr. K.S. Gupta
Director
School of Management and Technology
Jaipur National University
Jagatpura, Jaipur-302025
India
   93-52088033
   email: ksgupta37@gmail.com

Christine Hipple
11408 Elfstone Way
Columbia, MD 21044
   (410) 852-5742
   email: Christine.hipple@gmail.com

Homer H. Johnson, Ph.D.
Department of Management
School of Business Administration
Loyola University Chicago
820 North Michigan Avenue
Chicago, IL 60611
   (312) 915-6682
   email: hjohnso@luc.edu

M.K. Key, Ph.D.
Key Associates
1857 Laurel Ridge Drive
Suite 100
Nashville, TN 37215
   (615) 665-1622 or (615) 343-6182
   email: keyassocs@mindspring.com

Donald L. (Don) Kirkpatrick, Ph.D.
842 Kirkland Court
Pewaukee, WI 53072
   (443) 856-4500
   email: Dleekirk1@aol.com
   website: www.kirkpatrickpartners.com

Susan Landay
Trainers Warehouse
Natick, MA
   (800) 299-3770
   website: www.TRAINERSwarehouse.
   com

Deborah Spring Laurel
917 Vilas Avenue
Madison, WI 53715-1509
   (608) 255-2010
   fax: (608) 260-2616
   email: dlaurel@
   laurelandassociates.com

Mitu Mandal
DIPR, DRDO, Timarpur
Delhi – 54
India
   011-23917377
   fax: 011-23916980
   email: mitumandal@gmail.com

Rick Maurer
Maurer & Associates
P.O. Box 50142
Arlington, VA 22205
   (703) 525-7074
   email: Rickmaur@aol.com

Mohandas Nair
A2 Kamdar Building
607 Gokhale Road(s)
Dadar, Mumbai, Maharashtra 400028
India
   91-22-24226307
   email: nair_Mohandas@hotmail.com
   or MKnair@vsnl.net

Julie O'Mara
President
O'Mara and Associates
2124 Water Rail Avenue
North Las Vegas, NV 89084
   (702) 541-8920
   fax: 702-541-8830
   email: Julie@omaraassoc.com
   website: www.omaraassoc.com

Margie Parikh
BK School of Business Management
Gujarat University
University Road
Ahmedabad, 380009
India
(+91) 79 2630 4811 (office)
(+91) 79 25832971 (fax)
email: margie_parikh@yahoo.com

Paul H. Pietri, D.B.A.
Professor of Management
Mitchell College of Business
University of South Alabama
Mobile, AL 36688
(251) 460-6130
fax: (251) 460-6529
email: ppietri@usouthal.edu

David Piltz
CapitolMed, Inc.
1719 East SR 10, Suite 229
Parsippany, NJ 07054
(862) 203-3310
fax: (973) 749-6329
email: david.piltz@capitolmed.net
website: www.capitolmed.net

Dr. Sethu Madhavan Puravangara
P.O. Box 908
Abu Dhabi
United Arab Emirates
+971-50-6673021
email: drsethu@drsethu.com
website: www.drsethu.com

Linda M. Raudenbush, Ed.D.
7201 Kindler Road
Columbia, MD 21046
(410) 381-2747
email: drlmr2004@yahoo.com

Anne H. Reilly, Ph.D.
Department of Management
School of Business Administration
Loyola University Chicago
820 North Michigan Avenue
Chicago, IL 60611
(312) 915-6537
email: areilly@luc.edu

Shri S.S. Roy, MBA
Addl. General Manager/HRD
BHEL HRD Institute
Plot 25, Sector 16A
Noida – 201031 UP
India
91 120 2515434, 2416346
email: ssr@bhel.in

Lou Russell
Russell Martin & Associates
9084 Technology Drive
Suite 500
Fishers, IN 46038
(317) 475-9311
email: lou@russellmartin.com
website: www.lourussell.com

Jan M. Schmuckler, Ph.D.
Lignum Vitae Ltd.
1625 16th Street
Oakland, CA 94607
(510) 562-0626
email: jan@janconsults.com
website: www.janconsults.com

Rajinder Kaur Sokhi, Ph.D., Sc.E.
DIPR, DRDO, Timarpur
Delhi – 54
India
  011-23917377
  fax: 011-23916980
  email: rajindersokhi@yahoo.co.in

Steve Sugar
1314 Quarry Lane
Lancaster, PA 17603
  (717) 291-9010
  email: steve.sugar@verizon.net

Michele L. Summers
Purdue University
College of Technology at Indianapolis/
  Lafayette
5500 State Road 38 East, AD 2900
P.O. Box 5689
Lafayette, IN 47905-9405
  (765) 269-9631
  email: msummers@purdue.edu

K.M. Tripathi
DIPR, DRDO, Timarpur
Delhi – 54
India
  011-23917377
  fax: 011-23916980
  email: kmt.mani@gmail.com

Teresa G. Weldy, Ph.D.
Mitchell College of Business
University of South Alabama
Mobile, AL 36688

Gregory R. Williams, Ed.D.
Director and Clinical Associate
  Professor
Instructional Systems Development
  Graduate Program
University of Maryland, Baltimore
  County (UMBC)
Baltimore, MD 21250
  (410) 455-6773
  email: gregw@umbc.edu
  program website: www.umbc.edu/isd
  faculty website: www.gregwilliams.net
  Twitter: gregwilliams123 or ISDNow

Gary G. Wise
Chief Learning Architect
Myca Multimedia & Training Solutions
210 Arlington Drive
Batesville, IN 47006
  (317) 437-2555
  email: gwise@mycagroup.com

Contents of the Companion Volume, *The 2012 Pfeiffer Annual: Consulting*

Experiential Learning Activities

†Cutting-Edge Topics
**Learning in the Moment Topics

Editor's Choice

Inventories, Questionnaires, and Surveys

Articles and Discussion Resources

Pfeiffer Publications Guide

This guide is designed to familiarize you with the various types of Pfeiffer publications. The formats section describes the various types of products that we publish; the methodologies section describes the many different ways that content might be provided within a product. We also provide a list of the topic areas in which we publish.

FORMATS

In addition to its extensive book-publishing program, Pfeiffer offers content in an array of formats, from fieldbooks for the practitioner to complete, ready-to-use training packages that support group learning.

FIELDBOOK Designed to provide information and guidance to practitioners in the midst of action. Most fieldbooks are companions to another, sometimes earlier, work, from which its ideas are derived; the fieldbook makes practical what was theoretical in the original text. Fieldbooks can certainly be read from cover to cover. More likely, though, you'll find yourself bouncing around following a particular theme, or dipping in as the mood, and the situation, dictate.

HANDBOOK A contributed volume of work on a single topic, comprising an eclectic mix of ideas, case studies, and best practices sourced by practitioners and experts in the field.

An editor or team of editors usually is appointed to seek out contributors and to evaluate content for relevance to the topic. Think of a handbook not as a ready-to-eat meal, but as a cookbook of ingredients that enables you to create the most fitting experience for the occasion.

RESOURCE Materials designed to support group learning. They come in many forms: a complete, ready-to-use exercise (such as a game); a comprehensive resource on one topic (such as conflict management) containing a variety of methods and approaches; or a collection of like-minded activities (such as icebreakers) on multiple subjects and situations.

TRAINING PACKAGE An entire, ready-to-use learning program that focuses on a particular topic or skill. All packages comprise a guide for the facilitator/trainer and a workbook for the participants. Some packages are supported with additional media—such as video—or learning aids, instruments, or other devices to help participants understand concepts or practice and develop skills.

- *Facilitator/trainer's guide* Contains an introduction to the program, advice on how to organize and facilitate the learning event, and step-by-step instructor notes. The guide also contains copies of presentation materials—handouts, presentations, and overhead designs, for example—used in the program.

- *Participant's workbook* Contains exercises and reading materials that support the learning goal and serves as a valuable reference and support guide for participants in the weeks and months that follow the learning event. Typically, each participant will require his or her own workbook.

ELECTRONIC CD-ROMs and web-based products transform static Pfeiffer content into dynamic, interactive experiences. Designed to take advantage of the searchability, automation, and ease-of-use that technology provides, our e-products bring convenience and immediate accessibility to your workspace.

METHODOLOGIES

CASE STUDY A presentation, in narrative form, of an actual event that has occurred inside an organization. Case studies are not prescriptive, nor are they used to prove a point; they are designed to develop critical analysis and decision-making skills. A case study has a specific time frame, specifies a sequence of events, is narrative in structure, and contains a plot structure—an issue (what should be/have been done?). Use case studies when the goal is to enable participants to apply previously learned theories to the circumstances in the case, decide what is pertinent, identify the real issues, decide what should have been done, and develop a plan of action.

ENERGIZER A short activity that develops readiness for the next session or learning event. Energizers are most commonly used after a break or lunch to stimulate or refocus the group. Many involve some form of physical activity, so they are a useful way to counter post-lunch lethargy. Other uses include transitioning from one topic to another, where "mental" distancing is important.

EXPERIENTIAL LEARNING ACTIVITY (ELA) A facilitator-led intervention that moves participants through the learning cycle from experience to application (also known as a Structured Experience). ELAs are carefully thought-out designs in which there is a definite learning purpose and intended outcome. Each step—everything that participants do during the activity—facilitates the accomplishment of the stated goal. Each ELA includes complete instructions for facilitating the intervention and a clear statement of goals, suggested group size and timing, materials required, an explanation of the process, and, where appropriate, possible variations to the activity. (For more detail on Experiential Learning Activities, see the Introduction to the *Reference Guide to Handbooks and Annuals*, 1999 edition, Pfeiffer, San Francisco.)

GAME A group activity that has the purpose of fostering team spirit and togetherness in addition to the achievement of a pre-stated goal. Usually contrived—undertaking a desert expedition, for example—this type of learning method offers an engaging means for participants to demonstrate and practice business and inter-personal skills. Games are effective for team building and personal development mainly because the goal is subordinate to the process—the means through which participants reach decisions, collaborate, communicate, and generate trust and understanding. Games often engage teams in "friendly" competition.

ICEBREAKER A (usually) short activity designed to help participants overcome initial anxiety in a training session and/or to acquaint the participants with one another. An icebreaker can be a fun activity or can be tied to specific topics or training goals. While a useful tool in itself, the icebreaker comes into its own in situations where tension or resistance exists within a group.

INSTRUMENT A device used to assess, appraise, evaluate, describe, classify, and summarize various aspects of human behavior. The term used to describe an instrument depends primarily on its format and purpose. These terms include survey, questionnaire, inventory, diagnostic survey, and poll. Some uses of instruments include providing instrumental feedback to group members, studying here-and-now processes or functioning within a group, manipulating group composition, and evaluating outcomes of training and other interventions.

Instruments are popular in the training and HR field because, in general, more growth can occur if an individual is provided with a method for focusing specifically on his or her own behavior. Instruments also are used to obtain information that will serve as a basis for change and to assist in workforce planning efforts.

Paper-and-pencil tests still dominate the instrument landscape with a typical package comprising a facilitator's guide, which offers advice on administering the instrument and interpreting the collected data, and an initial set of instruments. Additional instruments are available separately. Pfeiffer, though, is investing heavily in e-instruments. Electronic instrumentation provides effortless distribution and, for larger groups particularly, offers advantages over paper-and-pencil tests in the time it takes to analyze data and provide feedback.

LECTURETTE A short talk that provides an explanation of a principle, model, or process that is pertinent to the participants' current learning needs. A lecturette is intended to establish a common language bond between the trainer and the participants by providing a mutual frame of reference. Use a lecturette as an introduction to a group activity or event, as an interjection during an event, or as a handout.

MODEL A graphic depiction of a system or process and the relationship among its elements. Models provide a frame of reference and something more tangible, and more easily remembered, than a verbal explanation. They also give participants something to "go on," enabling them to track their own progress as they experience the dynamics, processes, and relationships being depicted in the model.

ROLE PLAY A technique in which people assume a role in a situation/scenario: a customer service rep in an angry-customer exchange, for example. The way in which the role is approached is then discussed and feedback is offered. The role play is often repeated using a different approach and/or incorporating changes made based on feedback received. In other words, role playing is a spontaneous interaction involving realistic behavior under artificial (and safe) conditions.

SIMULATION A methodology for understanding the interrelationships among components of a system or process. Simulations differ from games in that they test or use a model that depicts or mirrors some aspect of reality in form, if not necessarily in content. Learning occurs by studying the effects of change on one or more factors of the model. Simulations are commonly used to test hypotheses about what happens in a system—often referred to as "what if?" analysis—or to examine best-case/worst-case scenarios.

THEORY A presentation of an idea from a conjectural perspective. Theories are useful because they encourage us to examine behavior and phenomena through a different lens.

TOPICS

The twin goals of providing effective and practical solutions for workforce training and organization development and meeting the educational needs of training and human resource professionals shape Pfeiffer's publishing program. Core topics include the following:

Leadership & Management

Communication & Presentation

Coaching & Mentoring

Training & Development

e-Learning

Teams & Collaboration

OD & Strategic Planning

Human Resources

Consulting